Assessing Student Learning in General Education

Assessing Student Learning in General Education

Good Practice Case Studies

Marilee J. Bresciani
San Diego State University
Editor

Anker Publishing Company, Inc.
Bolton, Massachusetts

To my father and mother, George and Helyn Ludvik, who helped me at a very early age to understand that learning takes place in many forms and that the transference of that learning requires skills and abilities that can be obtained by anyone, as long as your environment is conducive to such and as long as you have the opportunities to exercise those skills and abilities.

Assessing Student Learning in General Education
Good Practice Case Studies

ISBN 978-1-933371-20-7

Composition by Tanya Anoush Johnson
Cover design by Dutton & Sherman Design

Anker Publishing Company, Inc.
563 Main Street
P.O. Box 249
Bolton, MA 01740-0249 USA

www.ankerpub.com

Library of Congress Cataloging-in-Publication Data
Assessing student learning in general education : good practice case studies / Marilee J. Bresciani, editor.
    p. cm.
Includes bibliographical references and index.
   ISBN 978-1-933371-20-7
   1. General education—United States—Case studies. 2. General education—United States—Evaluation. I. Bresciani, Marilee J.

LC985.A88 2007
378.1'66—dc22
                                            2006100752

Table of Contents

About the Authors

The Editor

Marilee J. Bresciani has held higher education faculty and administrative positions for more than 19 years. In those positions, she has conducted enrollment management research, quantitative and qualitative institutional research, course-embedded assessment, and academic and administrative program assessment. Presently, Dr. Bresciani is associate professor of postsecondary education at San Diego State University, where she assists in students' preparation for careers in higher education. The master's and doctoral curriculum emphasizes student learning centeredness, integration of the curricular and cocurricular, and analysis, planning, and responsible practice in a socially just environment. In her previous positions as assistant vice president for institutional assessment at Texas A&M University and as director of assessment at North Carolina State University, Dr. Bresciani led university-wide initiatives to embed faculty-driven outcomes-based assessment in the day-to-day. She has led reforms in outcomes-based assessment program review, assessment of general education, quality enhancement, and cocurricular assessment.

Dr. Bresciani has been invited to present assessment workshops nationally and internationally, has a number of invited publications, and is a leading author of a book on assessing student learning and development and one on outcomes-based assessment program review. She has also developed and delivered several courses on assessment of student learning, and serves on the editorial board of the *NASPA Journal*. She is a reviewer for the Australian Quality Assurance Agency and is also a managing partner in an international assessment and enrollment management consulting firm.

Dr. Bresciani holds a Ph.D. in administration, curriculum, and instruction from the University of Nebraska and an M.A. in teaching from Hastings College.

The Contributors

Trudy W. Banta is vice chancellor for planning and institutional improvement and professor of higher education at Indiana University–Purdue University Indianapolis (IUPUI). She is a pioneer in the field of outcomes assessment in higher education, having established two centers focused on this topic, the first at the University of Tennessee and the second at IUPUI. The recipient of career achievement awards from seven national associations, Dr. Banta is the author or editor of 14 books and monographs and more than 200 articles and reports. Several of her publications focus on general education assessment. She has consulted with faculty and administrators in 46 states and addressed audiences in 18 other countries on the topic of outcomes assessment.

Susan L. Bosworth is associate provost for planning and assessment at the College of William and Mary, where she has worked extensively with faculty members and administrators to define a university-wide process of institutional effectiveness, develop a system of academic unit reviews, and integrate assessment into a broader planning model. She has been actively involved in assessment for 20 years and has presented assessment strategies and results of assessment research at regional and national conferences and for government organizations. Along with a research agenda in assessment, Dr. Bosworth studies and writes about the social responses to disasters. She has collaborated with faculty members to embed assessment and disaster research in graduate and undergraduate methods courses and independent research experiences. She earned her Ph.D. in sociology from the University of Virginia.

Paul A. Dale is vice president of learning support services at Paradise Valley Community College (PVCC). As the senior student affairs officer, he provides leadership for student development areas, learning support service areas, and learning technology services. Dr. Dale has been an administrator at PVCC since 1997, also working as vice president of student services and as associate dean of student development. From August 2003 through September 2004, he served as interim president of the college. PVCC is one of ten colleges in the Maricopa Community College District that collectively educates more than 250,000 students in the Phoenix metropolitan area.

Janice Denton is professor of chemistry in the Raymond Walters College at the University of Cincinnati, and director of the university's general education program. From 1994 to 2004, Dr. Denton chaired the Raymond Walters College assessment committee. She is recognized nationally for her work on assessment of student learning.

Mary E. Diez is dean of graduate studies at Alverno College, and former president of the American Association of Colleges for Teacher Education. She has served on the National Board for Professional Teaching Standards and is currently a member of the Board of Examiners of the National Council for the Accreditation of Teacher Education. Locally, she is vice chair of the City of Milwaukee Charter School Review Committee. She currently leads Project CALL, funded by the Joyce Foundation, which works with eight low-performing, low value-added Milwaukee public schools. Project CALL combines intensive coaching for school leaders with a focus on building capacity for effective formative assessment in the classroom. She is the 1995 winner of the Harold W. McGraw, Jr. Prize in Education.

Allen P. Dupont is director of assessment in the Division of Undergraduate Academic Programs at North Carolina State University (NCSU). In this position, Dr. Dupont coordinates and supports both undergraduate academic program review and assessment and general education assessment. Prior to joining NCSU, Dr. Dupont was director of institutional research, planning, and assessment and W. O. Duvall Professor of Business at Young Harris College.

David Eubanks is director of planning, assessment, and information services at Coker College. He earned a Ph.D. in mathematics from Southern Illinois University, and has been teaching mathematics and computer science at Coker College since 1991. His administrative duties currently include oversight for the library, information technology, and institutional research and institutional effectiveness. Visit his blog at http://highered.blogspot.com.

Teresa L. Flateby is director of university assessment at the University of South Florida (USF). She earned a B.A. at Capital University, and an M.A. and Ph.D. from USF. Dr. Flateby was director of evaluation and testing at USF for 15 years prior to her appointment as director of a new unit devoted exclusively to academic assessment. Her work in assessing writing and cognitive levels (cognitive level and quality of writing assessment) and with other institutions on how to assess learning outcomes has been published in a variety of venues. Her forthcoming book, *Assessment to Foster Effective Writing and Develop Thinking,* is a collection of studies about assessment and its linkage to improving learning outcomes.

Patricia L. Francis has served as assistant provost for university assessment and academic initiatives at SUNY System Administration since August 2004, and her major responsibilities include coordinating the SUNY Assessment Initiative for both general education assessment and assessment of academic majors. Prior to this position, Dr. Francis was executive assistant to the president and professor of psychology at SUNY Cortland, and she has also served as co-chair of SUNY's General Education Assessment Review Group since its formation in January 2001. Dr. Francis received her Ph.D. in lifespan developmental psychology from the University of Oklahoma and her B.S. and M.S. degrees in psychology from West Virginia University.

Matthew B. Fuller is assistant director of university assessment at Illinois State University (ISU). In this role, Matt supports the assessment of the ISU general education program using institutional portfolios and rubric-driven processes. He also oversees the administration of annual institutional surveys such as the Alumni Survey and the Survey of Student Engagement and consults with faculty, staff, and students on assessment methods. He received an M.S. in educational administration in student affairs administration from Texas A&M University and served as the university's program coordinator for institutional assessment. He is currently pursuing a Ph.D. in educational administration and foundations at ISU. Matt's research interests include studies in contemporary student engagement and learning issues in higher education, historiography, and meta-assessment of commonly used assessment methods.

Wayne Hall is vice provost for faculty development and professor of English and comparative literature at the University of Cincinnati. His earlier work in 19th-century Irish literature has given way to a more recent focus on the scholarship of teaching and learning.

Linda Cabe Halpern is dean of university studies at James Madison University, where she previously served as dean of general education for 10 years. She is also professor of art history and teaches art history courses in the general education program and also upper-level courses that focus on 17th- and 18th-century European art. She has published and presented on general education and on British garden design in the 18th century. She is currently a member of the Board of Directors of the American Conference of Academic Deans.

Sharon J. Hamilton is associate vice chancellor for academic affairs, associate dean of the faculties, chancellor's professor, and professor of English at Indiana University–Purdue University Indianapolis (IUPUI). As part of the Urban Universities Portfolio Project, developing the first generation of electronic institutional portfolios, she conceptualized and developed the IUPUI institutional portfolio, serving as director from 1998 to 2001. Since 2000, she has been serving as special projects director of the IUPUI Electronic Student Portfolio, which was chosen as the basis for the Open Source Portfolio Initiative 2.5 infrastructure. Her portfolio-related articles include "Snakepit in Cyberspace: The IUPUI Institutional Portfolio," "Institutional Portfolios for Quality Assurance and Accreditation" (with B. Cambridge and S. Kahn), "A Principle-Based Approach to General Education," "Enhancing Learning, Improvement, and Accountability through Electronic Portfolios" (with S. Kahn), and "Red Light Districts, Washing Machines, and Everything in Between: Constructing the IUPUI Institutional Portfolio."

Robert O'Brien Hokanson is associate professor of English and chair of Alverno College's communication ability department, which is responsible for the teaching and assessment of communication abilities in general education communication courses and across the curriculum. He has served as co-chair of the college's Council for Student Assessment, which sets policy and promotes good practice in the assessment of student learning. Dr. O'Brien Hokanson has presented at conferences on assessment, composition, and literature, and he serves as a consultant on student assessment. His publications include articles on poetry, multicultural literature, and, most recently, "Using Writing Outcomes to Enhance Teaching and

Learning: Alverno College's Experience," in *The Outcomes Book: Debate and Consensus after the WPA Outcomes Statement* (Utah State University Press, 2005).

Anne E. Huot joined the Office of the Provost at SUNY System Administration as associate provost for doctoral degree–granting institutions in February 2003 and became executive vice provost in June 2004. In that position, she has primary responsibility for the Offices of Institutional Research and Analysis, Academic Programs and Planning, Educational Opportunity Programs, and Campus and Academic Affairs, and she has played a major role in advancing the SUNY Assessment Initiative. Before joining SUNY, Dr. Huot served in several positions at the University of Vermont, including executive dean/interim dean of graduate studies, chair and professor of biomedical technologies, and director of the cell and molecular biology graduate program. Dr. Huot received her Ph.D. in cell and molecular biology and her M.S. in medical technology from the University of Vermont and her B.S. in medical technology from the University of New Hampshire.

Leslie Janac has taught English for nearly 15 years and has been teaching at Blinn College since 2001. She received a B.A. in journalism and an M.A. in English from Sam Houston State University, and a Ph.D. in English from Texas A&M University. At Blinn College, in addition to her teaching responsibilities, Dr. Janac served on the Core Curriculum Assessment Committee, which oversaw the Core Curriculum Assessment Study. Her participation in the Core Curriculum Assessment pilot study contributed to the success of the college's full implementation. In addition to her academic experience, Dr. Janac has four years' experience as an award-winning technical writer in transportation research with the Texas Transportation Institute and has served as the communications coordinator for the International Center for Aggregates Research.

Martha Marinara is co-director of the Information Fluency Initiative at the University of Central Florida (UCF), where she is an associate professor in the English department. From August 1998 until August 2006, she directed the First-year Writing Program at UCF, one of the largest programs in the country. Dr. Marinara received a B.A. in English and an M.A. in creative writing from

Southern Connecticut State University, and a Ph.D. in rhetoric from Lehigh University in 1993. She has published two textbooks and numerous articles on writing pedagogy, feminism, and queer theory. Dr. Marinara has also published poetry and fiction in notable and not so notable journals, and her first novel, *Street Angel,* was released October 31, 2006, published by Fine Tooth Press.

Marcia Mentkowski received her M.A. and Ph.D. from the University of Wisconsin–Madison in educational psychology. As professor of psychology at Alverno College, she directs the educational research and evaluation department, chairs the multidisciplinary research and evaluation council, and serves on the council for student assessment and the educational policies committee. *Learning That Lasts* (Jossey-Bass, 2000) and *Higher Education Assessment and National Goals for Education* (American Psychological Association, 1998) were named outstanding research publications by the American Educational Research Association (AERA); she has served on AERA's council and executive board. An American Psychological Association Fellow, she serves on editorial boards, has been an invited visiting scholar/fellow at Harvard (1975) and Oxford (2003), and speaks regularly at conferences on issues in learning and assessment.

Loraine Phillips is interim assessment director at Texas A&M University, where she works closely with the implementation and assessment of the university's quality enhancement plan (QEP). Dr. Phillips also assists faculty and staff with outcomes-based assessment efforts in the development of assessment plans, the identification of assessment methods, and the use of evidence for continuous improvement. Prior to her current position, Dr. Phillips served as director of program evaluation and the Southern Association of Colleges and Schools director of the QEP for Blinn College. Dr. Phillips earned her B.S. from Indiana University and her M.S. and Ph.D. from Texas A&M University with an emphasis in literacy and higher education administration.

Claudia Skutar received her doctorate in English from the University of Cincinnati in 2006. She has taught at Michigan State University and the University of Cincinnati, including introductions to creative writing and writing poetry, Shakespeare, Canadian literature, and composition. Her research areas of interest include contemporary American and British poetry, poetics theory, teaching and learning, and rhetoric and composition.

Donna L. Sundre is executive director for the Center for Assessment and Research Studies at James Madison University. She is also professor of graduate psychology and she teaches in the assessment and measurement Ph.D. program. She teaches courses such as Assessment Methods and Instrument Design, and Professional Consultation, and she supervises practica, internships, and dissertations in that program. Her research and publication areas include assessment practice, examinee motivation, instrument development, and validity issues. She is a frequent presenter in assessment and measurement topics and has consulted widely with many higher education institutions and public and private agencies.

Kristina Tollefson is assistant professor of theatre, specializing in costume and makeup design at the University of Central Florida. She holds an M.F.A. in costume design and technology from Purdue University and a B.A. from South Dakota State University in theatre and English. She serves as the undergraduate coordinator for the Department of Theatre, overseeing five undergraduate programs. She also serves as a commissioner for the Costume Design and Technology Commission of the United States Institute for Theatre Technology.

Nancy H. Womack is now retired. She served as dean of arts and sciences and chair of the assessment task force at Isothermal Community College. Having chaired the assessment task force since its inception in 1998, she helped guide the college in its development of an assessment culture. Her academic background includes a B.S. in education from Western Carolina University, an M.A. in English from the University of Central Florida, and a Ph.D. in English from the University of South Carolina–Columbia.

Foreword

Students and the public have a deep and abiding interest in what gets taught and learned in a college education. Too often, however, college is like a "black box"—walk in with what preparation and money you have, meet the requirements, and walk out with a degree, prepared for the rest of your life—or so we assume. Similarly, colleges and universities put forth noble goals for the education they provide, but then largely defer to autonomous faculty and disparate disciplines to meet these expectations—or so they hope.

Whether we ever really could, we no longer can afford sloppy thinking about the content of a college education. Knowledge and skill have become the foundation of the world economy, and rapid communications, population growth, and easy travel have made the world far more interdependent and far more fragile. Democracy, environmental sustainability, and world peace depend more than ever before on our capacity to help large numbers of people acquire the knowledge, skills, and understanding necessary for a productive, satisfying life and global citizenship. And in the United States, especially, the knowledge and skills of an authentic higher education are essential for full participation in our society. Why especially? Because Americans are the most expensive workers in the world; they have to be the best-educated people in the world or bear the risk of sustained unemployment.

In such a context, these short case studies make a real contribution. They examine the definition and assessment of collegiate-level *general education* in 13 higher education settings—12 diverse colleges and universities and 1 large multi-institution system. The editor and contributors deserve kudos; the case studies are descriptively engaging, well written and organized, and sufficiently brief and focused so as to make them valuable resources.

I hope readers will use these case studies as an opportunity to think, and think deeply, about what is taught and learned in our colleges and universities, and how institutions and faculty are organized for these purposes. Here readers will find many examples of how college-level general education needs to change, as well as good, experienced-based advice on tools or approaches available for improvement. In an era of increasing reliance on consumer information, market-based competition, and deregulation, it is particularly important to use such resources to move beyond a merely implicit understanding of what college involves. Both educators and students need more explicit criteria for making choices, allocating resources, and identifying quality.

Focusing on general education requires colleges and universities to look both inward to the core of their institutional mission and outward to the changing needs of society and the students they enroll. Of course, fundamental aspects of the human experience will always be at the core of higher education's mission. But with rapid changes in the world and the workplace, one cannot take for granted that long-standing approaches to our mission are consistent with the needs and expectations of society, nor that an institution's graduates are well prepared for the world they will face. Missions and institutional strategies must be reexamined periodically, and student outcomes must be examined continuously. Assessment of student-level general education outcomes is the lynchpin of this internal/external dynamic. To assess we must define, and in defining we are compelled to reexamine.

These 13 case studies demonstrate that significant improvements in the assessment of general education outcomes are possible. But these case studies were selected, in large part, because the institutions already are engaged in general education assessment and improvement. Further, those contributing the case studies did so because they recognized their efforts as worth writing about and conveying to others. We cannot from this collection judge how pervasive these good assessment practices are in higher education, but it is clear the public expects them to become widespread. Within the past two years three national reports, *Public Accountability for Student Learning in Higher Education* (2004) from the Business–Higher Education Forum, *Accountability for Better Results* (2005) from the National Commission on Accountability in Higher Education, and now *A Test of Leadership* (2006) from Education Secretary Spellings's Commission on the Future of Higher Education, have called for institutions to define learning goals and assess outcomes transparently in order to improve learning.

Fortunately, each of these national reports recognized that little of what these case studies demonstrate as good practice can be imposed from above. This applies whether that "above" is the federal government, state government agencies or governing boards, or institutional leadership. Top-down can easily suppress the authentic and effective bottom-up actions these case studies so clearly illustrate. But except for the volume editor's brief attention to the "context" for general education assessment, I am struck by the lack of attention to why these changes are important. Policymakers are clearly articulating the reasons and needs for a strong, well thought out general education component for college education. If faculty and campus leaders more explicitly demonstrate their understanding of the purpose and their ownership of the work, it will help assure the persistence of an appropriate division of labor.

Obviously, there is no single best way to integrate general education goals and assessments into the structure of an institution. These case studies demonstrate the value of a variety of approaches, assessment tools, and technical expertise; the complexity of the challenge requires pluralism in design along with rigor and unity of purpose. These emerging tools and strategies deserve wider adoption by those within institutions, and wider acknowledgment by those who set the policies and parameters in which higher education operates.

In the end, defining, assessing, and integrating general education has a single purpose—enhancing the knowledge and skills our students need for a satisfying, productive life. This volume is a useful tool for achieving that serious purpose.

Paul E. Lingenfelter
President, State Higher Education Executive Officers
Boulder, Colorado

Preface

Purpose

The purpose of this book is to outline case studies of good practice in the assessment of student learning in various types of delivery of general education. These case studies are intended to assist faculty and administrators in the evaluation of student learning as it relates to general education. In addition, the case studies are intended to provide readers with information about what was learned from evaluating general education and what may be avoided in the future.

The reader will note that there are several ways in which to evaluate general education. Each case study varies in its approach and each author shares some tips for implementing general education assessment as well as some challenges. While not a how-to book on engaging in general education assessment, this book is designed to give practical advice for consideration of implementation of general education assessment through the examination of each case study. Questions to guide the reader through each case study are posed in Chapter 1.

To further aid the reader, the book also contains some considerations to address when planning for general education assessment and a summary of good practice strategies for application. Strategies to consider when implementing general education within state guidelines are discussed in the final chapter.

Selection of Case Studies

Selection of the good practice case studies was based on Seymour Papert's (1991) constructionist learning philosophy. "Papert's philosophy was used in the context that those delivering the learning are learning about how to improve student learning when they evaluate the delivery of their teaching and evaluate the student learning" (Bresciani, in press). In this context, the concept of good practice emerges as those delivering the good practice engage in constructionist learning.

Good practice criteria were based on a set of criteria which emerged primarily from two key resources. The first is the *Nine Principles of Good Practice for Assessing Student Learning* (Astin et al., 1991) developed under the auspices of the former American Association for Higher Education's Assessment Forum. The second is taken from Principle 12 in the 1994 Association of American Colleges' publication, *Strong Foundations*, which outlines 12 principles for effective general education programs. Principle 12 illustrates the importance of evaluating general education. In the discussion of this principle, the authors emphasize the importance of ongoing and continuous assessment. Maki (2004) and Palomba and Banta (1999) echo the value of such a systematic review in order to refine teaching methods and curriculum in order to deliver quality student learning.

Making reference to these criteria, 23 of the most highly published assessment scholars in the United States were asked to identify institutions that they felt met these criteria in the practice of their general education assessment. A list of 23 institutions was generated and circulated to all the assessment scholars for further comment. No institutions were removed from the list and seven were added at a later date after the initial call for participation.

All institutions were asked to participate in this study. Each institution was asked to provide a 15- to 25-page case study that adhered to the following outline:

General Education Case Study Outline

I. Overview of the Institutional Culture

• Describe your institutional culture.

1) Briefly describe your institution (size, type, location).

2) What is your institution known for?

3) How is it arranged?

4) How does its special culture or peculiarities affect its view of general education?

II. Overview of the General Education Program

• Describe your general education program.

1) What is its purpose?

2) What do faculty expect to see as a result of having a general education program?

3) What are students expected to learn from general education?

4) How involved are the cocurricular professionals in the construction of the general education program?

III. Overview of Assessment of the General Education Program

• Describe your process of assessing general education.

1) How and when is general education evaluated?

2) Who is responsible for each step?

3) How flexible is the administration of the general education assessment?

4) What parts are required?

5) What can be adapted?

IV. Examples of Assessment and How Results Are Used

• Provide an example of your outcomes-based assessment process complete with outcomes, evaluation methods, criteria, observations, and decisions based on results.

V. Tips for Implementing the Process

• Based on how you construct general education and how you evaluate it, what recommendations would you make for other institutions who would want to implement your design?

1) What would you encourage them to replicate and/or adopt?

2) What would you recommend they avoid?

3) What general advice would you provide?

VI. Challenges to Assessing General Education and Strategies to Overcome Them

• Describe at least one challenge you encountered when implementing general education assessment and at least one strategy that you used to overcome that challenge. In describing this challenge, please recommend suggestions for adoption or strategies that should be avoided.

VII. References

Some good practice institutions elected not to participate in this study and others may have been inadvertently overlooked because they have not yet become known for their exemplary assessment practices in general education. I am indebted to those institutions who took the time to submit their work so that all can benefit from their current practice and the lessons they have learned in getting there.

This book is a compilation of the good practice case study submissions from those good practice institutions that elected to participate. Using grounded theory (Strauss & Corbin, 1998), I reviewed the case studies and compiled a list of recommendations to consider when implementing general education assessment. However, the reader should be cautioned that this book is not intended to be a one-size-fits-all, lockstep application of good practice. The contributing authors emphasize several points about the dangers of taking one institution's practice and trying to make it your own without tending to institutional culture and values. Thus, this book is intended to provide the reader with ideas to consider adapting to his or her own institutional culture.

This book is not intended to promote outcomes-based assessment of general education as a process established merely to sustain itself. Rather, it is intended to illustrate good practice in self-reflection that contributes to improved integration of and quality in student learning and development within general education. The process of assessing general education is not a means to its own end; rather, it is a way to systematically engage in daily critical inquiry about what works well and what needs to be improved (Maki, 2004).

Acknowledgments

I wish to acknowledge the aforementioned contributors of this book. Without their time and commitment to assessing general education and their willingness to write about it, there would be no book to help others think through the strategies the contributors have already thought through.

I would also like to acknowledge John Fackler, Matt Fuller, Martyn Gunn, Marty Loudder, Loraine Phillips, Kimberlee Pottberg, Doug Slack, Theresa Survillion, and Catherine Tonner. These fine professionals picked up the slack in the Office of Institutional Assessment at Texas A&M University so that I could enjoy the luxury of reflecting on these good practices and synthesizing the efforts of all who contributed.

In addition, I must thank my friends and family who have encouraged me to forge ahead with reflecting and writing. It would take me too long to name all those who would call with encouragement or drop me an email of understanding when I missed spending precious time with them in exchange for editing and researching. It is a wonderful gift to have people in my life who are so understanding and caring.

Finally, to all those whose good practices are not contained in this book, thank you for your commitment to student-centered learning. Your research and service, which ensures that learning is designed in a purposeful manner, that it is integrated with the discipline and the cocurricular, and that it is evaluated so that it may be improved, is indeed priceless. Thank you.

Marilee J. Bresciani
October 2006

References

Association of American Colleges. (1994). *Strong foundations: Twelve principles for effective general education programs.* Washington, DC: Author.

Astin, A. W., Banta, T. W., Cross, K. P., El-Khaswas, E., Ewell, P. T., Hutchings, P., et al. (1991). *Nine principles of good practice for assessing student learning.* Sterling, VA: Stylus.

Bresciani, M. J. (in press). *Exploring the epistemology of outcomes-based assessment.*

Maki, P. L. (2004). *Assessing for learning: Building a sustainable commitment across the institution.* Sterling, VA: Stylus.

Palomba, C. A., & Banta, T. W. (1999). *Assessment essentials: Planning, implementing, and improving assessment in higher education.* San Francisco, CA: Jossey-Bass.

Papert, S. (1991). Situating constructionism. In I. Harel & S. Papert (Eds.), *Constructionism* (pp. 1–11). Norwood, NJ: Ablex.

Strauss, A., & Corbin, J. (1998). *Basics of qualitative research: Techniques and procedures for developing grounded theory* (2nd ed.). Thousand Oaks, CA: Sage.

Chapter 1

The Challenges of Assessing General Education: Questions to Consider

Marilee J. Bresciani

The Context

Our nation has turned its eye toward conversations that concern the quality of higher education. There appears to be public confusion about what constitutes a discipline or a major and how the learning demonstrated in a degree may differ from that which is obtained through general education. Does satisfying general education requirements mean that every student, regardless of type of degree, is able to demonstrate certain skills and/or abilities? Or does it mean that every student will graduate with fundamental knowledge in broad areas? How does the learning obtained in general education differ from that gained through the discipline courses?

In addition, the question of how the out-of-classroom experience plays into this conversation causes further confusion. Does being engaged in the cocurricular mean that a student will be more liberally educated? Does the institution have to intentionally articulate the connection of the out-of-classroom learning to the in-classroom learning? Who is responsible for making the connections of learning from the curricular to the cocurricular and vice versa? How does the cocurricular contribute to general education learning goals or the institutional student learning principles?

Although these questions are not new, it seems that our ability to identify what students are learning from our general education efforts has still not been fully developed.

As regional reaccreditation agencies and national professional associations such as the Association of American Colleges and Universities (AAC&U) continue to focus on the assessment of student learning and the evaluation of core institutional learning principles, institutions desire assistance in understanding effective ways in which to evaluate student learning in general education. Furthermore, faculty need to understand how the investment in such evaluation can provide them with data to inform discussions about core learning principles in a manner that allows them to make decisions on how to improve general education offerings. While many resources exist on implementing general education, faculty need additional resources to help them discern how general education can be evaluated. This book provides faculty and administrators with needed examples of good practices in assessment for varying types of delivery of general education.

The Challenges

While many recognize the value of assessment of student learning in general education, the challenges posed by evaluating general education may still keep those who see its importance from engaging in the evaluation of it. In 1991, Hutchings, Marchese, and Wright articulately illustrated these challenges. Over a decade and a half later, these challenges remain, yet some institutions have been successful in addressing most or all of these barriers. However, apart from our learning about these success stories at conferences, many of these triumphs go untold or unnoticed by the majority of faculty and administrators seeking solutions. This book details some of these institutions' stories and outlines some of their struggles as well.

The following challenges taken from Hutchings, Marchese, and Wright (1991) are introduced with a brief explanation of each challenge and a few questions for the reader's consideration. The purpose of proposing these challenges and corresponding questions is to assist the reader with his or her own review of each case. These questions are intended to help the reader discern the application of ideas presented in each case study to his or her own institution.

In addition, specific suggestions and strategies for implementing outcomes-based assessment of general education are introduced in each case study, and overall items to consider when implementing outcomes-based assessment of general education are summarized in the final chapter.

1) Lack of Perceived Priority to Improve General Education

In an environment with increasing constraints on the economy, many ask the question of whether time spent on certain "activities" is time well invested. Leaving for just a moment the question of whether there are resources available to commit to general education assessment and/or its refinement, many faculty would rather spend time on their discipline. Therefore, investing time to improve student learning requires added incentive and understanding of its value, particularly in general education where many faculty are not at home in their own discipline expertise (Hutchings et al., 1991).

Outcomes-based assessment can help communicate the value of general education if the purpose of general education and the resulting design of the delivery of general education is well thought through and purposefully executed prior to evaluation (see number 3). In addition, the financing of general education must be clearly identified and articulated to the faculty so they can consider this in both the purpose of general education and the strategies to implement it. Furthermore, providing incentives for faculty and administrators to examine the purpose and learning value of general education is needed.

Determining the reasons for the ability of faculty and administrators to value the evaluation and refinement of student learning in general education is indeed a complex task. In order to seek clarification on your own institution, it may be helpful to answer the following questions. Many of the questions that may precede these questions are posed in item number 3; thus, for some institutions, it may be helpful to start with the questions posed there. For others, however, funding conversations drive purpose questions and it may be wise for them to begin the conversation here:

• How much is general education integrated into the requirements to achieve the discipline and integrated in the need to demonstrate competencies within the discipline?

- How much is general education integrated into the cocurricular or out-of-classroom experience?

- How is the delivery of general education funded? Is it a one-to-one student credit hour generation? If so, does the department providing the general education SCHs actually receive the money for generating the student learning in general education? If so, how do those contributing to the learning receive funding? In other words, how are dollars allocated if the learning is genuinely integrated learning? What is the funding motivation, for example, for those involved in writing across the curriculum initiatives or ethical leadership? Do they have to split one line of funding with their collaborative colleagues or do they receive equal shares as one would if one discipline was designing the learning by themselves?

- How are collaborations among faculty and across divisions and colleges funded or rewarded?

- How are faculty provided with opportunities to engage in conversation about improving general education learning, particularly since many of them are reviewed and promoted for their work within their own discipline?

- How are these faculty provided with opportunities to engage in collaborative learning with the cocurricular experts?

- Are the faculty given professional development opportunities to consider what general education should be about, how it can best be delivered within the institutional culture and context, and how it can best be evaluated so that improvements in student learning can be made?

- If faculty are provided with these professional development opportunities, how are they encouraged to allocate time to participate? How are faculty rewarded or recognized for doing so?

- Does the state or other governing body have financial expectations that compete with genuine conversations that faculty may desire to have in regard to general education? Such potentially competing expectations could be in regard to articulation agreements, progress toward degree, or limited number of credit hours within a degree. While these state or governing body requirements have their value, the requirements are often made with very little information about their contributions toward student learning. Faculty recognize this and may see these types of requirements to be in conflict with genuine learning outcomes conversations.

• Are faculty made aware of the results of outcomes-based assessment so that they can see that the results have been used to inform decisions or recommendations to improve student learning?

• Are the results and recommendations examined and/or reviewed by the faculty and administrative leadership signifying the importance of the findings and the resulting decisions?

• Are resources allocated for dissemination based on the results and recommendations or decisions of the outcomes-based assessment process?

2) Debate Over Ownership of General Education Offerings

Systematic evaluation of general education can be challenging if the ownership and delivery of general education spans varying departments (Hutchings et al., 1991). These very real turf issues, often associated with academic freedom, must be addressed in order for systematic, comprehensive assessment to occur.

When academic freedom is raised as a concern, it may be helpful to refer to the American Association of University Professors' *1940 Statement of Principles on Academic Freedom and Tenure*. This resource makes clear that it is not a violation of academic freedom for faculty to be held accountable for students' ability to achieve particular standards or principles of education, nor is it a violation for faculty to be held accountable for particular quality of student learning. Academic autonomy does not equate to academic freedom. Therefore, faculty are encouraged to break down barriers and join in the conversations that design the educational standards and learning principles for all students.

Once academic freedom concerns are addressed, what becomes a challenge, as illustrated in some of the cases within this book, is that faculty are not able to fully understand who is responsible for the delivery of general education. While faculty governing bodies may be responsible for approving what constitutes a general education course, it is sometimes confusing to faculty to know who is responsible for general education when the learning that was intended is not realized. Thus, it is extremely important for institutions to address the following questions when examining their general education:

• Who is responsible for articulating the purpose of general education?

• How does that body (the responsible body identified in bullet 1) interact with the body that articulates the overarching institutional learning principles?

• How do those bodies (the responsible body identified in bullets 1 and 2, if not the same body) interact with those who identify learning principles within the disciplines?

• How do those bodies (the responsible body identified in bullets 1, 2, and 3, if not the same bodies) interact with the body that identifies learning opportunities and outcomes in the cocurricular?

• How does each body engage with those who are responsible for delivering general education?

• How does each body engage with those who are responsible for evaluating general education?

• How do those who gather the results of student learning in general education interact with those who can make the improvements for student learning? Or inform conversations about financing general education? Or inform ideas for collaborations across departments, colleges, and divisions?

• Who is the keeper of the general education assessment plans and reports? How is that data integrated with institutional learning principles conversations and across the curriculum types of abilities and skills?

• Who is responsible for creating these opportunities for interaction and discourse around the:

  - Articulation of various outcomes

  - Design of the assessment processes

  - Gathering of evidence and interpreting of results

  - Review of results and making recommendations for improvement

  - Follow-up to ensure improvements have been made and to examine whether those improvements contributed to refined student learning

- If there are state or governing board requirements for general education attributes, do faculty feel empowered enough to have conversations about what those attributes could look like for their own students and how they would be delivered?

- Who facilitates the interaction and conversation when the state values appear to be in conflict with the faculty values for student learning within general education?

3) Clarifying the Goals of General Education

With faculty tied to discipline content and with the frequency of somewhat trendy conversations about institutional student learning principles and employers' vocal articulation of what they want every graduate to be able to know and do regardless of discipline, the purpose of general education can often be difficult to articulate (Ratcliff, Johnson, La Nasa, & Gaff, 2001). Establishment of an assessment plan can be seriously hindered if an institution is unclear about what it wants general education to accomplish.

It is important to first identify what the purpose of general education is, what the goals of it are intended to be, and then design the process for which those goals can be delivered. After the articulation of learning outcomes for general education, and the plan to deliver these outcomes, then and only then can come the ability to design the evaluation of whether those learning outcomes have been met.

In addition, it may be challenging to get faculty to consider a change in how they perceive general education. Some faculty may need to shift from focusing on the purpose of general education as students simply needing to meet specific requisites for general education—such as completing a certain number of courses or a certain number of student credit hours—to that of student learning. For example, historically in some institutions, general education may have been designed to "expose" students to other ways of thinking outside of their discipline. This kind of purpose for general education keeps faculty focused only on the delivery of general education, not on what students may be learning. Shifting the thinking from a purpose of requiring a certain number of credit hours to identifying student learning that is expected as a result of taking those credit hours may be needed before being able to evaluate student learning.

Given these challenges, some pertinent questions to consider include the following:

• What is the purpose of general education on your campus?

• How does your institutional culture contribute to the purpose of general education?

• How does your institutional mission contribute to the purpose of general education?

• How does your institutional context contribute to the purpose of general education?

• Is the purpose for general education clearly understood by all faculty, administrators, and students?

• Is the purpose for general education in the present different from how general education came into being? In other words, has the purpose of general education shifted, for example, from a faculty desire to "expose" students to various topics to that of desiring students to demonstrate competencies within their discipline via the spoken and written word? If the purpose of general education is now different from what it historically was, have you been able to engage all the necessary players in the conversations around the revised purpose? Have you planned time to build consensus?

• Are faculty and administrators in agreement as to the purpose of general education?

• Are faculty in agreement with the state or governing board as to the purpose of general education?

• How do across-the-curriculum-competency conversations play into the conversations regarding the purpose of general education?

• How do the overarching institutional student learning principles contribute to the purpose of general education?

• How does the governing board's or state's perspective of the purpose of general education contribute to the institutional faculty and administration's understanding?

• Are student learning expectations in general education only for the native students of the institution or do they also apply to transfer students?

4) Faculty and Student Disconnect Regarding Expectations for General Education

Even if an institution's faculty is clear on what they want general education to accomplish, it often remains a mystery to students (AAC&U, 2001). Students can be very helpful at evaluating their general education experience if they understand what they are supposed to learn from such an experience or if they can contribute to what that learning may look like (Mentkowski & Associates, 2000). There are multiple ways to involve students in the articulation of the purpose of general education and in the evaluation of it, and this involvement can be mutually beneficial for both faculty and students.

Sometimes, students desire different outcomes than faculty intend. Negotiating those value differences can be tricky and can therefore negatively affect the assessment process. However, in most cases, the misunderstanding may be based on unclear communication of student learning outcomes for general education, unclear connection of the general education learning outcomes to those of the institution and/or the discipline, or unclear connection of the outcomes to the way in which the learning is being delivered.

Questions to aid in the connection of expectations include the following:

- How clearly posted are the student learning outcomes for general education?

- Do students have a role in the articulation of general education student learning outcomes?

- Do students understand how that student learning is delivered and evaluated?

- Is the role of the student in the learning evaluation process made clear?

- How well articulated is the connection of general education learning outcomes to the core institutional learning principles?

- How well articulated is the connection of general education learning outcomes to the discipline outcomes?

- How well articulated is the connection of general education learning outcomes to the learning that occurs in the cocurricular?

5) Delivery or Organization of General Education and the Occasional Disconnect With General Education Goals

Many times, faculty and/or administrators expect that the general education experience will result in outcomes that are not embedded in the delivery of the general education process (Hutchings et al., 1991). For example, if administrators want students to graduate with global citizenship but deliver their general education in a course-based menu framework with no courses identified as teaching global citizenship outcomes, then a change in delivery, course design, or goals must occur prior to any assessment being implemented.

Discovering this disconnect and working toward its resolution is imperative prior to engagement in effective assessment. Often, simply mapping the delivery of your general education to the outcomes may provide you with a clear understanding of the disconnect (Maki, 2004).

Questions to aid in this self-examination include the following:

- Is the purpose for your general education clearly articulated?

- Do you have goals and outcomes that align with the purpose of general education?

- Is the way in which you deliver general education aligned with your goals and outcomes?

- Do you need different goals for different populations? For example, if you have a two-year general education program that prepares students to transfer into a four-year program, do the goals of that general education program need to differ from a general education that is based within the discipline or one that is pursued by lifelong learners?

- Can you map the delivery of your general education to your goals?

- Do you have courses, cocurricular experiences, and discipline courses mapped to the general education goals and outcomes?

- How does that mapping look when you consider transfer students?

- How does it look when you take into account articulation agreements?

6) Debate Over Knowledge Acquisition and Demonstration of Skill Within General Education or the Discipline

Similar to the previous point, some general education values can be delivered in general education as well as the discipline or cocurricular program. It is important to identify which is delivered where and how it is delivered prior to designing a meaningful general education assessment plan (Hutchings et al., 1991).

Sometimes, faculty assume that students will learn what they want them to learn out of general education without purposefully planning that learning experience and the means to evaluate it. Taking time to discuss learning expectations with all interested parties allows values to be articulated and can allow for the means in which faculty expect to see the competencies or abilities demonstrated. After faculty are able to identify what they want the general education learning to look like, they are able to determine where it is being delivered and to discuss the means to evaluate it.

Ask yourself the following questions:

• Do we want general education to be about our ability to identify transferable skills and abilities across the disciplines and through the cocurricular?

• Or do we want general education to be based on competencies or constructs demonstrated within a variety of disciplines for each undergraduate?

• Regardless of what we choose, even if we choose both, how are we ensuring that students are taught what we want them to know?

• How do we ensure the mapping of the learning experiences to the learning outcomes, regardless of whether they are competencies or abilities?

• How do we then go about evaluating that learning?

7) Establishing an Assessment Plan That Will Lead to the Improvement of General Education Offerings

Many institutions quickly adopt surveys or competency exams in an effort to demonstrate that they are engaged in assessment of general education (Forrest & Associates, 1990). While these methods may prove beneficial, implementing them without consideration as to whether informative findings will be generated may be destructive to future initiatives to improve student learning.

The use of results must be considered by institutions so that they can plan the most meaningful assessment of the student learning.

Results gathered in a manner that does not allow for areas of improvement to be made in the delivery of general education may be meaningful to some; however, it may also result in frustration to faculty when they are unable to identify opportunities to improve student learning based on the assessment results.

Furthermore, faculty may be hesitant to engage in general education assessment, particularly course-embedded assessment, if they believe that poor results will be factored into their teaching evaluations. Rather, poor results of student learning, if gathered with enough detail, may help provide professional development opportunities to faculty or help faculty better align evaluation materials to course planning and to intended learning outcomes.

Questions to consider include:

• How do administrators plan to use the results of general education assessment?

• How do faculty plan to use the results?

• Will faculty be assured that the results will not be used for personnel evaluations? Rather, will the results inform professional development opportunities?

• Who will see the results?

• Who will interpret them?

• Who will be involved in making recommendations or decisions based on the results?

• Is there a commitment to continuous improvement? Or is the institution only interested in gathering results for some sort of compliance initiative?

• What kind of requirements for comparability of data are there? How can those requirements be factored into the faculty and administrators' desires to improve student learning?

• What conversations need to take place to determine which results will be most meaningful to whom?

• How transparent will the results be to the public?

- Do faculty feel that their jobs are in jeopardy due to findings from the assessment of student learning?

- Do faculty feel that the funding of their program is in jeopardy due to findings from the assessment of student learning?

- Who will be involved in interpreting the results and making decisions for improving the course or design of general education?

- What role do each of the administrators, faculty, and students play in gathering, interpreting, and making decisions based on the results?

- How collaborative will the process be?

8) Debate Over General Education's Role in the Establishment of Institutional Undergraduate Learning Principles

Does general education contribute to the establishment of core institutional learning values? Can those core principles be delivered entirely within the discipline or will it be a combination of the discipline and general education (AAC&U, 2002)? Effective planning of curriculum and implementation of outcomes-based assessment can help address these questions and provide evidence for future decisions.

Some faculty and administrators are simply not clear about how their general education contributes to their core student learning principles. In other words, when institutions want their students to be able to demonstrate certain skills and competencies regardless of the students' major, are these skills and competencies to be delivered and evaluated in the general education, the discipline, the cocurricular, or a combination of all of these areas?

Building on the previously posed category questions, additional questions include the following:

- If your institution has goals for general education, but has not considered establishing student learning outcomes for the entire institution, how can they proceed to do so?

- How then will those conversations or the results of those conversations be coordinated?

- How will the results of the conversation affect the design of general education and its evaluation?

• How will the results of the conversation contribute to informing statewide conversation or governing board conversations where expectations may be in conflict?

9) Identifying and Clarifying the Role of Cocurricular in the Delivery and Evaluation of General Education

Many posit that learning occurs outside the classroom as well as within (American College Personnel Association, 1996; Kuh, Kinzie, Schuh, Whitt, & Associates, 2005; Mentkowski & Associates, 2000). The type of learning that transcends the classroom may very well be contributing to general education goals but without assessment, these types of conversations cannot be verified.

Furthermore, without an acknowledgment or commitment to have the cocurricular world brought into this conversation, opportunities to create and evaluate learning may be lost. Collaborations are imperative in order for these types of integration to occur.

Again, building on previously posed questions, the following may also be helpful to those seeking to engage in these types of integrated learning opportunities:

• How do cocurricular and curricular conversations occur on your campus?

• How are opportunities to promote these conversations introduced? Enhanced? Leveraged?

• Are there opportunities for integrated and collaborative learning?

• Do all departments (administrative and academic) understand how they contribute to the general education student learning outcomes?

• Are they evaluating how well they do?

References

American Association of University Professors. (1940). *1940 statement of principles on academic freedom and tenure.* Retrieved December 5, 2006, from www.aaup2.org/statements/Redbook/1940stat.htm

American College Personnel Association. (1996, March/April). The student learning imperative [Special issue]. *Journal of College Student Development, 37*(2).

Association of American Colleges and Universities. (2001). General education in the new academy. *Peer Review,* 5(4). Washington, DC: Author.

Association of American Colleges and Universities. (2002). *Greater expectations: A new vision for learning as a nation goes to college.* Washington, DC: Author.

Forrest, A., & Associates. (1990). *Time will tell: Portfolio-assisted assessment of general education.* Sterling, VA: Stylus.

Hutchings, P., Marchese, T., & Wright, B. (1991). *Using assessment to strengthen general education.* Sterling, VA: Stylus.

Kuh, G. D., Kinzie, J., Schuh, J. H., Whitt, E. J., & Associates (2005). *Student success in college: Creating conditions that matter.* San Francisco, CA: Jossey-Bass.

Maki, P. L. (2004). *Assessing for learning: Building a sustainable commitment across the institution.* Sterling, VA: Stylus.

Mentkowski, M., & Associates. (2000). *Learning that lasts: Integrating learning, development, and performance in college and beyond.* San Francisco, CA: Jossey-Bass.

Ratcliff, J. L., Johnson, D. K., La Nasa, S. M., & Gaff, J. G. (2001). *The status of general education in the year 2000: Summary of a national survey.* Washington, DC: Association of American Colleges and Universities.

Chapter 2

Alverno College:
General Education Case Study

Mary E. Diez, Robert O'Brien Hokanson,
Marcia Mentkowski

Overview of the Institutional Culture

Alverno College is an accredited, independent institution of higher education in Milwaukee, Wisconsin. Alverno offers a four-year liberal arts curriculum leading to bachelor of arts and bachelor of science degrees for women. Three graduate programs, the master of arts in education, the master of science in nursing, and the master of business administration, are available to men and women. In fall 2006 the student body numbered 2,480, with a full-time equivalent enrollment of 2,132. The student body is highly diverse (35% minority) and most commute to campus for their classes.

Alverno is known for its ability-based curriculum, its use of performance assessment across the curriculum, and its focus on self assessment. The distinctive feature of our ability-based approach is that the faculty at Alverno make explicit the expectation that students should be able to do something with what they know. Therefore, as students master content knowledge, they simultaneously hone the abilities related to that content, for example, developing critical thinking processes central to the disciplines, expressing their understanding of content in writing, and using frameworks from disciplines to guide problem-solving efforts. Classroom-based performance assessment is the primary vehicle for bringing content and ability together, and students complete literally hundreds of assessments in the course of their undergraduate programs. The faculty see self assessment as critical to a student's growth and have developed a model of self assessment that includes four components: the ability to observe oneself in action, analyze one's work, judge its quality, and plan for the next stage of growth.

Because of our dual focus on content and ability, the college faculty work in a matrix organization. Faculty are hired into disciplinary and professional departments and divisions and participate in teaching, assessment, curriculum development, advising, research, and service to the community. Most are also members of interdisciplinary ability departments, which serve the research and development function related to the abilities. For example, members of the social interaction department recently completed a three-year study of intercultural communicative competence, applying their interdisciplinary research in a revised set of outcomes for the ability and providing professional development workshops for faculty teaching for the ability in general education courses.

Our focus on ability-based education, performance assessment, and self assessment guides our approach to general education. Together, the content areas addressed in general education (history, English, philosophy, religious studies, arts, sciences, mathematics, psychology, and social science) and the eight abilities (communication, analysis, problem solving, valuing in decision-making, social interaction, developing a global perspective, effective citizenship, and aesthetic engagement) constitute a broad base of general knowledge that also becomes the foundation upon which a student builds the specialized knowledge associated with her major and support area. Through the performance assessments integral to general education courses and a set of assessments external to their courses, students are required to do something with what they know. Students receive extensive feedback from faculty, and they use the same criteria for their performances as faculty use to learn to self assess. Across general education and in their areas of specialization, students grow in sophistication in self assessment, using performance assessment to fuel their learning.

Our culture is marked by a collaborative style of inquiry and by a commitment to ongoing quality improvement and innovation. Because faculty work both in content area departments and in interdisciplinary groups focused on abilities, they approach curriculum as coherent and intersecting. Faculty and students are aware that, because all disciplines develop organizing principles and frameworks, their approaches to analytic thinking vary—even as they have similarities. Interaction across faculty, then, is a process that enriches their understanding and deepens their awareness of the connections between courses in general education.

Faculty use assessment information for multiple purposes—to gauge student mastery, to respond to student learning needs, to improve their teaching, and, with their colleagues, to develop and refine curriculum. Assessment information, therefore, is a key part of the quality improvement practice across the institution.

Overview of the General Education Program

In Alverno's general education program, students master the eight abilities that form the core of the college's ability-based education: communication, analysis, problem solving, valuing in decision-making, social interaction, developing a global perspective, effective citizenship, and aesthetic engagement. Through these abilities, contextualized by and integrated into disciplinary content, students demonstrate that they are able to do something with the knowledge they are learning in the arts, humanities, and the natural and behavioral sciences. Thus, knowledge and the abilities to apply it are learned simultaneously, one reinforcing the other. This broad base of knowledge and ability also serves as the foundation for the specialized knowledge and advanced abilities associated with the student's major.

In an effort to make these eight abilities teachable, we have articulated each one as a series of generic developmental levels corresponding to student progress across her college career, from beginning through intermediate levels in general education to advanced performance in the major. For each level of ability we have developed criteria for the ability being performed. These criteria provide students with a tangible goal for learning, and they give faculty across the curriculum a standard for judging and certifying demonstration of the ability. Faculty members who teach general education courses therefore use the college criteria for abilities at the beginning through intermediate levels to help shape the learning outcomes for their courses as well as the performance criteria for the classroom-based assessments they use.

While a student's general education continues throughout college, at Alverno it is concentrated in the first two years, where students develop and demonstrate the eight abilities through the intermediate level required of all graduates. Introductory courses in the arts and humanities both explore the ideas and viewpoints that have shaped history, literature, philosophy, religion, and the visual and performing arts and within that process develop students' communication, analysis, valuing, global perspectives, and aesthetic engagement abilities. Similarly, introductory courses in the sciences both advance students' understanding of key concepts in the behavioral, natural, and social sciences and help students develop communication, analysis, problem solving, social interaction, and effective citizenship abilities. Quantitative literacy and communication abilities are further reinforced by required courses in these areas, and all students take a course on citizenship in a global community as part of their general education. The distribution of learning and assessment opportunities among all general education courses as well as in the introductory courses in the majors assures students of multiple opportunities to demonstrate the eight abilities through the intermediate level required of all graduates. Each course beyond the introductory level carries ability prerequisites as part of course prerequisites, so students are also assured of taking courses when they are prepared to demonstrate the ability and level associated with the course.

Alverno faculty members have articulated their expectations for student learning and the development of abilities through general education in a variety of ways. In addition to the developmental levels of the abilities and the courses just described, faculty members have drafted outcome statements for general education that attempt to capture the combination of knowledge and ability we expect students to demonstrate. One version of these outcomes includes:

- Creatively applying and integrating the processes by which various liberal arts, behavioral, and natural sciences create expressions of human experience and knowledge

- Purposefully engaging varied perspectives and modes of inquiry in creating expressions of human experience

- Responsibly functioning as a global citizen and exercising appropriate leadership within various cultures and communities

• Critically analyzing and evaluating the effects of dynamic natural environments, cultural contexts, and technology

• Advocating for appropriate actions regarding events, issues, and ideas

Faculty members have also collaborated on creating a framework for the development of student self assessment, which aims to promote learning that is both active and reflective. This framework identifies four components of effective self assessment—the ability to observe oneself in action, analyze one's work, judge its quality, and plan for future improvement—and describes the characteristics faculty members expect to see in beginning, intermediate, and advanced performance.

Alverno's cocurriculum broadens students' general education experience beyond the classroom. Participating in a student organization, sports team, or a discussion group at the campus coffeehouse gives students the chance to develop and use the eight abilities that distinguish general education at Alverno. Cocurricular professionals also collaborate with faculty in the design and implementation of initiatives that enrich general education, such as events related to the first-year experience and the college's annual Community Day, when classes are suspended and students, staff, and faculty work together on community service projects.

Overview of Assessment of the General Education Program

There are really two senses in which one might talk about the assessment of general education at Alverno College. The first is the assessment of individual students with regard to the outcomes for general education; the second is the assessment of how well general education is working. At Alverno, we focus first on the assessment of individual students—to gauge mastery and to respond to their learning needs. Individual faculty members attend to the patterns of performance within classes to improve our teaching. And, because transfer of learning is important to us, we also attend to patterns of student performance across courses and in a set of external assessments that are part of general education. Using data from all these sources, we collaboratively develop and refine curriculum in response to the assessment of general education.

As described earlier, general education involves students in developing the eight abilities, contextualized by and integrated into disciplinary content. We define an *ability* as a complex combination of knowledge, skills, attitudes, values, and dispositions. The faculty, working in discipline and professional departments, identify which abilities capture the knowledge and skills integral to a course, whether in general education or in the major/support area. As an example, most courses address the ability of *analysis*, because it is so tightly tied to the ways in which the disciplines approach their content. But not all courses would address the ability we call *valuing in decision-making*, only those for which a focus on questions of values and ethical perspectives is a central issue.

Students are required to complete assessments within general education courses, and their successful demonstration of abilities, integrated and contextualized by content in these courses, is recorded by the registrar. Faculty are responsible for providing the assessment prompts and giving feedback to students, as well as for mining assessment results in order to improve teaching and learning and/or making adjustments to course design. The constant that provides stability within the flexibility of such an approach is the set of generic criteria articulated in terms of developmental levels for each of the abilities.

Because the abilities cut across courses, both the student and the faculty member are able to see her progress through the recording of the abilities she has demonstrated in the context of specific content. Alverno uses a system of recording that provides a picture of student success in demonstrating abilities within courses (the patterns of a class's performance in, say, Integrated Science I) and across courses for students (the patterns of a student's demonstration of her *analysis* ability across her general education coursework in a given semester, for example).

In addition to in-class assessments of the abilities in the context of the course content, students' general education is also assessed through external assessments taken at particular points in the student's program. External assessments provide a way to see how students, who have developed abilities across several courses and who have been assessed in particular content areas in relationship to the abilities, can demonstrate learning that transfers to new situations. Through external assessment, the student is required to integrate knowledge and abilities across courses and over time to demonstrate the outcomes being assessed. In external assessments, the assessment design, performance, and feedback help the student broaden her perspective beyond the immediate assessment context to consider future roles in the discipline, profession, and personal/ civic life.

External assessments are designed by teams of faculty and implemented through the Assessment Center, which organizes the assessment experience and manages the team of external assessors (which may include both faculty and trained community volunteers). The assessor role is to judge a self-contained performance based on public criteria for a student not in the assessor's own class. The assessor is expected to make judgments independently, without reference to the student's past performance.

External assessments illuminate differences as well as commonalities in student performance for improving student learning and strengthening the institution. The results of external assessments enable multidisciplinary observation, analysis, and interpretation of unique, individual differences, as well as developmental patterns in student performance(s). External assessments are also a resource for faculty consideration of the common understanding and application of criteria related to Alverno's eight abilities. The practice of external assessment provides a means of continually examining the validity of Alverno's educational assumptions, learning principles, and curriculum effectiveness by analyzing results of student performances on these assessments.

Adaptations of the assessment of general education occur in two ways. First, the generic criteria for the levels of the eight abilities are always refined and clarified in the context of the content of the course in which the specific ability is integrated. Because students participate in multiple demonstrations of the abilities across courses, they have multiple opportunities to learn and demonstrate their learning.

Second, the design of the external assessments also allows for adaptation over time. For example, in a mid-program external assessment the college is implementing an iterative inquiry process for examining student learning in general education in semesters 1 through 5 of course sequences. Through dialogues across the college, as a collective faculty and staff, we are identifying important questions about student learning in general education. Dialogues are occurring in discipline departments, in ability departments, among faculty who teach general education, and with staff involved in cocurricular activities. The Council for Student Assessment is responsible for facilitating this process and articulating the most pressing question(s) that emerges in the dialogues. The mid-program external assessment is then redesigned or adapted to address the question and another round of dialogues will be undertaken, involving faculty who teach specific general education and discipline courses that are related to the question. The educational research and evaluation department staff will also participate in designing the external assessment and identifying approaches for sampling and analyzing student performance data.

Examples of Assessment and How Results Are Used

Assessment of general education at Alverno is inextricably linked to the college's basic educational principles and its outcome-based curriculum. As noted previously, when we talk about assessment of general education at Alverno, we first think of the assessment of individual student performance with regard to outcomes for general education. Our assessment of how well general education is working as a program is therefore grounded in our observations of individual student demonstration of knowledge and abilities in the courses and external assessments that comprise our curriculum. For us, in its broadest sense, assessment means evaluating student learning outcomes on the basis of criteria for the sake of improvement and accountability. When applied to individual student learning, assessment means a process that involves observation, analysis/interpretation, and judgment of each student's performance on the basis of explicit, public criteria with resulting feedback to the student. In the context of general education, then, faculty use the information about individual students' demonstration of knowledge and abilities they gain from course-based and external assessments to refine pedagogy, improve curriculum, and (re)shape the general education program to better meet student learning needs.

What, then, does assessment of general education look like at Alverno? At perhaps the simplest yet most profound level, it means faculty members pay attention to student performance and are prepared to learn from it. This means, for example, that when an English professor notices that the students in her introductory literature course are struggling to do the kind of literary analysis that demonstrates a beginning understanding of the discipline and meets the college criteria for analysis as an ability, she revises her class schedule to devote more time to practicing the analytical steps involved in the process. Broader structural changes in curriculum and the general education program have also resulted from faculty members' expert observation of and judgment about patterns in student performance. Some 10 years ago, faculty members noticed that our approach to teaching communication abilities as discrete modes of performance via separate courses or "labs" in listening, reading, speaking, and writing skills was no longer working for our students. Faculty with a commitment to and expertise in the teaching and learning of communication (from what we call our communication ability department) led a group of faculty from across the disciplines in a major redesign of this component of the general education curriculum. The result was a sequence of integrated communication seminars that take a more thorough and comprehensive approach to communication abilities, helping students make connections among the various modes of communication rather than seeing them as discrete skills.

In addition to assessment based on direct, sometimes informal, faculty observation of patterns in student performance, Alverno has a number of structures and processes in place that contribute to the assessment of general education. The college's educational research and evaluation department collaborates with discipline and ability departments on program assessment in relation to general education as well as the major fields of study. For example, educational research and evaluation researchers recently worked with faculty from the effective citizenship and developing a global perspective ability departments to improve student performance in a general education course and related external assessment focusing on these abilities. Based on a review of student performance data, changes were made in both the course and external assessment, which involve learning about and developing informed perspectives on current issues in public policy. The course now offers students more opportunities to practice using the combination of knowledge and abilities required for the assessment, and the focus of external assessment was broadened to offer students the opportunity to draw on a wider pool of knowledge from the course.

The college's Research and Evaluation Council, which provides direction for program and institutional assessment, and the Council for Student Assessment, which provides direction for student assessment, also contribute to the assessment of general education on an ongoing basis. In recent years, for example, the faculty, staff, and administrators who serve on these policymaking groups have explored how we can continue to improve the ways we help our students become more reflective, self-aware learners. The ability to self assess one's own performance and development as a learner is a key general education outcome at Alverno, and members of the Council for Student Assessment have taken the lead in developing the college's Framework for the Development of Student Self Assessment. The picture of effective self assessment this framework provides, particularly at the beginning and intermediate levels, was shaped in large part by what we observed in student performance in general education, and the framework now serves as a benchmark for general education faculty to use in their approach to teaching self assessment skills. Members of the Council for Student Assessment and the Research and Evaluation Council have also collaborated in the review of a general education external assessment that prompts students to analyze their own development and set goals for future learning. Student performance data from this external assessment has in turn informed the development of a more comprehensive process for examining student learning in general education as described earlier.

Tips for Implementing the Process

Based on our experience at Alverno, we recommend that other higher education institutions develop general education as a coherent program leading to clear learning outcomes; that faculty across disciplines work together both to identify the learning outcomes and to develop meaningful in-class and external assessments of those outcomes; that in-class assessments support student learning as well as the improvement of teaching; that external assessments be designed by teams of faculty; and that general education learning outcomes be evaluated in an ongoing way, with results fed back into the design of the program.

Of particular assistance to our development of general education has been the development of cross-disciplinary faculty departments responsible for the eight abilities, as well as committees focused on experiential learning, the integration of technology, and internationalizing the curriculum. These departments meet on a regular basis and serve as think tanks for curriculum development and assessment design; they also provide ongoing professional development workshops for the faculty at large. When faculty work together across disciplines, they create a common language about student learning outcomes that all faculty can share.

We recommend avoiding general education as simply a collection of courses, without looking at the learning outcomes to be achieved in and throughout those courses. We also caution against using assessments of general education that are not connected to the learning outcomes of the courses within general education. As general advice, we recommend that faculty and staff responsible for cocurricular activities communicate in an ongoing way to assure that the learning outcomes for general education are supported and reinforced by student experiences with cocurricular activities.

Challenges to Assessing General Education and Strategies to Overcome Them

One challenge for us in implementing general education assessment has been assuring coherence in that assessment. We can address two strategies that we have used to overcome that challenge.

In assuring coherence, the most helpful strategy has been the development of common generic criteria for the levels of the eight abilities. Faculty use these criteria in the development of course-specific criteria for performance of course outcomes. Thus, as we assess across general education for student communication ability in reading, writing, listening, speaking, and quantitative literacy, for example, these communication abilities are contextualized by and integrated into disciplinary content. And yet we are also able to look across general education courses to track how students are demonstrating communication abilities as they progress through the general education curriculum.

An underlying strategy for assuring coherence in the curriculum is the development of cross-disciplinary faculty departments responsible for the eight abilities described in the previous section. These groups work on refining the meaning of the abilities and the student learning outcomes related to each, resulting in the common generic criteria for each level of a given ability. The cross-disciplinary groups also provide additional written resources, consultations, and professional development workshops that support faculty in their contextualization and integration of the abilities in general education course outcomes and assessments.

Chapter 3

Blinn College:
General Education Case Study

Loraine Phillips, Leslie Janac

Overview of the Institutional Culture

Blinn College is a public community college located in Brenham, Texas, with satellite campuses in Bryan, Schulenburg, and Sealy. The service area, as designated by the state legislature, consists of 13 counties in central Texas.

Founded in 1883 as the private Mission Institute for the purpose of training young men for the ministry, the school became coeducational in 1888. In 1889, the institution was renamed Blinn Memorial College in recognition of the substantial gifts and support from the Reverend Christian Blinn from New York. Over the next decades, the school developed into an academy offering a variety of academic and business courses, music programs, athletics, and residence halls. The institution was reorganized into a private junior college in 1927, and in 1937, the voters of Washington County created Blinn College, the Junior College District of Washington County, making it the first county-owned public junior college district in Texas.

By fall 2005, total enrollment for Blinn College was 14,360, including 2,328 students on the Brenham campus, 10,537 at Bryan, 329 at Schulenburg, 66 at Sealy, 937 high school dual-credit students, and 163 incarcerated students. The college's transfer rate is among the highest in the state.

The four Blinn College campuses offer distinct environments to their students. The Brenham campus is a residential college in a

small city with a population of 13,500. In addition to academic
transfer and technical courses, the campus offers such opportunities
as competitive athletic programs for men and women, performing
arts, and agriculture programs. The Brazos County campuses in
Bryan serve commuter students in a larger university community
with a population of 152,000. These campus's sizes and locations
allow them to offer extensive programs in academic transfer and
technical and workforce education, including numerous allied
health programs. The Schulenburg campus is located in a town with
a population of 2,800. This small commuter campus is expanding
its course offerings in response to demonstrated student needs. The
Sealy campus opened in spring 2005 and serves primarily dual-credit
students.

Overall, Blinn College, the 11th largest community college in
the state, is best known for being the first county-owned community
college in the state of Texas and having the highest transfer rate
among the state's 50 community colleges.

Overview of the General Education Program

In light of Blinn College having the highest transfer rate in the state,
the college's core curriculum is critical to accomplishing its institutional mission. As a community college, Blinn's core curriculum has
four important purposes:

1) The 42-hour core curriculum is used for students seeking associate of arts degrees and associate of science degrees.

2) A 15-hour core curriculum, which has as its selections the same
   courses in the larger 42-hour core, is used in the technical education degree programs that award associate of applied science
   degrees.

3) Students in the dual-credit high school program take core curriculum courses. This program focuses on the core.

4) The college offers a 42-hour core curriculum certificate that
   allows students to transfer the 42-hour core curriculum as a block
   to any public state university where the students are accepted.

When faculty members heard the call from the state to assess
the core curriculum, the first step in the process had been completed.

Due to the critical transfer mission of the institution, a 42-hour core curriculum was already well established. To assist institutions in reviewing their core curricula, the state's higher education coordinating board published a document in April 1998 titled *Core Curriculum: Assumptions and Defining Characteristics.* Upon review of that document by the Core Curriculum Assessment Committee, faculty agreed that the six identified intellectual competencies were, on the whole, important to student learning at Blinn College. Those six intellectual competencies are reading, writing, speaking, listening, critical thinking, and computer literacy.

As faculty and the Core Curriculum Assessment Committee began to consider assessing the core curriculum, the need for establishing and/or reviewing student learning outcomes in core curriculum courses was evident. For example, once various disciplines, including fine arts, humanities, mathematics, natural science, and social science, began to determine and document on a matrix which core curriculum courses encompassed the intellectual competencies, they realized the need for an ad hoc committee, which was created by the administration, to revisit the template for master course syllabi. The purpose of this ad hoc committee to review the template for master course syllabi included the need to incorporate appropriate intellectual competencies into the syllabus and to review and refine established student learning outcomes in core curriculum courses. Upon completion of this ad hoc committee's work, a statement of expected student learning outcomes for courses was included in the faculty handbook and was standard operating procedure for all divisions and the Curriculum Committee's work.

In addition, the ad hoc committee asked that all core curriculum courses be reviewed to determine the extent to which each core curriculum course aligned with the exemplary educational objectives listed in *Core Curriculum: Assumptions and Defining Characteristics.* Once the matrix was developed and approved by various faculty and administrative councils, such as the Curriculum Committee, the Core Curriculum Assessment Committee, the Council of Division Chairs, and Academic Affairs, all core curriculum courses were reviewed and updated with the new information. This process was key in setting a means of establishing and refining course-based student learning outcomes within the core curriculum that took into account the six intellectual competencies adopted from the Texas Higher Education Coordinating Board.

The college believed that the six intellectual competencies of reading, writing, speaking, listening, critical thinking, and computer literacy were expected to be developed by the end of students' core curriculum experience at the institution. The Curriculum Committee, the Core Curriculum Assessment Committee, and the college at large agreed with the Texas Higher Education Coordinating Board (2005, pp. 221–222) regarding the following:

> **Reading:** Reading at the college level means the ability to analyze and interpret a variety of printed materials—books, articles, and documents. A core curriculum should offer students the opportunity to master both general methods of analyzing printed materials and specific methods for analyzing the subject matter of individual disciplines.

> **Writing:** Competency in writing is the ability to produce clear, correct, and coherent prose adapted to purpose, occasion, and audience. Although correct grammar, spelling, and punctuation are each a sine qua non in any composition, they do not automatically ensure that the composition itself makes sense or that the writer has much of anything to say. Students need to be familiar with the writing process including how to discover a topic and how to develop and organize it, and how to phrase it effectively for their audience. These abilities can be acquired only through practice and reflection.

> **Speaking:** Competency in speaking is the ability to communicate orally in clear, coherent, and persuasive language appropriate to purpose, occasion, and audience. Developing this competency includes acquiring poise and developing control of the language through experience in making presentations to small groups, to large groups, and through the media.

Listening: Listening at the college level means the ability to analyze and interpret various forms of spoken communication.

Critical Thinking: Critical thinking embraces methods for applying both qualitative and quantitative skills analytically and creatively to subject matter in order to evaluate arguments and to construct alternative strategies. Problem solving is one of the applications of critical thinking, used to address an identified task.

Computer Literacy: Computer literacy at the college level means the ability to use computer-based technology in communicating, solving problems, and acquiring information. Core-educated students should have an understanding of the limits, problems, and possibilities associated with the use of technology, and should have the tools necessary to evaluate and learn new technologies as they become available.

More specifically, Exemplary Educational Objectives and Perspectives were further articulated to students in the college's catalog and master course syllabi so that students could identify what was expected of them.

The process involved in reviewing core courses to determine how closely they aligned with the exemplary educational objectives set by the coordinating board is essentially the same process and includes the same agencies involved in all changes made to the college's core curriculum. All courses in the core curriculum are developed through the following process, as set forth in the Blinn College Faculty Handbook (2004):

1) A faculty committee develops a course using the New Course Proposal Form and the Guideline to Developing Master Course Syllabi;

2) The proposed course is reviewed and approved by the program coordinator and division chairs;

3) The proposed course is submitted to the curriculum committee for consideration and approval;

4) The approved course is sent to the office of Vice President Academic Affairs for inclusion into the catalog and master course inventory.

Core curriculum courses in communications, mathematics, natural science, social and behavioral science, humanities, and fine arts must also identify all appropriate core curriculum perspectives as defined by *Core Curriculum: Assumptions and Defining Characteristics.*

The learning outcomes for each course in the core curriculum are identified by the faculty who teach the courses, and the educational objectives and intellectual competencies are detailed along with the means for measuring the achievement of these competencies and objectives. The Curriculum Committee will not recommend a course be included in the established core curriculum without the completion of the Core Curriculum Intellectual Competencies Form.

Overview of Assessment of the General Education Program

Table 3.1 illustrates the implementation phases of core curriculum assessment at Blinn College.

In 2001, Blinn College began an intensive review of all courses in the core curriculum. Initially, the focus of this review was to ascertain the extent to which each element of the intellectual competencies was represented throughout the core curriculum. The first step in the process was to carefully review the master course syllabus in each core course to determine which elements were being met and which could be reasonably added. By focusing on the strengths of each discipline and concentrating appropriate elements in logical and rational courses, the core would be more centered and, ultimately, stronger.

The first phase of the process involved designing matrices to illustrate and track which courses incorporated which intellectual competencies. Division chairs and all faculty members in each core component area reached consensus on the inclusion of the appropriate intellectual competencies in all core courses, regardless of teaching site or modality.

Table 3.1
Blinn College Core Curriculum Assessment:
Phases of Implementation

Phase 1	Phase 2	Phase 3
Fall 2001	Spring 2002	Fall 2002
Identify the intellectual competencies within the core curriculum and revise the master course syllabi format	For each course in the core curriculum, identify strategies and methods of measure for the intellectual competencies	Pilot test the model for collecting and analyzing student learning outcomes

Phase 4	Phase 5	Phase 6
Spring 2003	Fall 2004	Annual
Conduct first full implementation of core curriculum assessment	Document the use of results for improving educational programs	Process review by the Core Curriculum Assessment Committee and the Curriculum Committee

The division chairs and the teaching faculty for each core course then met to determine the strategies used to deliver appropriate student learning outcomes and the methods of measure to be used for each strategy. Additional discussion led to the premise that multiple assessment methods should be defined so as not to impose undue restrictions on faculty appraisal of student performance.

In the fall 2002 semester, the college launched the third phase of its core curriculum assessment, the pilot evaluation process, in which 12 English classes taught by full-time faculty members were selected to gather data on the level at which students mastered the intellectual competencies listed on the assessment form for each respective course. For each method of measure, artifacts of student work were collected to analyze the levels of achievement.

The pilot study focused on the following English courses:

• English 1301: Composition and Rhetoric

- English 1302: Composition and Introduction to Literature
- English 2307: Introduction to Creative Writing Prose
- English 2311: Technical Writing
- English 2322: Survey British Literature I
- English 2327: Survey American Literature I

Four full-time faculty (two each from the Brenham and Bryan campuses) were assigned to collect data for two sections of each course. The data collected included the matrices and identified the competencies taught in the course, the strategies used to deliver appropriate student learning outcomes, and the methods of measure to be used for each strategy along with the results (the number of students achieving 70% [C] or higher in the competency measured), as well as student artifacts collected by each instructor.

Samples of high, medium, and low quality of student artifacts were selected for each strategy used in the specific course. For example, faculty members teaching English 2311: Technical Writing can use a 20-page formal report to measure computer literacy and critical thinking skills.

The pilot study allowed the college to identify potential challenges with the assessment process that could be refined prior to launching the college-wide study in spring 2003. For example, due to the time-intensive aspects of the process and the large number of course sections for many of the core curriculum courses across all campuses, a plan was needed to manage the process while still collecting meaningful information for the assessment. The Core Curriculum Committee determined that including 20% of all core course sections from all campuses would provide an accurate representation of how the intellectual competencies were being achieved on a college-wide basis but still allow the study to be conducted in a manageable fashion.

Other issues that were resolved following the pilot study included the Core Curriculum Assessment Committee's decision to document the number of students enrolled in the course at the end of the semester, instead of the number of students enrolled on the official 12th-day roster, and to include both part-time and full-time faculty in the assessment, since community colleges often employ a large number of part-time faculty. It was determined that this would give a more accurate picture of the quality of student learning across the institution's core curriculum by including both faculty groups.

With these issues resolved, the college launched full core curriculum assessment in the spring semester of 2003. Each division chair determines the number of sections of each core course being taught each semester and identifies 20% of those sections to participate in core curriculum assessment. The selected faculty members often participate in a division meeting at the beginning of each semester in order to clarify the assessment procedures with their division chair and ensure what is expected.

Faculty choose a method of measure from the identified choices to measure a class's performance on a given strategy and competency. For example, Figure 3.1 presents a sample of the English 2311: Technical Writing matrix. The intellectual competencies of reading, writing, speaking, listening, critical thinking, and computer literacy have been further broken down into strategies. For example, the writing competency for English 2311 is defined as "the ability to produce clear, correct, and coherent prose adapted to purpose, occasion, and audience-above 12th grade level." This competency is measured through the strategies 1) "produce short professional-level documents," 2) "demonstrate correct language usage and style," and 3) "produce extended researched formal report on technical topic."

Each of these strategies is measured by the class's performance on a certain assignment that was set out in the meeting at the beginning of the semester. For the English 2311 strategy of "produce short professional-level documents," it was determined that an accurate measurement of the success of that strategy would be a student's performance on a written assignment.

The core curriculum assessment process continues to be evaluated on an annual basis and refinements are made. Many process refinements are suggested by faculty, such as the rotation of participating faculty, with no faculty member being included in the study for two consecutive semesters (except in the most exceptional circumstances) and including no more than two sections per faculty member.

Examples of Assessment and How Results Are Used

Several departments have begun to incorporate the results of core curriculum assessment for program improvement. Those decisions

Figure 3.1
Sample of the English 2311: Technical Writing Matrix

Core Curriculum Assessment

Core Curriculum Course: **ENGL 2311**　　　　　　Instructor: _____
Section: _____　　　　　　Semester: _____ Year: _____

Competency: _Reading_　　　　　　　　*Note: Circle only one measure for each strategy*

--the ability to analyze and interpret a variety of printed materials, books, document, and articles – above the 12th grade level.

Strategies/Course Requirements	Outcomes		Methods of Measurement							
	Number Students Assessed	Number Students Passing	Post-Test Score	Lab Assignment Score	Research Paper Score	Written Assignment Score	Classroom Presentation Score	Other Test Score	Class Participation Score	Other Measure Score
Read assigned chapters from the textbook			X			X				
Read assigned technical passages						X				
Analyze and use primary and secondary sources					X	X				

Competency: _Writing_

--the ability to produce clear, correct and coherent prose adapted to purpose, occasion and audience – above 12th grade level.

Strategies/Course Requirements	Outcomes		Methods of Measurement							
	Number Students Assessed	Number Students Passing	Post-Test Score	Lab Assignment Score	Research Paper Score	Written Assignment Score	Classroom Presentation Score	Other Test Score	Class Participation Score	Other Measure Score
Produce short professional-level documents						X				
Demonstrate correct language usage and style					X	X				
Produced extended researched formal report on technical topic					X	X				

Competency: _Speaking_

--the ability to communicate orally in clear, coherent, and persuasive language appropriate to purpose, occasion, and audience.

Strategies/Course Requirements	Outcomes		Methods of Measurement							
	Number Students Assessed	Number Students Passing	Post-Test Score	Lab Assignment Score	Research Paper Score	Written Assignment Score	Classroom Presentation Score	Other Test Score	Class Participation Score	Other Measure Score
N/A										

Core Curriculum Assessment

Core Curriculum Course: **ENGL 2311**　　　　　　Instructor: _____
Section: _____　　　　　　Semester: _____ Year: _____

Competency: _Listening_　　　　　　　　*Note: Circle only one measure for each strategy*

--to analyze and interpret various forms of spoken communication, possess sufficient literacy skills of writing, reading – above 12th grade level.

Strategies/Course Requirements	Outcomes		Methods of Measurement							
	Number Students Assessed	Number Students Passing	Post-Test Score	Lab Assignment Score	Research Paper Score	Written Assignment Score	Classroom Presentation Score	Other Test Score	Class Participation Score	Other Measure Score
Demonstrate ability to follow directions					X	X				
Build on skills learned in previous assignments					X	X				

Competency: _Critical Thinking_

--to apply qualitative and quantitative skills analytically and creatively to subject matter to evaluate arguments and to construct alternative strategies. Problem solve.

Strategies/Course Requirements	Outcomes		Methods of Measurement							
	Number Students Assessed	Number Students Passing	Post-Test Score	Lab Assignment Score	Research Paper Score	Written Assignment Score	Classroom Presentation Score	Other Test Score	Class Participation Score	Other Measure Score
Analyze and synthesize primary and secondary sources					X	X				
Learn library use for research in major study field					X	X				

Competency: _Computer Literacy_

--to understand our technological society, use computer based technology in communications, solving problems, requiring information.

Strategies/Course Requirements	Outcomes		Methods of Measurement							
	Number Students Assessed	Number Students Passing	Post-Test Score	Lab Assignment Score	Research Paper Score	Written Assignment Score	Classroom Presentation Score	Other Test Score	Class Participation Score	Other Measure Score
Produce graphics					X	X				
Incorporate graphics into formal report					X	X				
Develop professional computer-generated documents					X	X				

Figure 3.2
Action on Results Documentation Form

BLINN COLLEGE

Action on Results Documentation Form
Institutional Research and Effectiveness

This document is designed to report actions taken as a result of analysis of the data and reports supplied to instructional administrators and faculty by the Office of Institutional Research and Effectiveness. Completion of these reports demonstrates how data results are used to improve the effectiveness of the College's programs and services.

Please complete one form for each effectiveness process you are addressing.

Report or Data Collection: (double click on box to check)

- ☐ Pre- and Post Test Report
- ☐ Final Grades Report
- ☐ Course Tracking
- ☐ Core Curriculum Assessment
- ☐ Student Evaluation of Instruction
- ☐ Other ____________

Effectiveness Issue	*Reviewers*	*Improvement Action Plans*	*Follow-up Schedule*	*Success Measures*

Office of Institutional Research and Effectiveness (rev 9-04)

are reported on the Action on Results Documentation Form delivered to the academic deans on an annual basis (see Figure 3.2). For example, the Bryan kinesiology department made significant changes in courses, moving to a new textbook and incorporating more/improved technology into teaching core courses.

Three examples of how results of core curriculum assessment have been used for program improvement will be discussed. They include core curriculum changes for speech, made early on as a result of mapping the intellectual competencies throughout the core curriculum; embedding strategies and methods of measure that design learning experiences for students in science courses with the intellectual competency of reading; and adding a much-needed technology element for computer literacy uniformly throughout the mathematics division.

As part of the initial assessment process, all core curriculum courses were reviewed to ensure that they aligned with the intellectual competencies set out by the coordinating board. During the review of Speech 1318: Interpersonal Communication, it was determined that the course did not meet the speaking competency because there was no performance-based component in the course. Rather than attempting to radically adapt the course to make it fit the competency, the curriculum itself was changed. Speech 1318 was removed from the core curriculum. All other speech classes in the core curriculum were reviewed with a specific eye to the speaking competency and the performance-based component of the courses. Changes have also been made to all the core courses to bring them in line with the other competencies, so that students are conducting more research and improving computer literacy, reading, writing, and critical thinking skills.

Some members of the Brenham natural science division, having long been concerned with students reading their textbooks, began using open-book tests prior to major exams to cover material not discussed in lectures (Phillips, 2006). Developed as an expansion of the open-book test concept, members of the department instituted the use of two- to three-question open-book Reading Assessment Tests (RATs) as a method of measuring reading competency in entry-level biology courses. RATs are used at the beginning of each class period and focus on the reading to be discussed in each day's lecture. To find the answers, the students must use the textbook and must have read the material prior to coming to class. Those students who are not familiar with the material are, of course, less successful than those who have done the reading and who are prepared.

In addition to providing a quantifiable method of measuring reading competency, RATs have also provided faculty with a teaching strategy that encourages students to use the textbook and improves study skills. Students must be familiar with the typographical signposts in the textbook to be able to follow the contextual clues given in the open-book questions; thus, faculty must teach reading and study skills in addition to teaching their subject matter field. RATs were initially being used only in biology courses, but the method has now been expanded to other disciplines in the department, including physics and geology.

As a final example, the mathematics and engineering division across all campuses gave careful consideration to the computer/technology literacy intellectual competency. The graphing calculator was used broadly across classes taught by various professors but not consistently for courses, particularly for math courses in the core curriculum. In the beginning, as the division analyzed master course syllabi, the faculty decided to enhance students' technology skills through the use of the graphing calculator without sacrificing the students' abilities to learn and perform basic skills, as well as to learn the skill without the calculator. This was in line with the exemplary educational objectives embraced by the division and with the expected student learning outcomes for students taking core curriculum math courses. Initially, students in the freshman-level core curriculum math courses were required to complete at least one graphing calculator lab. The lab consisted of the following: an example that included the step-by-step process for the students, then students being asked to perform the lab assignment. These assignments are collected as evidence of student learning within the core curriculum assessment for the computer literacy intellectual competency. Not only were the master course syllabi adjusted to reflect the graphing calculator labs, but the syllabi of developmental mathematics courses were also changed to omit the use of calculators on major tests and final exams in order to stress basic number sense prior to higher-level math skills.

Faculty were supported in several ways as calculator labs were developed for core curriculum math courses. First, the division's leadership stressed to faculty that the calculator is not the driver for the quality of math learning, but the checker for the quality of the math learning. Faculty less comfortable with the graphing calculators could attend brown-bag lunch demonstrations where they shared ideas for incorporating the graphing calculators into their courses. Graphing calculator sessions outside of regular class were also offered to students if they were not familiar with the technology. Ultimately, the division's leadership noted that the use of graphing calculators over the last several semesters had increased. Where they started with small steps, asking all core curriculum courses to incorporate at least one calculator lab, now several uses for the graphing calculators are in place to enhance students' computer/technology literacy.

Tips for Implementing the Process

A success of the implementation can be seen in the faculty-driven approach to designing the procedures and process of core curriculum assessment and made the experience a generally positive one for faculty. This positive experience was furthered because the faculty members who would be participating in core curriculum assessment were involved in the process from the very outset, beginning with designing the strategies that would be measured and selecting appropriate methods of measure. By including as many faculty as possible, the participation was strong and faculty were committed to the success of the assessment.

Faculty concerns about the issues involved in collecting artifacts were particularly important. In the pilot study, faculty were asked to provide sample documents/artifacts representing a high, average, and low score on the paper/sample/method of measurement being used for each individual strategy. This led to an excess of documentation that faculty and division chairs sometimes had difficulty managing. Although this may seem like a minor problem, the time and resources needed for the collection of student artifacts needed clarification. This issue was dealt with in later semesters when the numbers of student artifacts collected by faculty were decreased (e.g., in some departments faculty divided the document samples among themselves so that, together, they produced one complete set of samples) and others developed rubrics to measure the quality of student learning.

Challenges to Assessing General Education and Strategies to Overcome Them

The college's major challenge in core curriculum assessment can be tied to issues of a multicampus institution. In the case of Blinn College, there are several campuses in Brenham, Bryan, Schulenburg, and Sealy. In addition, 32 high schools in the college's 13-county service area are engaged in the college's core curriculum. To add to this challenge, the college is owned by 1 of the 13 counties, Washington County, which houses the Brenham campus, yet the bulk of the college's operations occur in Brazos County on the Bryan campus near Texas A&M University. Operational decisions are made on a campus-by-campus basis, yet policy decisions for the institution at large come from the Brenham campus in the county where the college is owned. Obvious blurs between policy and operations occur, which can contribute to inconsistencies in the college's interpretations and applications of policies and programs.

Relating to this important part of the Blinn College culture and climate, certain structures were purposefully placed within the core curriculum assessment model. The model included areas where the entire college was expected to act in a like-minded way and areas where faculty members from various campuses could capitalize on their strengths in order to assess their courses. For example, all core curriculum courses are expected to follow the institution's master course syllabus. The master course syllabus states the expected intellectual competencies and exemplary educational objectives included in the course. Core curriculum courses offered on all campuses are guided by the same master course syllabus. In addition, as the divisions and departments that deliver the courses determined the strategies used to deliver appropriate student learning outcomes, it was decided that these must be embraced by faculty members on all campuses. However, so as to not limit faculty in regard to particular assessment methods, the institution determined to allow for flexibility in using methods of measure for each of the strategies that capitalized on faculty strength and alignment with the faculty member's course information sheet distributed to students at the beginning of the semester. Faculty in various disciplines agreed on several appropriate methods of measure that could be used to assess any particular strategy. In other words, every faculty member participating in core curriculum assessment had to apply the same competencies and strategies, but flexibility was used in selecting appropriate methods of measure.

This part of the assessment model's structure was seen as a more flexible avenue for faculty members to align their learning experiences and course assignments with the student learning outcomes determined in the master course syllabus. In addition, faculty leaders within departments and divisions have been key in guiding their colleagues in meaningful assessment methods that are in line with the competencies.

Inconsistencies between campuses have been a sustaining challenge. While faculty flexibility has been encouraged, some campuses have chosen to limit faculty options for aligning methods of measure with strategies and competencies in the core curriculum. In order to continue the alignment of intellectual competencies with appropriate and meaningful methods of measure, results, and use of results, more common and focused professional development relating to assessment methods and rubrics is recommended across all campuses.

Another challenge the college faced was determining the criteria for success. In other words, if a percentage of students meeting the intellectual competency is identified, how can that number be the most accurate and fair number possible? Adding to the challenge is the nature of a community college, which is that of an open-door institution. In light of our current attendance policies and after much deliberation within the Core Curriculum Assessment Committee and the Curriculum Committee, it was determined to identify the number of students assessed and the number of students who achieved success. Presently, the college's attendance policy is being revised, which may, again, help initiate this conversation.

References

Blinn College. (2004). *Blinn College faculty handbook.* Retrieved December 5, 2006, from the Blinn College web site: www.blinn.edu/facultyhandbook/

Phillips, G. (2006, April). Using open-book tests to strengthen the study skills of community-college biology students. *Journal of Adolescent & Adult Literacy, 49*(7), 574–582.

Texas Higher Education Coordinating Board. (1998). *Core curriculum: Assumptions and defining characteristics.* Austin, TX: Author.

Texas Higher Education Coordinating Board. (2005). *Lower-division academic course guide manual.* Austin, TX: Author.

Chapter 4

Coker College:
General Education Case Study

David Eubanks

Overview of the Institutional Culture

Coker College in Hartsville, South Carolina, attracts most of its students from the surrounding region. With about 165 employees, one can still know just about everybody else's name. Classes are small, and a professor who teaches service courses gets to know a significant number of the approximately 1,100 undergraduates. Courses follow a fall/spring/summer semester schedule for traditional students, and eight-week terms for evening nontraditional programs, which account for about half the student population. Evening courses are taught on campus and at three remote locations.

The college began in 1908 as a women's college, and officially became coeducational in 1969. Although once affiliated with the Southern Carolina Baptist Convention, it is now independent. The college has a long history of accreditation with the Southern Association of Colleges and Schools.

Coker College's mission has seen minor revisions in recent years, but the liberal arts core has always remained: "The College's goal is to graduate students with the ability to think analytically and creatively, and to write and speak effectively" (Coker College, 2006). These four abilities—to think analytically and creatively, and to write and speak effectively—have been enshrined as the four *core skills* in our lexicon, and assessment of them is systematic. This has been made possible by a faculty who see value in a liberal arts education and have been willing participants in the assessment process.

Strong support for general education also means that faculty members see themselves as stakeholders in the specification of the program. This has made curriculum change a sometimes slow and difficult process. In 2004, the college changed the way general education is administered.

Overview of the General Education Program

The general education program is now called the Liberal Arts Studies Program (LASP). The academic catalog prefaces the course specifications with a statement of purpose:

> Coker College is a place where the liberal arts are taken seriously.
>
> For us liberal arts education is essentially practical in nature. By teaching students how to learn, we are providing not just "job skills," but "life skills." This is especially important in an economic climate where individuals are likely to change careers several times over a lifetime.
>
> Although the basic liberal arts skills are invariant, the way they are taught is not. Coker's liberal arts approach is prospective rather than retrospective. It is designed to serve the needs of students who are moving into the next century rather than the habits of those trained by the methods of the past one.
>
> To be successful, an individual must be flexible, adaptable and confident in his or her ability to learn. To be successful, a college must help its students to lead productive and rewarding lives. Liberal arts education, done properly, instills these abilities and produces these results. Our product is education, not diplomas. (Coker College, 2002, p. 48)

LASP comprises general skills and specific knowledge areas we call baskets. The term *basket* is used as a metaphor to suggest interaction between a learner and a marketplace of ideas. The skills and knowledge baskets are:

- *General skills.* Writing: Nine semester hours of English with the chance to exempt one or more courses through placement. Public speaking: Three semester hours. Mathematics/computer science: Three semester hours. Non-native language: Demonstrated competence in a non-native language at the 102 level. Physical education: Three semester hours.

- *Knowledge in the arts.* Six semester hours from two different disciplines. The goal of this requirement is an understanding of Western cultural heritage as expressed in artistic achievements and an understanding of the contribution of the creative process to the life of the individual and to society. These courses are surveys of recognized macro-fields of scholarship treating the defining areas enumerated here: the principal themes, periods, cultures, or peoples of Western civilization.

- *Knowledge in the behavioral sciences.* Six semester hours from two different disciplines. The goal of this requirement is an understanding of the forces shaping contemporary societies and individuals as revealed in the social and behavioral sciences. These courses are broad surveys from social or behavioral sciences, including vocabulary, methods, history, or some combination thereof.

- *Knowledge of the humanities.* Six semester hours from two different disciplines. The goal of this requirement is an understanding of the major elements of Western cultural heritage as revealed in philosophy, religion, literature and theatre, and history. These courses are surveys from recognized macro-fields of scholarship treating the defining areas enumerated here: the principal themes, periods, cultures, or peoples of Western civilization.

- *Knowledge in the natural sciences.* Seven semester hours. Students must select one biological science, one physical science, and one hour of laboratory practice. The goal of this requirement is the application of the methods of science to the acquisition of knowledge and an appreciation of the major contributions of science to the Western cultural heritage and to the solution of contemporary problems. These courses must be broad surveys from natural sciences, including vocabulary, methods, history, applications or a laboratory, or some combination thereof.

- *Knowledge of the United States.* Three semester hours. This requirement explores the cultural and intellectual foundations of American civilization. Courses are surveys from recognized macro-fields of scholarship treating the principal themes, periods, cultures, or peoples of the United States of America.

- *Knowledge of the wider world.* Three semester hours. The goal of this requirement is an understanding of the diversity of other cultures and societies. These courses must be broad geographical, cultural, and chronological surveys that reach beyond Western tradition.

LASP is administered by a director who works with a faculty committee. Curriculum changes to the program must be submitted using course proposal forms that solicit information about assessment methods to be used in the course and the core skills rubrics.

The existence of a standing committee and formalized administration of the general education program enables it to cope more easily with changes while preserving the philosophy of the program. It also centralizes the coordination of assessment activities.

Overview of Assessment of the General Education Program

The design of the LASP assessment program is the result of a process best understood with a short narrative of its genesis.

In the "dream" phase of designing our assessment program we naturally started with what was already on hand. Mainly, that consisted of the Academic Profile, an instrument (since discontinued) from the Educational Testing Service that purported to assess certain general education skills, such as critical thinking. It was administered to freshmen and seniors. Although this gave us good internal and external comparative data, the problem was that since we had no control over the design of the instrument, there was no guarantee that it was actually valid for the questions we wanted to ask. What does a low score or a high score mean? How can it be translated into curricular changes, for example?

We then went back to the beginning and decided that the overarching goal should be: *A graduate of Coker College should demonstrate abilities in the core skills that are judged to be college-graduate level by educated supervisors.* When our graduates attend graduate school or get a job, we would like their work to be seen as exhibiting the qualities we value in liberal arts. If a supervisor shakes her head at a graduate's work and asks, "Where on earth did you learn to think?" we have failed. Although subjective, this is quite testable. This approach has led us to consider the broadest type of validity. What good would it do to design our own custom measure of success if the rest of the world doesn't agree? Instead of claiming that we teach writing (as defined by the general educated population), we would have to claim that we teach writing*—the asterisk denoting some special definition provided in the fine print, like "valid only at participating colleges." This seems at odds with the philosophy of a general education.

With the goal solidly in place, we proceeded to figure out how to assess it. Ideally we would send out surveys to employers and graduate school advisors to directly ask how our students are doing. But this is impractical and invasive. A more direct (pre-graduation) assessment is needed if it is going to be of any use in making changes while a student is still enrolled. So we next imagined a platoon of consultants descending on the campus, sitting in classes and reviewing student work for a few weeks or so, and then generating a rating for each student's ability in the four core skills we have identified. While this sounds like fantasy, we realized that we were already doing most of the work. Course instructors, including adjuncts, have ample opportunity to review and understand the abilities of their students. We had just never bothered to ask instructors to judge these (grades being something else). If you had visited the dining hall at lunch, you'd have heard them talking about it, but we had never systematically consulted our own assessment experts! Since the largest class at the college is about 25 students, the task of rating each student formally would not be overwhelming.

But what exactly would they rate? We tried out the idea of having faculty in each discipline contribute to the definition of each core skill (such as analytical thinking) to create a master rubric for the whole college. This turned out to not work very well for us because there are just too many ways to think about analytical thinking, for example, to create a universal definition. After more debate, we latched on to an idea we call Assessing the Elephant, named for the poem by John Godfrey Saxe about blind men exploring a large animal.

Rather than trying to administratively reduce effective writing to a list of specific rubrics that includes essays, poetry, laboratory reports, mathematical writing, advertisements, news writing, and so on, we decided to adopt a democratic model. To this end, each course instructor decides which of the skills are being observed (not necessarily taught—an important distinction) in his or her class. The course syllabus must include a rubric that describes what the criteria are for these three ability levels: freshman/sophomore, junior/ senior, and graduate. Figure 4.1 presents an example from a Linear Algebra class.

Figure 4.1
Sample Rubric Criteria

Analytical Thinking
We will think of analytical thinking in this course as the skill of mastering rules and applying them. There are many definitions, theorems, and procedures involved in learning linear algebra. These include the notions of dimensionality and span of a vector space, and the processes of reducing matrices to a particular form, or performing algebra with these mathematical objects. Some of these are easy to master, and some require more sophistication.

Graduate Level:	*Can check correctness of proofs for results that are unfamiliar, use novel notation, or advanced concepts. Understands eigenvectors/values, vector spaces, and inner product spaces and can solve straightforward problems on paper and using Maple.*
Junior/Senior Level:	*Can correctly apply matrix multiplication and do matrix algebra, understands the notational differences between matrix algebra and scalar algebra, under- stands use of transpose, inverse, and commutativity properties. Understands and can check correctness of basic proofs.*
Freshman/ Sophomore Level:	*Can perform mechanical processes of row reduction, solving linear systems using a pencil and on Maple. Knows basic properties of vectors and matrix algebra.*

Note that "Graduate Level" means that the student meets the professor's criteria described in Figure 4.1 as the general goal of the program— we can be proud to give them a diploma and send them out into the wide world. Ideally, every student would reach this level in each of the core skills before we certify him or her as a graduate of Coker College.

Near the end of the course, instructors log into the administrative web portal and enter ratings for each student. There are four possible ratings: the three just described and a fourth—remedial—for students who don't measure up to freshman/sophomore-level work. The web interface is shown in Figure 4.2.

Figure 4.2
Administrative Web Portal

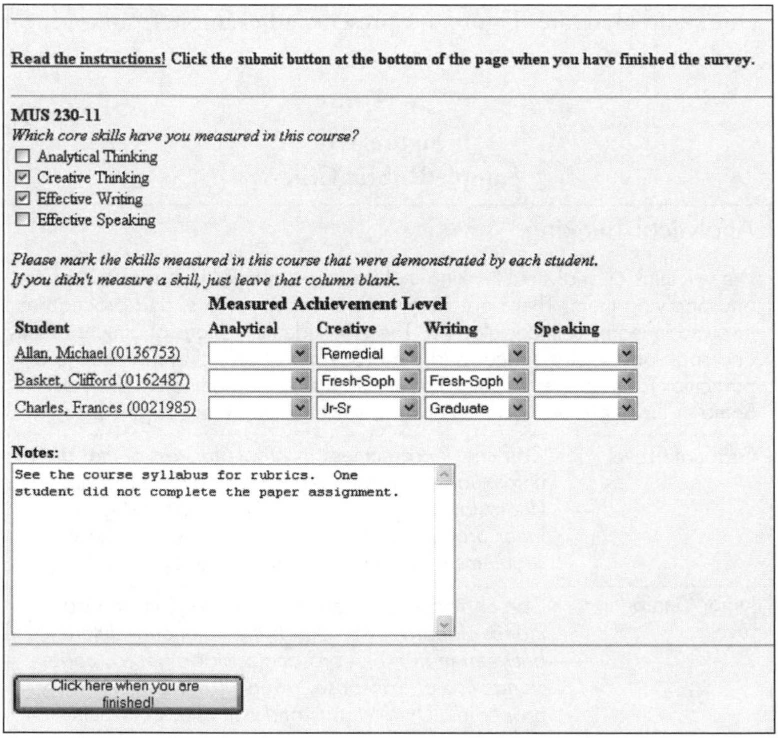

Note. Student names and ID numbers are fictitious.

We call this assessment the Faculty Assessment of Core Skills (FACS). Since a typical student takes four or five classes, FACS generates thousands of ratings each year. These are recorded with a 0–3 scale and used for research purposes.

Our first question was: Are we wasting our time? By letting each instructor decide what constitutes effective writing, are we simply gathering a bunch of random numbers? We tested statistical reliability by comparing one instructor's ratings to another and found that there is a tendency to rate students similarly (inter-rater reliability). The likelihood of agreement is not nearly as high as a standardized test would provide, but reliability has to compete with validity. We are trying to judge student abilities in very general and complex modes of behavior. Palomba and Banta (1999) describe this sort of tradeoff between validity and reliability:

> An . . . issue related to the reliability of perform-ance-based assessment deals with the trade-off between reliability and validity. As the perform-ance task increases in complexity and authenticity, which serves to increase validity, the lack of stan-dardization serves to decrease reliability. (p. 89)

The method of assessment certainly has face validity, considering our general goal. We compared FACS scores to grade point average, where it correlated at 0.64. Another test was to check FACS writing assessments against students' circulation histories at the library. One would guess that students who write better check out more books, which is upheld in the FACS scores (see Figure 4.3).

Figure 4.3
Writing vs. Library Use

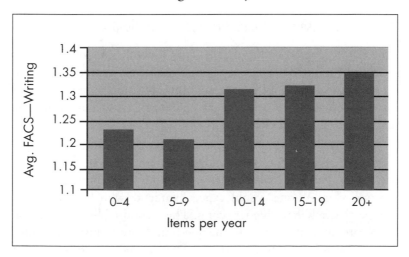

In Fall 2005 we began using an online student portfolio system. We again checked the validity of the FACS by sampling portfolios, scoring them using a rubric, and comparing FACS scores to portfolio ratings. They correlated weakly, but significantly at 0.37.

Our experience with assessing portfolios taught us some valuable lessons. It's very difficult to create a rubric that applies to the many varieties of written coursework that will be found in portfolios. We are exploring the idea of having more standardized written assignments given at particular points, such as in Freshman Composition, Sophomore Seminar, and Senior Seminar. This would no doubt increase inter-rater reliability for assessing portfolios and allow a rubric to focus on very specific kinds of writing issues, such as style problems with commas and the like.

For more specialized kinds of work, we are exploring the idea of creating discipline-specific reviews within an academic department.

The method of measuring skills based on an instructor's own definition of analytical and creative thinking and effective speaking and writing has proven to be a good general assessment of student skill levels. It does not allow for more specific assessments, so we plan to use the portfolio reviews to get a finer resolution, both for skills and knowledge. One benefit of having student work archived is that retrospective investigations are possible.

Examples of Assessment and How Results Are Used

The FACS generates a lot of data. This allows us to look for trends at a fairly high resolution. For example, academic departments compile reports showing the relative standings of students in their major programs. See Table 4.1 for an example (the actual name of the area has been changed to Generic).

Table 4.1 shows skill rating averages as assigned by course instructors. More than 8,000 individual ratings are summarized in the tables. The first table shows FACS scores for Generic majors by starting year. As one would expect, students who have attended longer generally have higher scores. The second table is a check on inter-rater reliability and asks the question: How do instructors outside of Generic rate those students? The smaller sample size creates more variability in the averages, but generally the same pattern

Table 4.1
Sample Department Report of Student Standings

FACS for Generic Majors

Class	N	Analytical	Creative	Writing	Speaking
2001	38	1.67	1.70	1.84	1.96
2002	167	1.69	1.71	1.63	1.88
2003	88	2.00	1.88	1.90	2.05
2004	96	1.30	1.29	1.31	1.32

FACS External Ratings for Generic Majors

Class	N	Analytical	Creative	Writing	Speaking
2001	22	1.65	2.00	1.94	2.00
2002	91	1.52	1.49	1.54	1.81
2003	30	1.83	1.75	1.71	2.00
2004	65	1.29	1.11	1.25	1.29

FACS for All Other Majors Combined

Start	N	Analytical	Creative	Writing	Speaking
2001	239	1.42	1.55	1.31	1.46
2002	1216	1.48	1.48	1.43	1.54
2003	1691	1.31	1.34	1.28	1.36
2004	911	1.33	1.26	1.23	1.34

holds. What we see is that the 2003 class appears to be particularly strong academically (for students in Generic). The third table shows averages from all majors excluding Generic. Generally speaking, Generic majors tend to score significantly higher in all skill areas.

The obvious general question to be answered is: Are our students learning? Figure 4.4 shows the average FACS scores for students based on the number of semesters in attendance.

These data show that instructors believe more senior students to be demonstrating higher ability than less senior students, but even the average of the most senior is still well below the ideal (3 = graduate level). This is now baseline data that we will judge future improvements against.

Because the college has a large evening school program, we are interested in learning differences between traditional and nontraditional students, as shown in Figure 4.5.

Figure 4.4
Core Skills vs. Semesters of Credit

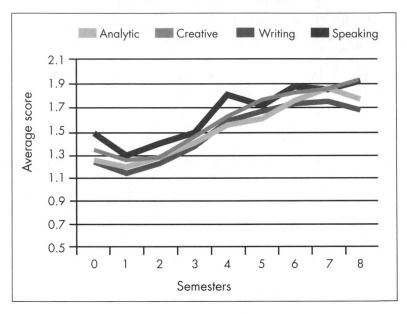

Figure 4.5
Day/Evening Comparison of Composites

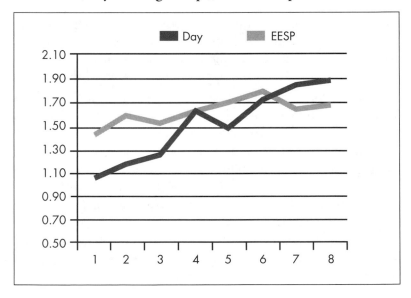

The averages show different characteristics of the two populations. Note that these are ecological rather than longitudinal data. This means that there are more sources of variability in interpreting the graphs. Although we try to isolate and account for that variability, there's no substitute for a real longitudinal study, which we will conduct for the first time at the conclusion of the 2006–2007 academic year.

The information from FACS, surveys, and focus groups convinced us in 2003 that we needed to design a program to increase writing effectiveness skills for our students. Thus, the *Write On!* Initiative became the centerpiece of the college's quality enhancement plan, required by our accrediting body.

Programmatic changes include a new type of in-class student writing tutor, more resources allocated to the writing center, faculty workshops on the assessment of writing, a partnership with the local high school, and the creation of an online portfolio system called {iceBox} for archiving student work. The {iceBox} system immediately became popular and has had some positive secondary effects. For example, off-campus students no longer have to rely on floppy disks or other portable media to submit their work.

Other instruments used for assessing LASP/core skills include an exit survey, alumni survey, an "Assessment Day" attitude survey, portfolio review, and periodic use of the National Survey of Student Engagement and the Faculty Survey of Student Engagement. Secondary information includes student course evaluations and library records (number of transactions for printed and electronic materials).

Because we "pushed" the liberal arts mission, embodied in the core skills, out to the whole curriculum, it established a common language for instructors and students to talk about this part of the college's mission. Each syllabus refers to the core skills, and many instructors have incorporated this language into their instruction, for example, by identifying a homework problem as requiring analytical thinking. The art program has incorporated the core skills into its sophomore and senior review process. In general, major programs' capstone experiences are expected to define a relationship to general education through the core skills.

Tips for Implementing the Process

The success of the adoption of FACS by faculty relies on their support of the basic idea that liberal arts skills are valuable. If our general education goals had been out of line with what the faculty actually believe to be important, it would have likely been impossible to implement the survey.

Ease of use is very important. To complete the FACS survey, faculty simply log on to their web portal (where they can access class portfolio files, email, reports, etc.) and click. Each student's name is hyperlinked to a photo, and the form is very simple. Faculty can fill in a form partially and then complete it later. They can even change their minds and override previous ratings (until the survey closes). The portfolio system is similarly very simple to use for both faculty and students.

Creating an appropriate scale was another issue that needed a second look. If we were to redesign the assessment procedure, we might consider going to a 1–10 scale instead of the four ratings we have now (0–3). We chose the four ratings to make it possible to describe them each in a syllabus, but there are other ways to approach that. For example, a sliding scale that allowed a 2.3 rating would retain the ease of description but allow more reporting flexibility.

The most important political decision is what the surveys will be used for. We decided not to give individual ratings back to students. Ratings are not part of a student's grade, and they are not used for instructor evaluation. The idea is to take away all incentives for raters to be less than candid. By integrating this with the portfolio system, however, it will be natural to rate individual pieces of evidence using a core skills rubric. This will be an important step in closing the communications loop with students.

Challenges to Assessing General Education and Strategies to Overcome Them

Initially, the primary obstacle we confronted was the lack of an obvious linkage between off-the-shelf standardized assessment solutions and student learning. We concluded that standardized measurement of complex skills results in oversimplification that can invalidate the metric. Our solution was to go from standardized assessment to customized assessment.

This customized approach has its own drawbacks. One is that it doesn't allow for external comparisons with a peer group. We have found the National Survey of Student Engagement useful for such a comparison.

Confidentiality in reporting is an issue that both creates and causes problems. On the one hand, it is easy for public reports to be abused or misinterpreted. If we used FACS to create a department rating system and published it, faculty would be motivated to rate artificially higher and invalidate the results. On the other hand, complete confidentiality means that the reports aren't useful at all. In finding a middle ground, we have tried to err on the side of confidentiality.

References

Coker College. (2002). *2002–2003 academic catalog.* Hartsville, SC: Author.

Coker College. (2006). *The college mission.* Retrieved October 20, 2006, from www.coker.edu/about/mission.htm

Palomba, C. A., & Banta, T. W. (1999). *Assessment essentials: Planning, implementing, and improving assessment in higher education.* San Francisco, CA: Jossey-Bass.

Chapter 5

James Madison University: General Education Case Study

Donna L. Sundre, Linda Cabe Halpern

Overview of the Institutional Culture

James Madison University (JMU) is a comprehensive public coeducational institution of higher learning in the Shenandoah Valley of Virginia. Founded in 1908 as a state school for women, JMU has grown to a current student body of 16,938 on a campus of 647 acres. Seven colleges comprise the university: College of Arts and Letters, College of Business, College of Education, College of Integrated Science and Technology, College of Science and Mathematics, College of Visual and Performing Arts, and College of Graduate and Professional Programs. JMU is considered more selective in the most recent Carnegie classification system and offers 67 undergraduate degree programs, as well as 30 master's, 2 educational specialist, and 4 doctoral programs.

JMU is dedicated to the belief that an enduring and meaningful educational experience must be future-oriented, grounded in knowledge of one's cultural heritage learned from study in the liberal arts and sciences. The goal of the university is to become the finest undergraduate institution in the country, and it has been identified as a quality institution in numerous national publications, including *U.S. News & World Report, Kiplinger's Personal Finance, Money, Changing Times, Guide to 101 Best Values in America's Colleges and Universities, Careers and Colleges, The Black Students' Guide to College Success, USA Today,* and *The New York Times.* JMU has also been cited in *Barron's, Peterson's, The Princeton*

Review, and *Yale Daily News* college guides as one of the nation's best choices among undergraduate public universities. It is known for the quality of its academic programs and for the level of student involvement across a wide range of experiential activities from undergraduate research and study abroad to student government and community service. For example, JMU was recently ranked second nationally among mid-size universities in the number of students entering the Peace Corps.

While JMU enjoys recognition from many external publications and agencies, the evaluations most carefully attended are those designed, implemented, and continuously supported from within. These evaluation methodologies extend beyond our well-developed assessment practices to include regularly scheduled academic program reviews for all academic programs, program reviews for all programs across the other divisions of the campus, strategic plans for administrative units, and a planning database for the entire campus. This case study will focus on the assessment and evaluation procedures dedicated to the JMU General Education Program.

Overview of the General Education Program

The General Education Program, called The Human Community, is considered a signature program at JMU. Its overall purpose is described in program material as promoting "the cultivation of habits of the mind and heart that are essential to informed citizens in a democracy and world community." It has been the subject of numerous national and regional academic presentations as well as scholarly publications (i.e., DeMars, Sundre, & Wise, 2002; Lee, 2002, 2003; Reynolds et al., 1998). The overall program comprises 41 credit hours of lower-division courses, or just over one-third of the 120 credit hours required for graduation from JMU.

Initiated in 1997, the JMU General Education Program and the process through which it was designed represent a revolution in the conceptualization of general education and how it is delivered. A set of primary premises have guided the development and maintenance of the program since its inception: an insistence on specific learning objectives; clear linkages of objectives to courses; nonproliferation of approved courses; clear communication among teaching faculty; ongoing assessment; and action based on assessment results

(Reynolds et al., 1998). Initially, more than 140 faculty members from 30 different academic programs responded to a call for student learning objectives; more than 1,300 objectives were submitted for consideration. A faculty committee worked for more than a year to distill these objectives into a set of 100 that were assigned to five general education areas that we termed *clusters*. The five clusters are organizational categories that generally reflect standard categories within higher education in the U.S., but are clearly understood as clusters of learning objectives and therefore are characterized by what students learn rather than the discipline or department in which a particular course is taught.

- Cluster One: *Skills for the 21st Century* includes courses in freshman composition, oral communication, and critical thinking, and competency tests in basic technology skills and information literacy. Completion of Cluster One is required of all students by the end of their freshman year.

- Cluster Two: *Arts and Humanities* includes courses in historical and philosophical foundations, appreciation of the fine arts, and appreciation and analysis of literature.

- Cluster Three: *The Natural World* includes one course addressing mathematics and at least two courses representing different approaches to science, and incorporate a laboratory component.

- Cluster Four: *Social and Cultural Processes* includes two courses based in those aspects of social science that address groups and institutions, one focused on the United States and one focused on global content.

- Cluster Five: *Individuals in the Human Community* includes two courses, one based in social science focused on the individual and one addressing college-level health and wellness.

In the formative years of the General Education Program, agreement on the student learning objectives for each cluster preceded a campus-wide solicitation of courses to fulfill these expectations. All courses were reviewed to assure balanced and complete coverage of learning objectives. While the objectives themselves and the program both have undergone continuous refinement, careful maintenance has continued to ensure that courses approved for general education credit reflect the student learning objectives of the cluster. For example, Cluster Three: The Natural World consists of 10–12 credit hours of collegiate courses mapped to eight objectives, with each course expected to address about four of the objectives in depth. The current list of learning outcomes can be found as part of the cluster descriptions at www.jmu.edu/gened/.

In its first iteration, the program was designed so that coursework in each cluster was organized into *packages*—groups of courses sharing some thematic content that collectively met all the learning objectives of the cluster. Students were expected to complete one package in each cluster. It quickly became clear that such groupings of courses were impossible to administer well at a university as large as JMU, and that not all students were well served when they had to choose an entire group of courses at once. As the program matured, each cluster developed a tier or group organization, with the learning objectives of the cluster becoming aligned with one or more specific area within it. This in turn engendered further refinement of the outcomes statements. In 2005–2006, the program completed the process of rethinking its structure and all five clusters are now organized by groups of courses sharing a subset of the cluster's learning outcomes rather than by packages of courses that collectively meet the cluster outcomes. Because there has been consistent commitment to the outcomes themselves, the refinement of structure and organization has been accomplished as a set of incremental decisions rather than instigating the sort of institutional upheaval that often accompanies general education curricular changes.

Decisions about inclusion of courses in the program are made on the basis of faculty judgment about the alignment between the course and the cluster objectives. This is built into the general education approval process. Furthermore, the program has adopted the practice of periodic review of each cluster, so that each course will be reviewed for continuing alignment with the cluster objectives and evaluated using data from the cluster assessment procedures. The standards for evaluating courses for inclusion in the program explicitly reference the analytical standards by which we use assessment data to evaluate program effectiveness.

During its initial development and in ongoing refinement and governance, the General Education Program has worked closely with the Center for Assessment and Research Studies (CARS) on the clarification of objectives and on the development of assessment design and instruments. It is through the unique and long-term collaboration between faculty in CARS and the faculty teaching within general education that our assessment instruments were developed and refined.

Program governance is accomplished through five cluster committees, each incorporating faculty representing the various academic areas that contribute to the cluster. Some committees have student representatives and representatives from other university units that have some relationship to the cluster. For example, the Cluster One Committee includes library faculty connected to the information literacy requirement, and the Cluster Five committee has a representative from the University Recreation Center, since some courses require students to participate in recreation activities. Each cluster has a dedicated CARS liaison who is closely involved in the assessment activities of the cluster and is a member of the cluster committee. The program-wide decision-making body is the General Education Council (GEC), with representatives from the General Education Program administrative staff as well as from each cluster, each undergraduate academic college, CARS, advising, libraries, the Faculty Senate, and the Student Government Association. All changes to learning objectives or to program requirements are made following votes by both the cluster committee and the GEC.

Overview of Assessment of the General Education Program

The Center for Assessment and Research Studies has been active on the JMU campus since 1987. CARS is currently staffed by eight full-time faculty who hold dual appointments with the Department of Graduate Psychology. The CARS mission is to be

> a nationally recognized standard of excellence for assessment programs in higher education through its doctorate in assessment and measurement, through practitioner work on campus, through professional organizations, and through writing in national publications. As part of this national model, the Center

will design sophisticated and innovative assessment
instruments that meet the needs of higher education
communities. (JMU, 2006)

JMU and CARS have been formally recognized for their excellence in assessment practice. Three examples of this recognition
come from external accreditation bodies: the most recent two
Southern Association of Colleges and Schools and the most recent
National Council on Accreditation of Teacher Education visiting
teams awarded JMU commendations for excellence in assessment.
Moreover, CARS has been contracted to conduct external assessment workshops for many other institutions and held an Assessment
Institute in summer 2005 for approximately 70 participants from
across the nation and beyond on the JMU campus. Furthermore, in
2006, JMU and CARS received the CHEA award for Institutional
Progress in Student Learning Outcomes.

JMU has a culture of assessment, not a climate. We have been
collecting institution-wide data through two annual, formal
Assessment Days at JMU for more than 15 years. This assessment
design rests on a firm scientific foundation by which important
research questions can be posed and answered. Every entering first-
year student participates in an Assessment Day in late August just
before classes begin. Students are assigned to testing rooms on the
basis of the last digits of their JMU student ID number, and various
rooms are assigned different assessment instruments (e.g., developmental inventories, science and mathematics, fine arts, history, and
global studies). Specific assessment tests for each general education
cluster have been developed and refined over time through effective
collaboration between faculty teaching in each area and the assessment experts in CARS.

In this way, we gather baseline data for every student prior to
their entry into a classroom. As a result of these procedures, large,
representative, and random samples are generated. In the spring
semester of every year, all undergraduate classes are canceled for one
day, and all students with a cumulative count of 45–70 credit hours
are assigned to participate in Assessment Day. This represents the
midpoint of their undergraduate academic career. Because all
undergraduate classes have been canceled, there are no time or room
conflicts. Further, students who do not participate in assessment

activities will find their registration for the next semester blocked until they complete their assigned assessment test. Since students are assigned to assessment locations on the basis of their student ID and because these numbers do not change, we can collect repeated measures of general education outcomes for each student. Our student participation rates exceed 95% on all Assessment Day activities; thus, our data collection procedures provide a scientific foundation for our work. The spring Assessment Day is also used by academic departments for assessment of their graduating seniors and for faculty development activities. These policies and procedures provide compelling evidence that JMU's administration and faculty are committed to quality assurance and institutional accountability.

The goal of assessment of the General Education Program is to provide results that can inform our faculty about the growth and development of JMU students in all areas of the program. JMU has designed analytic strategies to be employed with general education assessment data. Four important educational research questions frame the basis of our analytical strategies. These research questions focus on the following:

- *Differences.* Do students learn or develop more if they have successfully completed courses when compared to students who have not (i.e., no coursework completed compared to those that have completed one course or two courses)?

- *Relationships.* What is the relationship between assessment outcomes and relevant program indicators (i.e., course grades)?

- *Change.* Do students change over time?

- *Competency.* Do students meet our expectations?

Using these analytic strategies and our assessment process, we have created a continuous feedback loop that allows us to further improve our assessment instruments and to ask more penetrating research questions with confidence. We can also demonstrate program impact in all five clusters of the General Education Program. We have been able to share this information with faculty teaching general education courses at JMU and with many external audiences.

In addition to the pretest/posttest model described above, which is used for most General Education Program assessment, other methods utilized to evaluate the effectiveness of general education coursework include portfolio review for freshman writing and a standardized final exam for general education oral communication courses. Each year, sample student portfolios are gathered from all sections of the freshman writing class, and they are rated in the summer by JMU writing faculty. Each portfolio is rated by two readers according to a rubric designed by faculty in the JMU Writing Program in collaboration with representatives from CARS, and if the ratings disagree by more than one point then a third reader also rates the portfolio. The Writing Program uses the annual portfolio rating project as a faculty development activity to encourage a shared understanding of writing standards across the program.

The faculty who teach oral communication classes have developed a standardized final exam used in all sections in order to evaluate student achievement of the communication outcomes. Since this is one part of the final exam for all sections, it also serves as the assessment test for oral communication. In addition, faculty from the School of Communication Studies have worked in collaboration with CARS faculty to develop a competency test for oral communication in alignment with the standards of the National Communication Association. This test is used at JMU primarily to provide credit-by-exam in oral communication for transfer students and was piloted in other institutions in 2006.

Another approach to assessment is the two information literacy tests that all students must pass as part of Cluster One. The first test (Tech Level I) is a basic computing test and requires students to demonstrate their competence in using word-processing software, presentation software, and spreadsheet software. All freshmen must pass this test in their first semester at JMU. They may take the test multiple times, but if they do not pass it, they are unable to register for courses in the second semester. Students take the Tech Level I test in a dedicated assessment computer lab with a proctor. Students who have made a good faith effort to pass the test but have not been able to do so may register for courses after signing a contract with the general education technology coordinator. The second test is the Information Seeking Skills Test (ISST) developed by library faculty in collaboration with CARS. This test is based on the nationally recognized Go for the Gold learning modules found on the library web site (www.lib.jmu.edu/gold/default.aspx). Each module contains practice test items, but students must also past the ISST in a proctored computer lab by the end of their first year at JMU. The same penalties and contract procedures used for the Tech Level I test apply to the ISST.

Examples of Assessment and How Results Are Used

We are currently using the eighth version of our two locally developed instruments that measure quantitative reasoning (QR) and scientific reasoning (SR). These instruments are used for program assessment in Cluster Three, the area of the General Education Program that addresses science and mathematics. We believe these instruments may have important utility for many other institutions. Indeed, JMU has been approached by several institutions and has marketed the instruments on a limited basis. Table 5.1 provides the recent administrative history of the two instruments and how they have been improved over time. Working collaboratively with science, technology, and mathematics faculty teaching in Cluster Three, we have learned a great deal about what general education is and how to create appropriate items. We have eliminated items deemed to be assessing discipline-specific factual information, rather than student ability to understand and use mathematics and science as ways of knowing. We have conducted both quantitative and qualitative studies to gather information about item quality. For example, we interviewed students to determine which items they found confusing, intriguing, or interesting. We have conducted "think-aloud" studies with students to determine the strategies used to solve problems. We engaged Cluster Three faculty in several summer Faculty Institutes in which we guided them following Cobb's (1998) principles in writing more innovative and interesting items that address higher levels of cognition than the previous versions. We are pleased with the continued improvement of the instruments. However, we maintain that they can still be improved, and we will continue to work on new revisions.

We have conducted many studies exploring the validity of the test scores we have produced. These research procedures are consistent with the professional standards of the educational research, psychology, and measurement fields (American Educational Research

Table 5.1

Sample Sizes and Reliability (a = Cronbach's alpha) for the Scientific and Quantitative Reasoning Tests (SR and QR), Fall 2000 through Fall 2005

Academic Year	Test Form*	Semester	First-Year Students			Sophomores/ Juniors		
			N	SR a	QR a	N	SR a	QR a
2000–2001	5	Fall 2000	994	.54	.50			
		Spring 2001				978	.65	.58
2001–2002	5	Fall 2001	746	.56	.52			
		Spring 2002				801	.69	.60
2002–2003	5	Fall 2002	1084	.61	.50			
		Spring 2003				1174	.67	.59
2003–2004	6	Fall 2003	1304	.75	.64			
		Spring 2004				902	.84	.75
2004–2005	7	Fall 2004	839	.77	.68			
		Spring 2005				770	.83	.75
2005–2006	8	Fall 2005	1158	.73	.62			
		Spring 2006				526	.85	.73

*Note. Four versions of the SR and QR were administered during the academic years 2000–2001 through 2005–2006. The number of items comprising each test was as follows:

Form 5: SR–27; QR–23   Form 6: SR–57; QR–44
Form 7: SR–65; QR–30   Form 8: SR–50; QR–24

Association, American Psychological Association, & National Council on Measurement in Education, 1999). All items included in the test have been successfully mapped to JMU's quantitative and scientific reasoning objectives by our Cluster Three faculty and independent raters. This process is referred to as back translation and represents a form of content validity. We have also employed the analytical strategies described earlier. Some of these results are described below.

We have identified students with different course-taking histories to determine if the number of courses taken in Cluster Three courses impacts test performance. We have correlated student test performance with grades in science and mathematics courses. In addition, because we had the use of the fifth version of the instruments over several years, we were able to conduct a number of analyses involving repeated measures (i.e., assessment of the same students with the same instrument as entering students and again as sophomores). It is important to note that these interpretive reports were generated through the collaboration of assessment and measurement experts working closely with the Cluster Three faculty who teach in mathematics, science, and technology programs. In the following bulleted list, we provide a summary of some of the research questions we have posed and answered via assessment analysis. These results provide compelling evidence not only of the utility of this instrument, but also the efficacy of our General Education Program. Several of our full reports have been posted on the Center for Assessment and Research Studies web site at http://www.jmu.edu/assessment.

Selected Quantitative and Scientific Reasoning Assessment Findings

• The reliability estimates for both quantitative and scientific reasoning appear stable even with reduction in items; reliability is higher for sophomores than first-year students.

• Sophomores and juniors with 45–70 credit hours taking the exam do not score differently from one another across academic years; however, sophomore samples consistently score significantly higher than entering first-year student samples.

• Scores on the scientific reasoning and the quantitative reasoning tests rise significantly with increasing numbers of Cluster Three courses completed.

• Multiple regression analyses reveal that Cluster Three–related advanced placement and JMU courses both significantly predict scientific and quantitative reasoning scores. In contrast, cluster-related transfer credits do not. Of additional interest, cumulative credit hours across subject areas negatively predict scientific and quantitative reasoning scores. In other words, test scores are not enhanced via academic maturation through undifferentiated course taking.

- More than 90% of correlations between relevant course grades and scores on scientific and quantitative reasoning were positive. This is a strong indicator of the close alignment between the cluster learning objectives measured by assessment testing and the course content and assignments measured by grades.

- A repeated measures multivariate analysis of students completing their Cluster Three coursework revealed significantly higher overall posttest scores with no interaction by package. In other words, for package completers, Cluster Three performances were significantly higher on their sophomore posttest than their first-year entering pretest, but no significant differences were observed when the packages students completed were compared. This is a very powerful finding and it supported the recent Cluster Three decision to abandon packages in favor of the group structure already in place in other clusters.

The systematic collection of assessment data using solid sampling designs combined with assessment instruments with psychometric integrity has allowed us to confidently monitor and report on the quality of our educational enterprise. Faculty reflection and interpretation of our findings has enabled us to modify our course offerings and sequencing. As noted earlier, our academic program review process mandates reporting of assessment results and use for program improvement.

Tips for Implementing the Process

Based on our experiences, we offer the following recommendations for implementing and assessing a general education program:

- *Use your institution's mission statement to frame your work in general education.* Every institution of higher education has developed a mission statement that fully embraces the importance of general education, but very few institutions match that semantic commitment with a structural and ongoing commitment.

- *Get commitment from the very top and sustain it.* This is crucial to the success of a general education program, but it is even more essential for an assessment program. There are many campuses where assessment was launched then faltered, sputtered, and suffered an untimely and early death due to neglect. These failed attempts create legitimate skepticism and inertia that is difficult to overcome. Remember, some of the most important resources don't cost anything. For example, a consistent message of the importance of general education to faculty, students, parents, employers, legislators, and others with an interest in higher education costs nothing but provides valuable momentum and support for these core programs. This message must filter down from the president, provost, vice presidents, deans, and department heads. Faculty are already deeply committed to student growth and development; we just need to demonstrate that assessment is a means by which we can work together toward this shared value.

- *Take an institutional view and be bold.* Particularly at the beginning planning stages, dare to dream. Carefully explore successful models in use at institutions similar to your own. The excellent model employed at Alverno College could not be transplanted successfully to JMU. Each campus has its own culture, and you must identify a model that fits your institution. You may never again have the opportunity to ask for substantive change once a program is in place. Dare to demand quality from the start; compromises will jeopardize long-term impact. Your institution and your students deserve the very best. You will experience resistance; change is difficult. Be resolute. You will find that resistance recedes over time, and the quality of the sampling plan and the instruments you use will be key to your success.

- *Build an administrative infrastructure for general education.* We have been so grateful that when we initiated our new General Education Program in 1997 the administration had the foresight to develop the infrastructure we now take for granted: a dean of general education, a General Education Council, and the faculty committees that review and monitor each of the general education clusters. Our General Education Program has a home, yet general education belongs to the entire university. Our dean of general education has a staff to support coordination of all this important work, and there are reporting structures built into this design. This leads to our next recommendation.

- *Design a program that will allow for incremental change.* By virtue of the general education cluster areas with administrative oversight by faculty that teach in those areas, assessment and other important data can be reviewed on a regular basis. This allows these bodies to use this information in a timely fashion; they are able to trim their sails much more effectively. Further, incremental change has allowed us to implement program changes without the chaotic and disruptive environment that often accompanies general education review at most institutions.

- *Design a general education program and assessment practice that are appropriate for the size of your institution and the nature of your student body.* Much of the national literature on higher education practice emphasizes the pedagogy, curriculum structure, and assessment practice appropriate for smaller institutions. Larger institutions must adapt these practices in order to implement appropriate curricula and use their size as a benefit. At JMU, our large student population made up primarily of traditional college students who enter as freshmen makes it possible to conduct assessment using a pretest/posttest model with large representative samples of our student population. Our transfer students simply enrich our analyses by providing meaningful comparison groups and very useful feedback for the institutions that provide transfer students to us. Because of our confidence in our assessment results, we plan to use our findings to inform our articulation agreements with these institutions.

- *Use locally developed assessment methodologies that are clearly aligned with the learning outcomes of the program.* The learning goals and objectives of your programs must be directly linked to the assessment methods employed. We have found that development of our own instruments provides the best alignment and the most useful information for our programs. This takes time and expertise, but most colleges and universities employ individuals with these very skills and talents. Content experts are needed, and every college has made it its business to recruit and retain the very best individuals across academic areas. Qualified assessment practitioners who are capable and eager to guide faculty in collaborative teams are equally important. These professionals are in shorter supply; however, many of the necessary skills and competencies do exist on your campus right now. As demonstrated earlier with the examples of our quantitative and scientific reasoning instruments, assessment methods will evolve and improve over time. The best advice is to get started knowing that your assessment instruments are not perfect. They never will be, but as you improve them you will also gather some very important information that your faculty will value and utilize in program development.

Challenges to Assessing General Education and Strategies to Overcome Them

One of the greatest threats to the assessment model we have employed pertains to *examinee motivation.* Many of our assessments are conducted in what are termed *low-stakes* testing conditions. This means that there are no personal consequences for individual students in regard to their performance. While we can mandate their participation, we cannot force students to try hard on the assessments. This threat to the validity of inferences we wish to make about student learning and development is shared by many testing programs across the nation and the globe. In fact, this threat impacts every norming study, every research study, and many large-scale testing programs.

This has led to considerable scholarly inquiry about this important phenomenon and to the formal recognition by our administration of the Motivation Research Institute within the Center for Assessment and Research Studies. We have developed an instrument for gauging examinee motivation: the Student Opinion Scale (Sundre, 1999; Sundre & Moore, 2002). Those interested can freely download the 10-item scale from our web site (www.jmu.edu/assessment/). We have carefully explored student motivation, and we can answer our faculty when they ask about it. We now know that our students exhibit the same level of motivation during our Assessment Day activities as that observed in classroom embedded assessment activities that do not count toward grades. We can identify the few students (less than 1%–2%) who are "blowing off" the test. We know that examinee motivation is not correlated with SAT scores; the correlation is less than +.05. This means that it is not necessarily a weak student that is not expending effort—it could just as easily be your National Merit Scholar. We also know that the most important factors to enhance student motivation are related to allowing any form of choice in the testing room. For example, we have evidence that allowing students choice as to whether or not music should be played during testing results in an increase in both motivation and performance. We also know that the proctor assigned to conduct the testing administration accounts for considerable variance in student motivation and performance. Knowing that this factor increases examinee motivation, we have spent considerable time with the selection and professional training of these individuals. In 2007, we plan to invite emeriti faculty to serve as proctors at our Assessment Days. They have a strong affiliation with the university, and their love for students is everlasting. We know that these "retired" and honored faculty members have just the classroom experience that communicates immediately to students who is in charge and what is important. We believe they will want to return to campus to work with our new students.

Many campuses have elected to use course embedded assessment data collection strategies to overcome this motivation problem. We have remained steadfast in our commitment to the value of our large-scale Assessment Days because of the scientific foundation it provides for the quality of our assessment data. Our data collection design also strongly communicates the shared value of assessment and what it means to be a member of this community.

An additional barrier that all institutions will experience regardless of the methodologies they employ is *faculty resistance*. Let's face it: The professoriate is among the most autonomous of all professionals. You will need to employ a number of creative strategies to enhance faculty and student understanding of assessment. Communication about the positive impact of general education and its assessment is of paramount importance. Some of the strategies we have employed include the following:

- Development of the administrative infrastructure for general education to enhance communication and meaningful input and oversight by faculty and students in our program, its curriculum, and assessment.

- Implementation of a campus-wide Assessment Advisory Committee to advise CARS on assessment practice. This group formed two subcommittees to focus on procedural and communications issues and has generated several excellent recommendations that have been implemented with success. For example, we instituted collection of a simplified Assessment Progress Template for annual reporting. This template is submitted for each academic program with the department's annual report. We have now identified several exemplar assessment programs that we can highlight within and beyond our campus.

• Recruitment of students to participate in assessment-related committees at all levels—they will then be able to understand what this is, why it's important, and their insights are unique and powerful. Every department benefits with a student leader on its committee to help design and implement its assessment program. We try to have two student representatives on our General Education Council. Their contributions to our recent academic program review were immensely useful.

References

American Educational Research Association, American Psychological Association, & National Council on Measurement in Education. (1999). *Standards for educational and psychological testing.* Washington, DC: American Educational Research Association.

Cobb, G. W. (1998, April). *The objective-format question in statistics: Dead horse, old bath water, or overlooked baby?* Paper presented at the annual meeting of the American Educational Research Association, San Diego, CA.

DeMars, C. L., Sundre, D. L., & Wise, S. L. (2002). Standard setting: A systematic approach to interpreting student learning. *Journal of General Education, 51*(1), 1–20.

James Madison University. (2006). *The Center for Assessment and Research.* Retrieved December 4, 2006, from the James Madison University, Center for Assessment and Research web site: www.jmu.edu/assessment/

Lee, J. S. (2002). *An institutional profile of James Madison University's General Education Program, "The Human Community," and the history of general education at James Madison University from 1978 to the present: A comparative analysis.* Harrisonburg, VA: James Madison University.

Lee, J. S. (2003). *Trends in the liberal arts core and James Madison University's "The Human Community."* Retrieved November 30, 2006, from the James Madison University, General Education Program web site: www.jmu.edu/gened/powerpointgened/Lee.ppt

Reynolds, C. W., Allain, V. A., Erwin, T. D., Halpern, L. C., McNallie, R., & Ross, M. K. (1998). Looking backward: James Madison University's General Education Reform. *Journal of General Education, 47*(2), 149–165.

Sundre, D. (1999). *Does examinee motivation moderate the relationship between test consequences and test performance?* (Report No. TM029964). Harrisonburg, VA: James Madison University. (ERIC Document Reproduction Service No. ED432588)

Sundre, D. L., & Moore, D. L. (2002). The Student Opinion Scale: A measure of examinee motivation. *Assessment Update, 14*(1), 8–9.

Chapter 6

Indiana University–Purdue University Indianapolis: General Education Case Study

Trudy W. Banta, Sharon J. Hamilton

Overview of the Institutional Culture

Indiana University–Purdue University Indianapolis (IUPUI) is an urban research university established in 1969 as a partnership between Indiana and Purdue Universities, with Indiana University as the managing partner. Consequently, IUPUI is a campus of Indiana University (IU) that grants degrees in some 185 programs offered by 20 IU schools and 2 Purdue schools (science and engineering and technology). More first professional degrees are conferred at IUPUI than at any campus in Indiana and IUPUI is a national leader in this area. With almost 30,000 students, the campus is home to the largest nursing school and the second largest medical school in the U.S. In addition to medicine and nursing, IUPUI is also the primary campus for statewide programs in dentistry and social work.

IUPUI serves as a model worldwide for institutional collaboration. Geographically centered between its two Big Ten parent institutions, IUPUI provides the site for significant interdisciplinary work across the three campuses. IUPUI is Indiana's academic health sciences campus and is consistently in the top 10 institutions in the country in the number of health-related degrees it confers. IUPUI also ranks among the top 15 in the country in the number of first professional degrees granted. The campus has received national awards and recognition for the quality of its programs for first-year students, community-based learning, academic success of student athletes, and outcomes assessment based on institutional research. Located in the heart of downtown Indianapolis, the campus is just three blocks from the state capitol and the Indiana Government Center, the site for important student internships and faculty research.

Close linkages are maintained between most academic units at IUPUI and their counterparts at Indiana University and Purdue University. Nevertheless, there is no single model for collaboration. As noted previously, IUPUI is the home campus for statewide programs in medicine, nursing, dentistry, and social work, but faculty in education, public and environmental affairs, and business are considered members of coequal faculties based at Indiana University Bloomington. Curricula in the sciences, engineering, and technology mirror those at Purdue University West Lafayette. The Schools of Law and Liberal Arts, while granting IU degrees, work independently of counterparts in Bloomington.

Offering programs from two sizable universities has resulted in the formation of an unusually large number—22—of academic units at IUPUI. Moreover, the adoption in 1989 of responsibility center management—a system in which every unit is in charge of generating and balancing its own revenues and expenses—has tended to emphasize the distinctive nature of each of these units. Not surprisingly, prior to 1991, the approach to general education at IUPUI was unique to each of the schools enrolling undergraduates and consisted almost exclusively of distribution requirements.

Overview of the General Education Program

The purpose of the general education program at IUPUI is to provide for our students a common set of curricular and cocurricular experiences that develop a shared foundation of intellectual skills, dispositions, and modes of inquiry for a lifetime of further learning and application.

Prior to 1991, the general education curriculum had been the responsibility of each school and, as aforementioned, consisted primarily of a course-based distribution model. In 1990–1991, as part of our preparation for our decennial reaccreditation visit from the North Central Association in 1992, campus leaders established a Commission on General Education to oversee the development of a centrally coordinated approach to general education for IUPUI. In its earliest deliberations, the commission identified three possible approaches to general education:

• *Distributive approach.* Defining required areas and specific requirements within those areas that would be consistent across all IUPUI schools.

• *Core curriculum approach.* Involving the identification and/or development of a set of courses required of all majors.

• *Process approach.* Focusing on student learning experiences and coordinating those experiences across disciplines to provide all students with knowledge and skills considered appropriate by the faculty.

Although the campus had been employing primarily a distributive approach, there was no guarantee of a common general education experience. The Schools of Liberal Arts and Science had already explored and then rejected a core curriculum approach, since they could not agree on which courses needed to be included and every department wanted to protect its student enrollment-based tuition income. The commission therefore chose the process approach, not because it seemed most likely to succeed, but because it seemed least likely to fail on a campus as diverse as IUPUI.

A process approach to general education necessitates widespread and ongoing involvement of faculty. Consequently, within the first two years of its formation, the commission involved more than 200 IUPUI faculty in the following events:

• *First Annual Symposium on General Education* (April 1992). More than 150 faculty attended, and they developed a list of core values that most agreed should be included in any general education program.

• *Commission Report to the Faculty* (September 1992). This report synthesized the core values identified by the faculty and set up a faculty study group for each core value, involving almost 200 faculty.

• *Faculty Study Groups on General Education* (1992–1993). These study groups explored the pedagogical and curricular implications of their respective core value and developed a considerable body of teaching and evaluation strategies and suggestions.

• *Second Annual Symposium on General Education* (April 1993). More than 200 faculty attended to hear presentations from each of the study groups and to provide feedback on their work.

During the summer of 1993, the commission synthesized the two years of deliberations by faculty and administrators. An initial set of eight Principles of Undergraduate Learning (core communication and quantitative skills; critical thinking; intellectual adaptability; self-awareness; collaborative learning; engagement in cocurricular activities and learning; understanding culturally and ethnically diverse societies; and service beyond the self) resulted from these deliberations. Based on the work of the faculty study groups, the commission published a manual outlining curricular, pedagogical, and assessment suggestions and recommendations for each of the eight principles, providing a copy for every faculty member. Although a few schools and academic units began the challenging work of integrating these principles into their curricula, notably nursing and allied health sciences, whose accrediting agencies had requirements that closely matched the principles, most schools did not adopt them in this first iteration.

At this time, the chief academic officer appointed a Council on Liberal Arts and Sciences, representing two of our largest under-graduate schools, to discuss the possibility of a merger into a School of Liberal Arts and Science. While the council rejected the proposed merger, the members began to design a common curriculum for the two schools, basing it on the proposed principles. During discus-sions, the deans of the two schools decided that eight principles were too many and reduced them to five (core communication and quantitative skills; critical thinking; intellectual breadth, depth, and adaptiveness; integration and application of knowledge; and under-standing society and culture). The Principled Curriculum, as it came to be known, based on these five principles, was approved by the faculty assemblies of both schools in 1998. Concurrent discus-sions across the campus added a sixth principle, values and ethics, and these six principles were approved by the IUPUI Faculty Council also in 1998. Subsequent amendments adapted the Principled Curriculum to include this sixth principle.

This Principled Curriculum, while officially applying only to the Schools of Liberal Arts and Science, was an important docu-ment because it signaled an underlying faculty value about the role of general education in relation to the major. Rather than a set of introductory courses taken prior to the major and independent of the major, these principles were intended to permeate the major from the first year to the senior year. This model of implementation was unique for a large, comprehensive urban university, and proved a catalyst for documenting and assessing learning in ways previously unimagined by most of our faculty.

Prior to the adoption of the Principles of Undergraduate Learning (PULs) in 1998, IUPUI faculty saw general education primarily as a set of courses to prepare students to do well in the major and to broaden their learning beyond the major. They envisioned general education taking place during the first two years of undergraduate learning. A review of syllabi at that time revealed that very few faculty not teaching a general education course referenced the goals of general education or explicitly integrated general education learning meaningfully into the major.

The "principle" behind the Principles of Undergraduate Learning, which in themselves are simply categories of intellectual skills, dispositions, and ways of knowing, is that they permeate the undergraduate experience, providing a seamless yet explicit integration of general education with the major. While faculty subscribe to this principle in theory, they find it challenging in practice.

With the model of the Principled Curriculum as one form of implementation guide, the next step was to make explicit the integration and role of the PULs in curricular and cocurricular learning across the campus. An institutional approach to assessment of student learning provided the mechanism for ensuring that this integration was taking place. The Program Review and Assessment Committee (PRAC), formed in 1994 with two faculty members from each school to initiate and strengthen assessment of student learning in the major, has become the campus body for shepherding the PULs. PRAC encouraged schools to document the integration of the PULs into each academic major and asked for evidence of student mastery of the PULs in the annual report to PRAC expected from each school (see www.planning.iupui.edu/prac/prac.html).

The next step was to gather specific information on how the PULs were being taught, learned, and assessed in each school. In spring 2000, three faculty associate positions were created to work with the director of campus writing to collect and collate this information campus wide. These faculty associates met with every school and academic unit serving undergraduates to determine how their curricula advanced student understanding of the PULs in relation to specific course and program requirements. Their work resulted in the document *Phase I of a Study on Student Learning: A Working Document for the Campus*. This document is truly a portrait in time of the faculty view of general education at IUPUI in 2000. Like a cubist painting, it presents a fragmented and somewhat off-kilter perception of general education, where more is going on beneath the reported surface. In essence, it shows a faculty in transition from a traditional model of general education to, in theory, our more integrated model of the PULs, with faculty at different stages in this transition and therefore at different stages of their expectations for general education.

Typically, general education is offered through either a core curriculum or a distribution method, wherein students take a specified number of courses in the humanities, social sciences, and sciences. Additionally, most general education programs occur during the first year or two of study. The IUPUI PUL program represents a fresh approach in both areas.

First, it departs from the conventional distribution and core approaches by specifying abilities and ways of knowing intended to be part of all curricular and cocurricular programs. This requires an epistemological shift in faculty and student conceptions of what constitutes learning in a course. For example, a geography course now engages students explicitly in critical thinking, in integrating and applying their learning to other contexts, in understanding society and culture, and in seeing the values and ethics inherent in various approaches to the physical environment. Students are similarly explicitly engaged with these ideas in history, biology, and so on. Students connect their learning through concepts that integrate the specific content of their various courses.

Second, most approaches to general education involve a one-time engagement with a skill or concept, with expectations for transference to other courses. An institution might require Western Civilization, for example, as a proxy for understanding the development of our current society and culture. Once the course is taken, knowledge and transference of that knowledge are assumed. The IUPUI approach to general education, on the other hand, is based on the assumption that students improve in the PULs by having multiple opportunities to practice them throughout their full range of undergraduate curricular and cocurricular experiences. For example, the English department created developmental grids from freshman year to senior year. Education established PUL-related professional goals showing development not only from the freshman to senior year, but also during the first three years of teaching. Engineering uses a grid that articulates ABET (Accreditation Board for Engineering and Technology) outcomes with the PULs throughout its degree programs.

Student engagement with the Principles of Undergraduate Learning occurs in the following ways:

• From orientation through graduation, students learn about the significance of the PULs and are provided curricular and cocurricular opportunities for intellectual engagement with the PULs. University College plays a key role for entering students by organizing the first-year seminar and working with the schools to offer 108 learning communities for more than 2,000 students, or 85% of all new freshmen. University College personnel also have embedded the PULs in first-year seminars, painted the PULs on the stairwells and in classrooms, and developed a laminated PUL bookmark for all students and faculty.

• The Office of Campus and Community Life provides a rich array of cocurricular activities integrating the PULs, which are described in the following section.

• The Center on Integrating Learning is developing an electronic student portfolio (ePort) to enable students to track, document, reflect on, and share their growth and achievement in the Principles of Undergraduate Learning. The ePort is discussed in detail in a later section of this chapter.

Integration of the Principles of Undergraduate Learning with cocurricular activities is a priority for our Office of Campus and Community Life. Our vice chancellor for student life and diversity and dean of students provides support and encouragement at the highest level of administration for this integration. Examples of cocurricular programs that support the PULs include the following:

- Cultural heritage months support Understanding Society and Culture (Hispanic Heritage Month; GLBT Awareness Month; Native American Heritage Month; Black History Month; Women's History Month; Asian Heritage Month).

- Cultural programs and diversity trainings challenge students to analyze information and ideas from multiple perspectives, explicitly supporting critical thinking (see www.life.iupui.edu/culture/index.asp).

- Leadership development programs include workshops and community service activities to develop values and ethics in civically minded students (see http://life.iupui.edu/volunteer/index.asp). Leadership workshops provide opportunities for students to use new knowledge and apply it to specific issues and real-world problems, reinforcing the integration and application of knowledge (see http://life.iupui.edu/leadership/index.asp).

- Campus and Community Life oversees more than 160 undergraduate student organizations that engage students as they develop and refine their leadership skills as well as their core communication and quantitative skills and their understanding of diverse societies and cultures (see http://life.iupui.edu/groups/index.asp).

Overview of Assessment of the General Education Program

The 1998 Principles of Undergraduate Learning document did not specify a plan for implementation. In the absence of a campus-wide curriculum committee, it was not immediately clear which standing committee should assume leadership for advancing the PULs. Nevertheless, given the emphasis during their development on the goal of integrating the PULs within the learning outcomes of each discipline, and given that the proof of that integration would come logically through assessment of student learning, the Program Review and Assessment Committee stepped up to the plate and began to guide the diffusion and evaluation of the PULs. Now annual assessment reports from every school document the curricular and cocurricular integration of the PULs as well as related changes in curricula and pedagogy made on the basis of assessment findings.

For a decade the annual assessment reports from the schools have followed the format specified in the matrix depicted in Figure 6.1. Prior to 1998, the learning outcomes and assessment methods reported each year pertained only to student learning in the major. After 1998, faculty in each school were encouraged to integrate the outcomes associated with the PULs with outcomes developed for the major and to devise assessment strategies that would test learning in both realms; separately in some cases, but for the most part, in an integrated fashion.

Figure 6.1
Planning for Learning and Assessment

1) What general outcome are you seeking ?	2) How would you know it (the outcome) if you saw it ? (What will the student know or be able to do ?)	3) How will you help students learn it ? (In class or out of class.)
4) How could you measure each of the desired behaviors listed in #2 ?	5) What are the assessment findings ?	6) What improvements have been made based on assessment findings ?

In 2000, four senior faculty members undertook a semester-long study, meeting with faculty and administrators from all schools and analyzing curricula and syllabi to determine the extent of the PUL implementation. The results of their study, which showed almost universal awareness but at varying degrees of implementation, were posted on our electronic institutional portfolio (www.iport.iupui.edu) in the form of an interactive matrix. Anyone may click on a school and one or more PULs to learn how that school is integrating and assessing the PULs and how those assessments are improving teaching and learning. Having this information available to everyone has increased interest on the part of units with empty cells in the matrix to take actions that enable them to fill those cells. It also has produced a forum for sharing effective practices, thereby making it more likely that such practices will be tried elsewhere and that integration and assessment of the PULs will increase and improve. The visiting team representing the North Central Association that reaccredited IUPUI in 2002 found the interactive matrix quite helpful in gauging the status of general education implementation across the campus.

While each department is responsible for articulating the learning outcomes for each principle for its majors at the senior level, the PUL implementation is furthered by a multidisciplinary Community of Practice for each principle to develop specific learning outcomes for the PULs at the first (Introduction) and sophomore (Intermediate) levels. For example, the Understanding Society and Culture Community members have developed the following learning expectations for the Introductory and Intermediate levels, explicitly leading toward growth and development:

Introductory

- You have identified and explored some aspects of the range of diversity and universality in human history, society, and culture.

- You have recognized some aspects of interconnectedness of local and global concerns.

- You have interacted, in person, in literature or film, or through academic reading, with people and ideas in a culture different from yours.

Intermediate

• You have investigated in depth an area of diversity or universality in the human experience.

• You have analyzed and understood some aspect of the correlation between community affairs and globalization.

• You have engaged in intercultural communication (face to face, through technology, performance, etc.) on a level that shows appreciation and knowledge of diverse societies and cultures.

Sample assignments are being developed in each Community of Practice to model the integration of these expectations into discipline-specific concepts. It is important to note, however, that these rubrics are being developed more as starting points for departmental and programmatic discussion than as definitive expectations for every program. They are available as "default" rubrics for departments to use, but it is expected that each department or academic program will modify them according to programmatic expectations and emphases.

In fall 2004, the Center on Integrating Learning began the design of the IUPUI student electronic portfolio (ePort) to provide evidence of both achievement and improvement in each of the PULs as they are learned within the context of the student's major. Authentic evidence of individual student learning, as well as aggregated information about learning at the course, department, program, and campus levels (see Figure 2 below) increasingly will be available as the ePort moves to full implementation over the next four to five years.

Every student will have opportunities to provide evidence of learning in each of the Principles of Undergraduate Learning at the Introductory (first 26 credit hours), Intermediate (first 56 credit hours), and Advanced (junior and senior) levels. Additionally, throughout their undergraduate careers, students will be able to upload examples of cocurricular and extracurricular learning in relation to each of the PULs.

Across the top of the cube in Figure 6.2 are the possible objects for which aggregated information will be available in relation to each of the principles at each level. Listed are objects such as artifacts (the actual student work), reflections, course grades, and interactions between faculty and students, advisors and students, or students

Figure 6.2
Diagram of the ePort Assessment of Learning Model

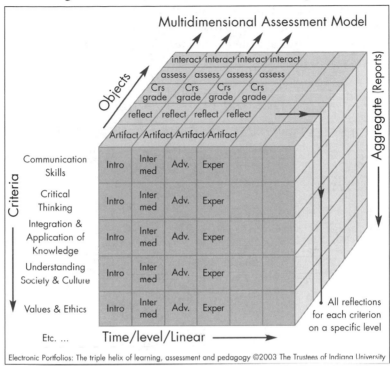

with clients (depending on how each program customizes the objects for assessment). However, the bases for documentation of learning for assessment purposes will be artifacts—actual student work, already graded within the academic program—and student reflections on that work in relation to the PULs at each of the three levels: Introductory, Intermediate, and Advanced.

The learning matrix for each student, illustrated in Figure 6.3, is the repository for the aggregated information described above. The matrix provides access, in one screen, to all the relevant undergraduate experiences of each student in relation to the PULs. The PULs form the left column of the matrix, and levels of student progress form the column headings. As students complete work in their majors, they upload graded assignments that demonstrate knowledge in the major and proficiency in one or more of the PULs. Faculty committees have developed learning expectations for each cell and a process for writing and reviewing reflections has been established. Student committees have developed expectations for experiential learning, providing opportunities for students to document cocurricular and extracurricular learning that applies, enhances, or integrates their curricular learning with their experiences beyond the classroom.

Figure 6.3
The IUPUI Learning Matrix

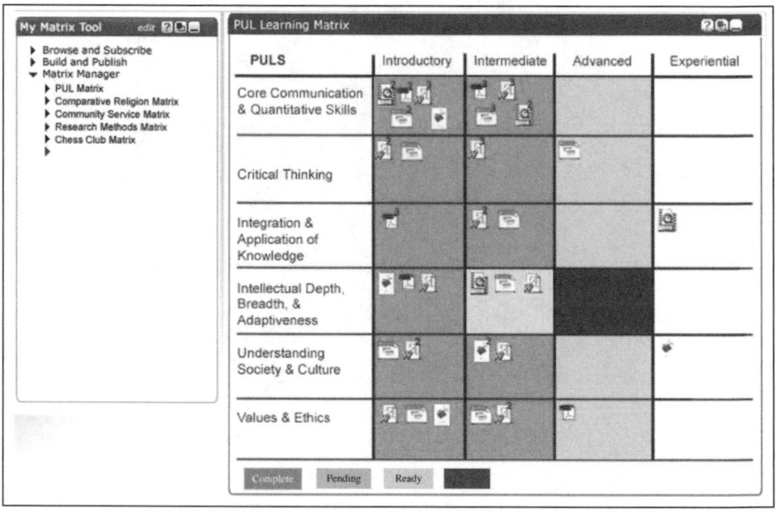

Each student uploads artifacts from coursework (or from cocurricular and extracurricular learning in the "experiential" cells) into the appropriate cell (each square of the matrix is a cell). When the student has met the campus- or department-determined expectations for learning in one of the cells, he or she writes a reflection, showing how understanding of that principle has been demonstrated and enhanced by the creation of these artifacts of learning. Each reflection has three parts: evidence of learning, connection of the evidence to campus/department learning outcomes, and intellectual growth (the articulation of increased understanding).

In its earliest design, the reflections are read and assessed by trained readers (initially emeritus faculty who are members of the Senior Academy) who provide written responses to each student. Readers rate the student's artifacts and reflections on a scale from 1 to 3 and these numbers are aggregated for instantly available assessment information. A 3 indicates that the student has exceeded campus expectations, a 2 indicates that the student has met campus expectations, and a 1 indicates that the student has made a start at meeting campus expectations. While individual students receive written comments, these numbered equivalents are accessible only on an anonymous, aggregated basis.

Once the technological infrastructure matures beyond this earliest stage, student learning outcomes may be aggregated according to any demographic or programmatic variables required so that, for example, one could learn how honors students are performing in relation to Quantitative Reasoning or Values and Ethics. Similarly, one could compare how majors in biology are achieving in Understanding Society and Culture in comparison to philosophy majors. The ability to gather meaningful assessment data on student learning of the PULs will meet academic and administrative needs and will provide useful information to improve curriculum and pedagogy at IUPUI.

Completing the matrix will provide students, faculty, departments, and the campus with a rich source of information about growth and achievement of the PULs in relation to academic and professional programs. That's the goal. The reality is that at IUPUI, as at most institutions, academic success is defined in terms of courses completed and grades on a transcript. Looking at broad and enduring goals for learning, such as critical thinking, values and ethics, or understanding society and culture, across a range of courses does not come naturally to most students or even to most faculty. While both faculty and students appreciate the importance of broad goals for learning, the first reaction is that documenting growth and achievement in the PULs is additional work with no spaces in established courses for that additional work to take place. A considerable reorientation (not to mention time, resources, and collective commitment) is required to find ways that both course/program goals and broader goals for learning may be explicitly taught, learned, and assessed.

Much work remains to be done to implement the technological requirements of the ePort, to put in place manageable means of evaluating student work in the portfolios, and then to institutionalize the ePort as a principal means of evaluating student achievement and progress in general education in all majors. Currently, there is no requirement that students in every discipline use the electronic portfolio and no expectation that faculty in every program will make the ePort a requirement for their students. If the experience of the students and faculty who try out this new technology is sufficiently positive, IUPUI administrators anticipate that acceptance of the ePort as a primary assessment tool will spread throughout the institution. Our goal is to make completion of an ePort a requirement for completing every undergraduate major by 2010.

The Program Review and Assessment Committee, with representation from every school, provides guidance for and disseminates information about programmatic developments and initiatives related to the PULs. The faculty governance system oversees any revisions of or curricular requirements related to the PULs. The Center on Integrating Learning was created in 2002 to support Communities of Practice and a PUL-related mini-grant program (CoPs).

Administration of the general education assessment is very flexible since faculty in every school are free to implement the PULs as they consider appropriate. Moreover, use of the ePort in this process is still in a pilot phase. No component of general education assessment is compulsory and only students in pilot sections are using the ePort to date. Our vision is to have students placing evidence of learning at Introductory, Intermediate, and Advanced levels in the ePort throughout their careers, both while they are students at IUPUI and throughout their lives. Nevertheless, a requirement for completion of the cells in the ePort will have to be enacted by the Faculty Council before all students can be expected to complete the ePort as all components of general education assessment are flexible at this point.

Examples of Assessment and How Results Are Used

The electronic student portfolio has been designed to integrate curricular and cocurricular growth and achievement in relation to the PULs. The PUL-based learning matrix specifies the learning outcomes developed by the Communities of Practice. This matrix is customizable, so that engineering students, for example, may complete a matrix that integrates the PUL learning outcomes with ABET outcomes. Education students integrate the PULs with the INTASC (Interstate New Teacher Assessment and Support Consortium) principles. The PUL-based learning matrix also encourages cocurricular learning of the PULs, with provision to document cocurricular experiences and to reflect on that learning in relation to the PULs.

Opportunities for cross-disciplinary dialogue associated with the development of the PULs have influenced the teaching philosophy of our faculty, departments, and schools. Analysis of our curricular offerings over the past five years demonstrates that our interdisciplinary, international, and service-learning programs—all indicative of a broader, more integrative teaching philosophy—have burgeoned within these networked initiatives.

Detailed evidence of the integration of the PULs is available in annual school assessment reports that outline curricular and pedagogical changes resulting from assessment of student learning of the PULs integrated into discipline-specific learning outcomes. The most significant of these changes are summarized in annual reports prepared for the Indiana Commission on Higher Education (http://planning.iupui.edu/527.html). The changes range from increasing emphasis on communication in the capstone course for physics majors to adding three new courses for seniors in business that are designed to increase students' understanding of values and ethics in business settings.

We have begun several additional initiatives to determine the impact of the PUL implementation on student learning, engagement, and retention. First, we have developed a series of items related to the PULs that are administered periodically in questionnaires for enrolled students and graduates of IUPUI. Respondents are asked to rank themselves on a 5-point scale on such abilities as solving mathematical problems; working effectively with people of different races, ethnicities, and religions; finding useful information on the Internet for work-related projects; and thinking critically and analytically. When one compares the responses of enrolled students surveyed in 2001, 2003, and 2005, students' self-ratings have remained stable or improved slightly. No rating has decreased significantly, and significant gains have been noted in four areas:

- Preparing a presentation that I will deliver to a group

- Using the computer applications that are most common to my work or field of study

- Doing research on an issue or topic before I plan a course of action

- Exercising my responsibilities as a citizen (voting, staying current with community and political issues)

In 2004, we were awarded one of five (of 105 submitted) NPEC/AIR grants to study the impact of ePort, a key aspect of our PUL Implementation Program, on student learning, engagement, and retention. We found a higher level of engagement in learning for the experimental group (those who used ePort) than for the control group (those who did not). Based on the many studies showing strong correlations between student engagement and student learning, these findings strongly suggest that our PUL Implementation Program is having a positive impact on learning.

Led by the Center on Integrating Learning, the IUPUI student electronic portfolio (ePort) is being designed to provide evidence of both improvement and achievement in each of the PULs as they are learned within the context of the student's major. Authentic evidence of individual student learning, as well as aggregated information about learning at the course, department, program, and campus levels will be increasingly available as the ePort moves from its pilot phases to full implementation over the next four to five years.

In 2006, the IUPUI Principles of Undergraduate Learning received two national awards in recognition of contributions to student learning: the Hesburgh Certificate of Excellence and the Council for Higher Education Accreditation's Student Learning Outcomes award.

Tips for Implementing the Process

We involved more than 400 faculty over eight years in discussing the approach to general education that resulted in the PULs. The extent of this involvement produced a campus-wide consensus that assisted later in the implementation of the PULs.

Having an established representative body like the Program Review and Assessment Committee to oversee the implementation and assessment of the PULs has been essential. The matrix employed by PRAC members for the past decade (see Figure 6.1, shown earlier) has been very helpful in initiating thinking about incorporating the PULs in courses and curricula and assessing student achievement thereof.

Provide adequate time for consensus to develop regarding the principles that will guide general education as well as methods for assessing student achievement of these. This is hard work, but we counsel others not to give up. Even if one group turns in a report and the members ask not to be involved further, appoint a new group the following year to finish the work.

Integrate general education with the major; don't separate the two. General education abilities should be enacted uniquely in each major and assessed there at the senior level. This integration should take place throughout the major, from freshman to senior year, so that students have multiple opportunities to practice the skills and abilities faculty consider most important.

Involve student affairs professionals in extending general education learning outside the classroom through guest lectures, art exhibits, and opportunities for students to learn speaking and organizational skills as they provide leadership for campus groups and activities.

Encourage linkages between general education knowledge and skills and those advocated by disciplinary associations such as ABET and NCATE. This will encourage faculty in professional schools to buy into the general education initiative since they will not have to do duplicative work.

Assess directly and indirectly; use various methods in capstone courses, senior projects, and electronic portfolios as direct measures of learning and periodically use locally developed as well as national surveys as indirect measures. In addition, peer review and broader evaluation studies should be applied from time to time.

Challenges to Assessing General Education and Strategies to Overcome Them

Our major challenge was that the PUL document approved in 1998 specified no plan for implementation, and there was no campus-wide curriculum committee to shepherd the development of the PULs. Neither of these absences was accidental; both were intentional responses of faculty governance to suggestions made by the Commission on General Education. The prevailing view was that these principles were the "apple pie and motherhood" of higher education, and that everyone would pay attention to them; hence nobody needed to ensure their curricular inclusion. Consequently, when the commission engaged eight senior faculty and more than 100 tenured and tenure-track faculty in developing curricular, pedagogical, and assessment approaches for the campus, the resultant publication, in 1999, was highly resisted and never implemented, except by the School of Nursing. The study conducted by the four senior faculty in 2000 highlighted these gaps in implementation and demonstrated that a campus-wide implementation plan was needed after all.

A plan did evolve, but we lost almost four years before we were fully organized with all the initiatives that we have described previously in this chapter. The PULs might well have become a paper document only, had it not been for the intervention of PRAC and later the Center on Integrating Learning. Nevertheless, both of these bodies exist outside the formal faculty governance structure and are eyed somewhat suspiciously by Faculty Council leaders. This means that making the electronic portfolio a requirement for all students faces an uphill battle. Similarly, service on curricular and pedagogical committees, such as our Communities of Practice, dedicated to improving and assessing the effectiveness of general education through our PULs, is still not as highly regarded or rewarded as more traditional aspects of faculty roles and responsibilities.

Even so, a dedicated core of faculty and academic staff is enthusiastically engaged in implementing and assessing the PULs, and the numbers in that core grow exponentially each year. Since 2000, new faculty in particular have increasingly seen the value of the PULs and willingly contribute their time and expertise to the implementation process. Providing funded faculty development opportunities that relate curricular and pedagogical change directly to the PULs has also had a significant impact.

In retrospect, the division between administration and governance has been difficult to overcome. Although the PULs were approved through the system of faculty governance, oversight of their implementation and assessment has been primarily the responsibility of the administrative arm of academic affairs. In order to mitigate the dichotomy between administration and governance, we recommend developing a plan for implementing general education initiatives that is overseen by faculty governance, preferably via a campus-wide curriculum committee.

Chapter 7

Isothermal Community College: General Education Case Study

Nancy H. Womack

Overview of the Institutional Culture

Isothermal Community College, located in Spindale, North Carolina, was chartered on October 1, 1964, just over one year following the state legislature's creation of the North Carolina Department of Community Colleges. Since it was designed to serve both Rutherford and Polk Counties, the original board of trustees wanted to give the college a name that encompasses the region rather than to use the names of the counties. For years the word *isothermal* had been used to describe the thermal belt climate the region enjoys. Protected by mountains, our foothills location is one of those areas marked on geological maps as being in the line of an isotherm. Hence, the name seemed fitting to the college founders.

From its early years, Isothermal has been a comprehensive community college with equal emphasis on preparing students interested in transferring to four-year colleges and on preparing those interested in applied sciences and business fields for the job market. The college also has an active continuing education department with a high school completion program that traditionally has the largest graduating class in the county. Since its inception, the college has sought to meet the educational and training needs of its constituency with a mix of traditional and nontraditional students. The service area is rural in nature. Until recently the economy was based largely on textile and furniture manufacturing. The closure of most of these plants has affected the college, with increased enrollment of displaced workers and a new challenge to retrain them while simultaneously helping them develop confidence in themselves as students with new career goals. Our current enrollment is around 2,000 curriculum students with an additional 16,000 enrolled annually in continuing education courses.

Since the mid-1990s, Isothermal Community College has made an all-out effort to become a "learning college." Several events came together to move the college in this direction. Among these were our 1995 accreditation reaffirmation with the Southern Association of Colleges and Schools; participation of the college in a series of Pew Roundtable discussions; a visiting speaker, Dr. James Anderson, who challenged the college to "become a cutting-edge" institution; an acceptance of that challenge by 85% of the faculty; a review of the college's mission, along with the addition of vision and values statements; and the involvement of several faculty members in the Hewlett Fellows initiative at North Carolina State University. All of this led to one of the most significant institutional changes in Isothermal's history—the foundation of the Team for the Advancement of a Learning College, commonly known as TALC. This team became an umbrella organization under which several task forces began to operate. These task forces, made up of all volunteers, currently cover the areas of professional development for both faculty and staff, learning strategies, enhancing systems and processes, campus life, institutional effectiveness, business and industry training, and assessment. Currently, Isothermal is known for its learning college commitment and the progress we have made in that effort.

Isothermal's curriculum program is organized into four academic areas: arts and sciences (including nursing), business sciences, applied sciences and technology, and developmental education. The arts and sciences program offers A.A. and A.S. degrees with 21 pre-majors, along with L.P.N. and A.D.N. nursing. Business sciences, which offers the associate of applied science degree, as well as several diploma programs, has nine areas of concentration, including three that deal with computer programming and information systems. Applied sciences offers an array of certificate, diploma, and A.A.S. degree programs ranging from its highly acclaimed broadcasting and production technology program to service-related programs such as criminal justice and early childhood education. Developmental education serves as the foundation of support for all the curriculum areas. The college has a firm belief that students, in order to be successful in curriculum courses, must have basic skills provided by developmental studies in math, English, and reading and that early enrollment in these courses is essential for students who place into them.

While the developmental education program helps those students in need of its services to attain some of the basic general education skills, these skills are reinforced and enhanced through the general education component in each curriculum program, leading to a diploma or a degree.

Overview of the General Education Program

Degree programs in business and allied sciences have a 15-semester hour general education requirement. Those in arts and sciences have a 44-hour general education core, as well as several hours of electives in most programs which are often filled with additional general education courses. A critical philosophical perspective at Isothermal is that all faculty are responsible for teaching general education competencies along with the content of their courses. Every curriculum course has a writing component, and most faculty members stress additional general education competencies in their syllabi. Diploma programs require at least one communication course and one math course.

The purpose of the general education component in degree and diploma programs at Isothermal is to provide students with important life skills. The student handbook (Isothermal Community College, 2006, p. 35) makes the following statement regarding the purpose of general education:

> Because we believe an education is more than an accumulation of credits earned through completion of a variety of courses, and because we want graduates of our programs to be successful at whatever their next step may be—either getting a job or transferring to another college—it is essential that they exhibit the general education skills . . . basic to getting along in the world of work. They are skills employers tell us they want most in people

they hire. They are skills necessary to success in daily life. Our expected general education outcomes are as follows:

- Communicate effectively through writing, reading, speaking, and listening and through demonstration of information literacy

- Analyze problems and make logical conclusions

- Demonstrate positive interpersonal skills through cooperative learning and group interaction

- Demonstrate quantitative competencies

- Demonstrate basic computer skills

In their first semester at Isothermal, students are required to take a success and study skills course (ACA 115). It is in this course that most students are first introduced to the general education emphasis at the college. In addition, the emphasis is reinforced in other curriculum courses through syllabi which have a required component titled "General Education Competencies Addressed in This Course." As instructors review their syllabi, students begin to grasp that this is an important concept at the college. They are provided with ample printed media and are encouraged to use the college web site for information about general education skills expected of them. Faculty members from all areas have ownership in the general education program, largely because they were involved in its development.

Overview of Assessment of the General Education Program

While Isothermal has always engaged in assessment practices of varying sorts and degrees, it was a rather fragmented process until quite recently. Soon after making the decision to become a learning college, based on the tenants of Terry O'Banion's work, *A Learning College for the 21st Century* (1997), it became apparent that the college needed a focused approach to learning outcomes assessment. In 1998, the Assessment Taskforce was formed and added to the previously mentioned Team for the Advancement of a Learning College. The composition of the original Assessment Taskforce was almost evenly mixed between administration and faculty. Today it is 80% faculty and only 20% administration.

In its first year, the Assessment Taskforce spent most of its energy researching assessment practices at other schools and looking for resources we thought would be helpful to the college. Taskforce members read works by major authors in the field, including Trudy Banta, Patricia Cross, and Tom Angelo, as well as publications from Alverno College. We participated in the teleconference "I Taught, but They Didn't Learn It," featuring Craig Nelson, James Anderson, and Tom Angelo. We also communicated with several of our peers. All of this resulted in two major events in 1998–1999: having Jeffrey Seybert of Johnson County Community College come to Isothermal as a consultant, and our sending two representatives to Alverno to attend their weeklong Assessment Institute. Seybert encouraged us to use our already adopted general education competencies as a starting point for an assessment plan, and Alverno gave us ideas on how to do it.

By Convocation Day in the fall of 1999, the Assessment Taskforce announced a structural framework that would involve 100% of full-time faculty, as well as selected professional support personnel, to begin work on establishing criteria for assessing learning outcomes of our general education competencies: communicating effectively through writing, speaking, reading, and listening; demonstrating problem-solving skills; demonstrating interpersonal skills through cooperative learning and group interaction; demonstrating quantitative competency; and demonstrating basic computer skills. (Information literacy was later added to the communications competency.) As noted earlier, our contention from the beginning was that teaching these competencies is the purview of the whole college, not just that of selected liberal arts disciplines. The goal has always been to integrate these skills into as many courses as possible.

The 1999–2000 academic year, modeled on the Alverno principles of involving everyone and keeping people talking about assessment, not only resulted in the development of our general education outcomes criteria and rubrics, but also advanced teamwork and leadership emergence among faculty. The structural framework we used required people from across disciplines to work together. At the fall convocation workshop, everyone was given an opportunity to select a competency team on which he or she wanted to work. Since the communication competency was so comprehensive, we divided it into two teams, one for reading and writing and one for speaking and listening. Altogether there were six sign-up sheets designed with only a given number of slots for each academic area. Team chairs, along with reporters and facilitators from the Assessment Taskforce, were already listed on each form. Senior administrators and academic deans were not included on the teams since we wanted this to be a faculty-driven project. However, as teams began to meet (once a month on Friday afternoons), administrators were present at all meetings as rovers going from one team to another to offer support and to observe progress. Of course, we faced some resistance, but most of it was overcome as faculty and professional support personnel began to see purpose in what they were doing. A lot of cross-campus conversation and interdependence as well as individual leadership skills emerged as teams began to learn from each other at the campus-wide report sessions we conducted periodically. The level of conversation advanced dramatically with each new session.

With the major objective of developing criteria and rubrics for our general education learning outcomes completed by the beginning of 2000–2001, the task force decided to cut back on the number of campus-wide assessment meetings and to begin field testing the use of the rubrics. Much of our meeting time was then devoted to troubleshooting problems faculty members had experienced with the rubrics. Teams reconvened and revised the wording until all seemed satisfied that they had created the best documents they could produce. Next, the Assessment Taskforce began to weave assessment into the fabric of the college. We began this cultural shift by including assessment language and references to the rubrics in course syllabi. To do this, the Assessment Taskforce sponsored workshops, again at campus-wide meetings, to train faculty in how to accomplish this goal. We published all the general education outcomes criteria and rubrics in a handout for students, and we also began to include an assessment and student portfolio session in our success and study skills class (ACA 115). In addition, we added an assessment vocabulary list to the student handbook.

In the following academic year, 2001–2002, we continued to advance the assessment initiative in two significant ways—by providing training to faculty in using the rubrics and by taking some first steps toward advancing assessment from the classroom level to the program level. To accomplish the first goal, the Assessment Taskforce planned two campus-wide meetings. The first was conducted by English teachers on using the writing rubric. In small groups, faculty members were given the chance to assess four examples of student writing (one representing each of the four levels of competency reflected on the rubric). They used the rubric first, then engaged in discussion designed to help non-English teachers realize that they do not have to have a degree in English to assess writing. The second workshop used a round robin format that included sessions on using all the other rubrics. Faculty members could select which three of these they wished to attend. To begin work on the second goal, the Assessment Taskforce sponsored a campus-wide meeting devoted to curriculum mapping using a form that contained all the general education competencies and their criteria. In breakout groups by curriculum area, we began the process of determining which competencies were being addressed in which courses, as well as how the competencies were being assessed. These findings were reviewed and addressed in each curriculum area the following year.

Curriculum mapping proved to be an important component of our general education outcomes assessment initiative. Some of the first "informed" changes we made in assessing our general education program came from realizing which competencies were emphasized the least and coming up with improvements we could make in specific courses to address these deficiencies. By focusing on specific courses within the framework of an entire program of study, we were actually taking the first steps toward formal assessment of general education outcomes as a part of program assessment.

To take Isothermal to the next stage of general education outcomes assessment, the college developed an assessment plan model. Components of this model include the following:

- Program mission statement
- Review of program-specific literature
- Expected program outcomes

- Program goals for a specific time frame

- Activities for achievement of goals

- Assessment of activities

- Follow-up: annual reports, setting new goals, continuing the process

Each curriculum area of the college has developed a program assessment plan based on the model described above. While each area uses the same template for creating its plan, there is adequate flexibility within the model to accommodate various approaches.

Examples of Assessment and How Results Are Used

Faculty members in all areas of the college use a combination of formal and informal assessment. The college encourages the use of classroom assessment techniques as outlined in Angelo and Cross (1993). The Assessment Taskforce has offered two workshops on informal assessment, and it surveys faculty on alternate years to determine the level of usage in the classroom. The college also provides quality improvement forms for individual faculty members to use when they make changes to their courses based on their own observation of needed changes or on student feedback on informal assessments. For formal assessment each program area has its own assessment plan based on the model previously discussed. For example, in business sciences faculty members have chosen to focus on no more than three programs in any given year. In 2004 they chose business administration, information systems, and office systems for program assessment. For each selected program they established not only program-related goals, but also general education goals. They collected artifacts which were analyzed and evaluated. From these they developed quality improvement plans that are in the process of being implemented. While follow-up studies are conducted on the results of the first round of program assessments, initial work is under way on three other programs.

As with most assessment plans, nothing is ever finished; with each closure, the loop opens again. Applied sciences is using a similar approach to program assessment with the general education component being one part of a larger plan. In developmental education the assessment focus is based primarily on measuring attainment of basic skills. In developmental math, for example, students are given a diagnostic test at the beginning of each course. These scores are compared to scores on exit exams. At the elementary algebra level instructors and students aim for 85% accuracy on unit tests. Students are then tracked to see how well they perform in higher-level math courses. In addition to the attainment of math skills, the program emphasizes clear communication and logical thinking, again bringing in two more of the general education competencies we expect our students to achieve.

The arts and sciences program not only prepares college transfer students for entry into baccalaureate degree programs, but also provides general education support courses for all areas of the college. The program assessment focus in arts and sciences is devoted entirely to general education. In addition to the six competencies previously listed, arts and sciences programs have added a competency statement on understanding diverse cultural and historical perspectives. Most courses in the humanities, and many in the social sciences, have embedded final exam questions which get to the heart of this competency as instructors ask students to synthesize what they consider the primary concepts and the value of their courses. This type of "unique assessment" (Ehrmann, 1998) gives students the opportunity to focus a response based on their own unique experiences with the content of the course. This is not quantitative assessment, but its qualitative value is immeasurable. Artifacts collected over time and periodically reviewed reveal trends in student thinking as well as insights into their ability to communicate effectively.

Responses also often provide instructors with insights into how they may more effectively structure questions and directions for better responses. Most faculty do not rely exclusively on unique assessment for measuring learning outcomes but instead combine it with what Ehrmann (1998) refers to as "uniform impact"—testing for certain knowledge the instructor expects all students to attain.

The Arts and Sciences Assessment Plan has a section for each of the general education learning outcomes. For each general competency, core outcomes based on the college-adopted criteria and rubrics are listed. For each of these, specific courses are identified as the major courses in which a specific competency will be emphasized. In addition, the plan includes the types of assessment to be used for measuring the competency, a timeline or schedule for assessing the competency, and a list of parties responsible for carrying out the plan.

In reality, arts and sciences faculty members try to integrate all (or most of all) the competencies into each of their courses. All courses have a writing component; most have a speech component; almost all require computer skills, interpersonal skills, and problem-solving skills. Some have developed assignments to measure reading, information literacy, and listening skills. The quantitative skills competency is not included in as many of the syllabi as other competencies, but it is not limited only to math classes—it is included in most science classes. However, for purposes of planning and monitoring the plan, arts and sciences designated three to four general education competencies for focused study each year.

In 2004–2005, the first full year of implementation of the Arts and Sciences Assessment Plan, faculty members began work on more focused assessment of writing, speaking, information literacy, and understanding diverse cultural and historical perspectives.

For writing, two activities were planned and implemented: a diagnostic grammar/mechanics test was administered in selected fall semester composition classes, and selected writing artifacts from classes other than English were collected and assessed by external evaluators using the college writing rubric. Analysis of the artifacts revealed a close parallel with the diagnostic test. Grammar/mechanics was the section of the rubric on which students scored lowest. Further analysis of the types of errors students were making in their writing revealed problems in the same areas in which they had scored low on the diagnostic test. Among these were problems with verb tenses, agreement problems (subject-verb and pronoun-antecedent), sentence structure, including sentence fragments, and punctuation problems. This information was fed back to instructors, who, incidentally, were not at all surprised. It just provided them with reason to focus more on these problems in writing instruction.

Another side benefit from the external assessment of the writing artifacts was a recommendation from the assessors that the rubric include more credit for content. As a part of our overall assessment plan, all general education outcomes assessment rubrics are scheduled for review and possible revision in 2006–2007. Undoubtedly, this recommendation will be taken into consideration at that time.

When arts and sciences first conducted curriculum mapping, an ad hoc group of faculty members reviewed the information on requirements in all arts and sciences courses and discovered that speech was one of the weakest areas in terms of assignment requirements. Our response to this was to initiate several new assignments involving oral communication. This was all done by faculty members who volunteered to make that addition to their classes. These included debates in history and political science courses, structured controversy activities in some biology and English classes, group project presentations in a number of different courses, poster presentations in anatomy and physiology, and a variety of other individual research reports that students present orally as well as in writing.

For the assessment of speech, the majority of faculty members who have speech components in their classes use the speech rubric (or a variation of the official rubric) on a regular basis. In 2005, for our arts and sciences assessment focus on speech, the speech instructor used the rubric in a variety of ways as a major part of the class. He videotaped his students' speeches for each assignment and then put the tapes on reserve in the library. Students were required to view the portion of the tape that contained their own individual presentations and fill out a rubric just like the one the instructor had used. Following this self-assessment activity, teacher and student compared rubrics, and students were given feedback for improvement or reinforcement for what they had done well.

Another activity designed to help students improve their speech skills involved peer assessment. The day before each set of individual presentations, the instructor had the students practice their speeches in small groups of three or four. Students assessed each other using the speech rubric and offered suggestions for improvement. Based on the instructor's review of the students' presentations from the beginning to the end of the class, all but two students made dramatic improvements in their speeches.

The other two general education competencies scheduled for special focus in 2004–2005 (information literacy and understanding diverse cultural and historical perspectives) were carried over to the next academic year. For the assessment of information literacy, faculty in the English department decided to assess students in the basic research classes using pretests and posttests. After creating and administering the first pretest, they found that the questions were too subjective and that the responses were impossible to tabulate in any fashion that provided concrete data. So, in essence, they started over by creating objective tests that were administered at the beginning and end of two research classes in spring 2006. One class showed a 95% improvement rate, while a smaller class had three students who did not show improvement and thus brought the class average down to 74%. The highest improvement rate per individual student was an increase of 22 points. English faculty have analyzed the overall test results on a question-by-question basis to determine areas where additional instruction may be needed.

The assessment of understanding diverse cultural and historical perspectives is still a work in progress. Several instructors in the humanities and social sciences are using embedded exam questions for assessing this competency and are currently field testing a rubric developed by an interdisciplinary subcommittee from the Assessment Taskforce. This rubric will be officially approved for campus-wide use in spring 2007.

Other areas of emphasis for the Arts and Sciences Assessment Plan call for special focus on assessing reading, problem solving, and quantitative skills. Faculty in the math department devised a tool for assessing problem solving and quantitative skills via an embedded exam question on graphing and graph interpretation that they used in six different courses ranging from Math Concepts to Calculus II. They set a 90% accuracy rate as their success goal. After piloting this approach, they realized some flaws in the grading point scale that made this figure difficult to reach. Students were either 100% accurate in their responses or much lower than 90% if they missed even a single part of a question. So the accuracy rate ended up at 76% based on the criteria they initially set. Still, it was a good experiment that will be repeated in spring 2007.

Since the reading rubric is currently under review, the development of an assessment plan for reading skills in arts and sciences courses has been tabled until spring 2007.

The third year of the arts and sciences general education assessment focused on listening skills, interpersonal skills, and computer skills. As stated earlier, the assessment of all these general education competencies is ongoing. However, in the years specified our goal is to attempt to quantify the effectiveness of our general education program by generating data based on the specific assessment of selected skills.

From the students' perspective, the college has recently begun incorporating portfolio development into at least two of their required courses. This form of authentic assessment is described by Zubizarreta (2004):

> The learning portfolio is a flexible, evidence-based tool that engages students in a process of continuous reflection and collaborative analysis of learning. As written text, electronic display, or other creative project, the portfolio captures the scope, richness, and relevance of students' learning. The portfolio focuses on purposefully and collaboratively selected reflections and evidence for both improvement and assessment of students' learning. (p. 16)

In spring 2006 arts and sciences piloted a capstone portfolio course designed to enable students to bring together artifacts demonstrating all the general education competencies they have learned or further developed during their work toward the A.A. or A.S. degree. The course selected for this project was Human Values and Meaning. The instructor incorporated the portfolio component throughout the semester. Portfolios were assessed by an interdisciplinary group of faculty members and were judged on predetermined criteria. Selected students were recognized publicly for their outstanding work. All students were provided feedback on their portfolios. This assessment endeavor will be repeated in the spring of 2007.

The purposes for all assessment practices at Isothermal Community College, whether formal or informal, are to improve instruction and to promote learning.

Tips for Implementing the Process

Based on experiences at Isothermal, the best advice we have to offer other schools that are starting a general education outcomes assessment initiative is to involve as many people as possible. Since Isothermal is a relatively small school, it was fairly easy for us to involve all faculty. Larger schools may have to use faculty representatives for plan development. Even so, there needs to be a vehicle for keeping everyone informed—newsletters, email, reports at larger meetings, and so on.

There also should be a vehicle for feedback and a willingness to listen to faculty concerns and/or suggestions. If faculty do not play a role in the establishment of an assessment plan, it will be very difficult to get the buy-in needed to implement it. Research into what other schools have done is also helpful, but each school still has to work through details on its own. It would be disastrous just to take someone else's plan and foist it on a different faculty. Equally disastrous is the administrative edict that imposes a plan without faculty participation.

It is also important to realize that creating a culture of assessment takes time. Faculty are accustomed to and generally quite adept at assessing student progress in their own courses, but when required to become part of a larger assessment plan, they tend to have more questions—questions not only about the "how to," but also questions about the "why." Thus, training becomes another significant part of the project. At Isothermal, our campus-wide assessment meetings (at least two per semester) frequently involve workshops on various aspects of assessment as well as updates on what different areas of the college are doing with assessment. We learned from the Alverno model that keeping people talking about assessment is one of the best ways to assure that assessment is taking place. People do not get comfortable with outcomes assessment practices over night. Give them time.

One caution is to avoid trying to do too much at one time. The tendency is to want to do everything until reality steps in and says you can't do it all. Be selective in what you assess and realize that random sampling works just as well.

Challenges to Assessing General Education and Strategies to Overcome Them

One of the most significant barriers Isothermal Community College has encountered in the process of implementing its general education assessment plan correlates with faculty turnover. Of the faculty who first developed the assessment criteria and rubrics, many have retired or moved on to other jobs. With each new hire, the process of assessment orientation and expectation starts over again.

The strategy we have used to help overcome this barrier starts with the job interview. The assessment focus and the learning college focus are discussed in both the initial interview with each candidate and in a follow-up session with the president and the vice president for academic and student affairs. Selected candidates are given printed information about our expectations and are encouraged to review our web site publications before they start their employment. Once on the job, area deans/directors provide each new faculty member with the general education criteria and rubrics as well as a syllabus template and an explanation on how to incorporate general education competencies into their courses. New faculty are also encouraged to participate in campus-wide assessment meetings and to utilize the expertise of their peers. Still, it generally takes at least a semester before most new faculty members feel comfortable speaking the language of assessment and incorporating it into their work.

Developing and implementing a plan for the assessment of general education skills is an ongoing and time-consuming task, and certainly not one that can be put on the shelf and labeled complete. Because it is a circular rather than a linear procedure, there is always a loop to close and another one to open. There are always new people to train and new students who have to become acclimated to assessment procedures and language, but it is an exciting journey, especially when viewed as another tool to aid and measure learning. It is an essential tool for any institution seeking to become a part of the learning college movement.

References

Angelo, T. A., & Cross, K. P. (1993). *Classroom assessment techniques: A handbook for college teachers* (2nd ed.). San Francisco, CA: Jossey-Bass.

Ehrmann, S. C. (1998, June). *What outcomes assessment misses.* Paper presented at the American Association for Higher Education Assessment Conference, Cincinnati, OH.

Isothermal Community College. (2006). *Student handbook.* Spindale, NC: Author.

O'Banion, T. (1997). *A learning college for the 21st century.* Phoenix, AZ: American Council on Education/Oryx Press.

Zubizarreta, J. (2004). *The learning portfolio: Reflective practice for improving student learning.* Bolton, MA: Anker.

Chapter 8

North Carolina State University: General Education Case Study

Allen P. Dupont

Overview of the Institutional Culture

North Carolina State University (NCSU) is a relatively large doctoral/research-extensive institution located in Raleigh, with approximately 22,000 undergraduate students. It is a unit of the consolidated University of North Carolina system. A land-grant institution, NCSU has been known primarily for its undergraduate and graduate programs in agriculture and life sciences, engineering, and textiles. More recently, programs in design, humanities, social sciences, and environmental sciences have gained prominence. Despite these recent developments, engineering programs are still the most popular with undergraduate students.

NCSU is led by a chancellor to whom the provost and executive vice chancellor for academic affairs report. Reporting to the provost are the deans of the 10 colleges, of which 9 offer undergraduate programs (the College of Veterinary Medicine only offers graduate programs). The colleges are somewhat autonomous, leading to the often lamented silo structure, but despite this there is a reasonable level of cooperation among them. In each college, an associate dean for academic affairs is responsible for undergraduate academic programs, including assessment and program review. The dean of the Division of Undergraduate Academic Programs has responsibility for administration of the general education requirements (GER) program with input from the Council on Undergraduate Education (CUE), a faculty committee. The division does not award degrees but provides numerous academic support programs for students, administrative support for the curriculum approval process, and oversees and supports the assessment of general education and academic programs through the Office of Assessment.

As a doctoral/research-extensive university, it is not surprising that NCSU rewards individual faculty members and departments for securing grant funding and producing publishable research. Presumably, this is typical at all similar institutions and institutions that aspire to the same classification. This is not to say that the faculty does not care about undergraduates. To the contrary, there are a surprisingly large number of faculty members across the university who have devoted and continue to devote a significant amount of time and effort to the issues surrounding undergraduate education and specifically general education. However, the prevailing attitude toward general education is shaped by the fundamental mission of the institution. For a large number of faculty members, general education is viewed as essentially "exposure to the disciplines" (or "civilizing the engineers," as some wags have stated it) and general education courses are viewed as synonymous with survey courses. This is not a universally held view, of course, and much progress has been made in explaining the purposes of general education as developed and monitored by CUE.

Overview of the General Education Program

The purpose of general education at NCSU is to provide students with opportunities to develop critical academic skills, including communication, research skills, and quantitative literacy, and to prepare graduates for productive lives as citizens through an understanding of the scientific method, social scientific methods, and an appreciation for and understanding of the humanities and the arts. Thus, there are two basic aims: preparation for study in the major, and the acquisition of skills deemed necessary for all graduates of NCSU. In conversations with faculty members, it appears that this is fairly widely understood and accepted.

Organizationally, the GER consists of 50 to 53 semester credit hours of work loosely divided into disciplinary categories (mathematics and natural science, humanities, etc.). Each category has a list of approved courses, and students choose courses from that approved list. There is one special category (science, technology, and society) that consists of interdisciplinary courses that provide students with opportunities to deepen their understanding of the ways in which science and technology impact society. Under certain circumstances courses on this list can also satisfy another GER requirement, but generally double counting is not allowed.

However, programs are allowed to require that their majors take only certain courses on each list or to choose from a subset of each list. This is partly a result of the cap on the total number of credit hours that can be required of students in any degree program (currently set at 128 for all students in the University of North Carolina system). This means that many of the GER courses are double counted with major requirements. For example, the calculus courses required of engineering majors are on the GER mathematics list and the required physics courses are on the GER natural science list. This can create an extra burden for a student changing majors, depending on the extent to which the major programs involved have "subset" the lists.

This system is, at 50 to 53 hours, larger than that at almost any other institution with a similar general education system. The average number of hours required at doctoral/research-extensive institutions with analogous general education systems is between 35 and 40 hours. Partly as a result of the size and partly as a result of the structure, students often see it as a checklist and not as a rational series of courses leading to a set of important skills, knowledge, and attitudes. Of course, the argument is frequently made that students view it as a checklist because it is, in fact, just that. However, a bit of history is in order here.

When the current GER was put in place at NCSU in 1993, there were no student learning outcomes or objectives associated with the categories. Neither the state of North Carolina nor the University of North Carolina System mandated any objectives, outcomes, or competencies for student learning, and that is still the case today. The only guidance for faculty members (and students) was provided by the broad goals of the GER itself. This was not a very satisfactory situation, as it left in doubt what the faculty expected students to learn from general education. Assessment was also very difficult, as anyone who has thought about the issue knows that it is hard to assess student learning when there is no clear expectation of what students should be learning. Finally, without a clear expectation of what students should be learning (by category), CUE had no clear criteria for recommending that a course be approved for addition to a list.

In 1999, the GER was dramatically improved without changing the essential structure. The members of CUE, working with assessment professionals and faculty members in areas represented by the various categories, devised student learning objectives for each category. These objectives were not meant to be measured directly but were meant to provide guidance to faculty members teaching GER courses. The process for approving courses for the list was changed accordingly, and new courses now must include measurable student learning outcomes that contribute to student achievement of the category objectives (at least one outcome for each category objective). Furthermore, the faculty member proposing a new course for the list, or substantially revising a course in the GER list, must detail how the GER outcomes for the course will be assessed. This ensures that each course on a list actually addresses the category objectives and that evidence of student achievement of the outcomes and objectives is developed.

Currently, NCSU has clear expectations about what students will learn from general education while ensuring that faculty members retain significant latitude in designing and delivering their GER courses. Additionally, there is evidence of student achievement of the general education objectives and evidence that faculty members are improving their courses based on the results of their assessment of their own courses. It should be noted that this approach does not easily lead to summative data. With this system is it very difficult to provide simple answers when asked if students across the university are achieving the general education objectives. However, it is an ideal approach for NCSU, where faculty, department, and college autonomy are highly valued and where the culture of assessment stresses designing and implementing processes that are formative (even at the expense of summative evidence).

Overview of Assessment of the General Education Program

Assessment of general education at NCSU is course-focused, meaning that it is situated in individual courses and is the responsibility of the faculty teaching the courses. The individual faculty members teaching multiple sections of a single course are expected to collaborate in setting outcomes and assessment methods, and in some cases the department offering a particular course will direct the course coordinator to take responsibility for outcomes assessment in that course. This is particularly likely when graduate teaching assistants teach some or most of the sections. The faculty members are responsible for using the results of their assessment to improve their own courses. They are also asked to provide a short report to the Office of Assessment outlining the results of their assessment activity and changes made to their course (if any).

As this process was implemented, a very important decision was made to provide training and support for faculty members who were asked to pilot the process. This training focused on the purposes of general education and assessment, how to write measurable student learning outcomes that foster the category objectives, how to assess student achievement of the outcomes, and how to navigate the new administrative process for getting a course approved for the GER list. A faculty member rather than an assessment professional led this training, and this was an important element in the success of the training. Faculty members from various departments that offered general education courses were asked to participate with the goal of "seeding" this knowledge throughout the university.

It should be obvious that utilizing this data for summative purposes is difficult because it is idiosyncratic and not amenable to aggregation. It is therefore very difficult to answer questions about the overall general education achievement of NCSU graduates, but this does not mean that the data are not available. The answers are there but they are not simple. On the other hand, NCSU has experimented with commercially available tests that are often used to evaluate student learning of general education outcomes. Those experiments were unsatisfactory in that faculty members found it difficult to relate the results to their own courses and students. In other words, they did not use the results to make changes in their own courses or, alternatively, to the general education program as a whole. The most prominent reason for this, as reported by faculty members who responded to survey questions on this topic, was that they did not perceive that the tests reflected what they thought were the most important student learning outcomes in general education. Since NCSU explicitly places a higher value on assessment practices that lead to improvements at the course and program level rather than at the institutional level, the course-focused approach is particularly appropriate.

However, recognizing that some institutional-level data for summative purposes is desirable, the Office of Assessment has begun work to pilot other general education assessment processes. These are viewed as additional processes rather than as replacements for the existing course-focused approach. Currently two pilot projects are under way, one in mathematics and the other in written communication. In mathematics, four courses were selected for assessment because they are large enrollment courses that are not prerequisites or precursors to calculus and thus are used to meet general education requirements by large numbers of students whose major programs do not require calculus. The course coordinators were asked to select sample questions from the course final exams (when there is a common final exam) or to ask those teaching the sections to select sample questions from their final exams (when the final exams are not common) that allow students to demonstrate their achievement of the mathematics general education objectives. Once these questions are selected, the course coordinators and the teaching faculty were asked to record student performance on these particular questions and to forward that data to the course coordinators and thence to the Office of Assessment. The Office of Assessment staff will tabulate and analyze the data in order to determine the extent to which these students have achieved the mathematics general education outcomes. While this approach presents some obvious drawbacks, it does provide summative data without infringing on the autonomy of the faculty. It is anticipated that this project will continue and that the trend data will prove illuminating.

The other pilot project is the assessment of the First Year Writing Program (FYWP). This assessment project is being carried out independently by the FYWP director and staff but will be reviewed by the Office of Assessment to determine its utility for providing information for the improvement of general education. The FYWP has developed a rubric that will be used to evaluate a random sample of freshman writing. In view of the fact that the only general education course required of all freshmen is Freshman Composition, it would be very surprising if the results of this assessment activity did not have implications for general education.

Similar projects in other general education areas are currently planned, with lessons learned from these pilot projects to be incorporated into future projects. However, it bears repeating that the primary assessment process for general education is the course-focused approach described earlier. These additional projects are not intended to replace that approach but only to enhance it by generating additional evidence by an additional means. It is expected that most improvements in a course-based general education system will take place at the course level rather than at the institutional level, and the course-focused assessment system is designed to provide data that will be used for that purpose.

Examples of Assessment and How Results Are Used

Several examples of category objectives, specific course outcomes that foster student achievement of the category objectives, and assessment methods for the outcomes are presented next. Each is followed by a summary of the changes made as a result of the assessment.

Natural Sciences Category Objectives

Each course in the natural sciences category of the general education requirements will provide instruction and guidance that help students to 1) use the methods and processes of science in testing hypotheses, solving problems, and making decisions; and 2) articulate, make inferences from, and apply to problem solving, scientific concepts, principles, laws, and theories.

Course Learning Outcomes: CH 100 Chemistry and Society

Students should be able to apply what they've learned about scientific methodology in one experimental situation to a different situation, to reason through the new situation scientifically and project likely results, to use a basic chemical principle to explain a specific chemical process, to state what the chemical process tells the students about the principle, and to identify various ways in which chemistry affects their everyday lives.

Evaluation Instruments for Assessing Course Learning Outcomes: CH 100

Test question. In class you observed an experiment that demonstrated X. Apply what you learned in experiment X to experiment Y. What would you hypothesize would be the results in experiment Y? Show how you used what you observed in experiment X to reach your hypothesis in experiment Y.

Test question. The concept of quantization of energy provides for an explanation of why certain materials burn in flames of certain colors. Apply the concept of quantization of energy to the burning of wood. What color is the flame of wood? Explain why it is that color. What does the color of wood flame tell you about the nature of reacting materials?

Assignment. Collect five articles from the popular press—newspapers, magazines, web sites, and the like—that show chemistry in the news.

Only minimal changes were made to this course as a result of the assessment process. The faculty member felt that the students generally met the expectations, although more in-class experiments and opportunities for interaction were built into the class as a result of indications that students found those elements more useful than pure lectures.

Humanities: History Category Objectives

Each course in the history category of the general education requirements will provide instruction and guidance that help students to 1) understand and engage in the human experience through the interpretation of evidence from the past situated in a geotemporal context (this objective must be the central focus of each history course); 2) become aware of the act of historical interpretation itself, through which historians use varieties of evidence to offer perspectives on the meaning of the past; and 3) make academic arguments about history using reasons and evidence for supporting those reasons that are appropriate to the field of study.

Course Learning Outcomes: HI 216 Latin America Since 1826 (The Struggle for Human Rights)

Students should be able to 1) identify human rights in the context of Latin American history through the interpretation of primary and secondary sources; 2) articulate the fact that all history is interpretive, founded in a wide range of motivations for constructing interpretations; and 3) make logical, historical arguments about Latin America.

Evaluation Instruments for Assessing Course Learning Outcomes: HI 216

Thought questions.

• Read the reactions of Christopher Columbus to people in the Caribbean, written in 1492–1493 (Primary Sources Page). You are a rival explorer, eager to get support for your voyages from the Spanish monarchs. Write a letter to King Ferdinand and Queen Isabella in which you critically question some of Columbus's descriptions and assumptions about peoples of the Caribbean. Give some examples of ethnocentrisms and errors you find.

• It's the year 1876. The feminist congress of Latin American women is meeting. You are a delegate. Prepare your remarks on how and why discrimination and machismo reduce opportunities for woman in both rural and urban society. Also identify any hopeful signs of change. Read Slatta, Gauchos (chapters 4–5), and the 1876 statement by an Argentine feminist on the Primary Source Page.

• Read Slatta, Gauchos (introduction, chapters 1–5). Last name Q–Z: Identify negative traits often attributed to gauchos. Note examples of ethnocentrism. A–H: Identify positive traits often attributed to gauchos. I–P: How and why did such conflicting views arise? Think creatively and sociologically. That is, consider the background and experiences of the people who are giving descriptions of gauchos.

Assignments.

• It is something of an unhappy irony that Las Casa, "Defender of the Indian," urged that Spain import African slaves in order to spare Native Americans. Role-playing: You are representatives to an international conference debating whether to abolish the African slave trade. Prepare you remarks. All students: On your Primary Sources Page, read the two anti-slavery poems and the conceptual overview of the varieties of racism. Please note that when a majority of individuals may not be racist, that institutions and social pressures can perpetuate racism for a very long time. Last name Q–Z: Read document 1, the essay by Fitzhugh, and summarize and critique his pro-slavery arguments. A–P: Read the anti-slavery documents 2, 3, and 4 and summarize and critique their arguments.

- Current events reports: Collect three articles from Latin American newspapers and discuss the peculiarly Latin American perspective you find in each article and how that perspective is different from a U.S. perspective on the same event.

Analytical essays.
- Gaucho Human Rights (read Slatta chapters 6–8 and the "International Declaration of Human Rights" from Primary Sources Page): Explain how and why Argentina's elites violated the gaucho's human rights as defined by the International Declaration.

- U.S. Responses to Human Rights: Using Cleary (chapters 5–7) and prior discussion and student reports, analyze the contradiction between U.S. support for military dictatorships and U.S. policy claims to promoting human rights and democracy.

- Review *all* the readings and your notes for the semester. Identify and categorize 1) the major reasons for (causes of) human rights abuses during the past five centuries in Latin America, and 2) the major types of abuses (nature of the actions, against whom). In both cases, provide specific evidence and quotations from primary sources.

This faculty member found that his expectations for his students were higher than they were likely to achieve, and that they required more instruction in basic college skills. He altered his course to focus more on basic research and learning skills. Overall, he found that his expectations were too high and that he needed to rethink the learning outcomes related to evaluating primary and secondary sources.

Tips for Implementing the Process

Implementing a general education assessment process is typically difficult, if only because general education is not often "owned" by a single department and therefore decisions are made more slowly and require more widespread discussion. It is important to plan the implementation process in addition to the assessment process itself.

It is just as important to understand and openly discuss the institutional culture as it relates to general education and assessment. The following questions may be useful for discussion:

• What is the real purpose of general education? Is it student learning of specific knowledge and skills, exposure to the disciplines, or a student-credit-hour generator?

• Who is in charge of general education? Who is in charge of assessment? Who will consider and make judgments about the assessment results? How will this be communicated?

• How will faculty members (and to a lesser extent, administrators) be rewarded for their work on general education assessment?

• What questions is the general education assessment process expected to answer? Is the purpose of assessment primarily formative or summative?

• What resources are available for general education assessment? Do senior administrators understand assessment and are they committed to supporting it? What is the overall level of assessment maturity at the institution?

• Where are the assessment professionals on the organizational chart? Is assessment centralized or dispersed across multiple units? What are the implications of this organizational style?

If the decision is made to implement a course-focused general education assessment as outlined in this chapter, there are additional issues that should be addressed. The course-focused approach starts with category objectives, which are broad statements of what students will learn that should guide faculty members in setting measurable student learning outcomes for their courses. It is critical that faculty members in the various general education disciplinary areas have ample opportunity to contribute to the discussion of these objectives. Without their support, the entire process will quickly falter.

Careful attention should also be given to the matter of assessment timelines or cycles and reporting lines. How often are faculty members expected to assess their general education courses and report on the results? Who will receive their reports, and what will happen to those reports? Will the assessment professionals get copies of the reports, or will they only get summaries prepared by the department or college? Will faculty members be willing to expose shortcomings in their courses to the assessment professionals? What happens if faculty members do not assess their courses and prepare reports of the results?

Challenges to Assessing General Education and Strategies to Overcome Them

The general education program at NCSU is heavily but equally weighted toward humanities and social science (21 hours) and mathematics and natural science (20 hours). However, there are more courses on the humanities and social science lists than there are on any other lists. Add to that the fact that the only course required of all freshmen is English Composition, and it becomes apparent that much of the burden of assessing general education using a course-focused approach falls on the humanities and social science faculty. The extent of the disparity in effort among the different faculties is difficult to quantify, but the perception of disparity can be undeniable. This can lead to serious problems, particularly if insufficient attention is given to rewarding faculty for their efforts in general education assessment.

The most efficient strategy for overcoming this problem is to avoid it altogether by developing rewards for faculty participation in general education assessment. This could take any number of forms and should probably encompass a range of rewards. Regardless of the approach taken, the senior leadership of the institution will have to support the process and should aggressively seek resources with which to do so. The assessment professionals can and should play a role in this process, by requesting resources and educating senior administrators about the importance of general education assessment.

It is important to remember that resources may not entirely ameliorate this obstacle. It is critical that the assessment professionals continuously engage in a dialogue with faculty members who are asked to assess general education. This means really listening to those who voice complaints, attempting to understand the issues raised, and working collaboratively and creatively to alleviate their concerns while continuing to promote student learning. This dialogue also serves to build trust between the faculty and the assessment professionals and can have long-term benefits for everyone. Developing an authentic assessment process is a cultural change, and for some institutions it is a wrenching and difficult process. Culture change is easiest when there is strong leadership and a trusting environment in which the threatening aspects of change are dealt with openly and honestly.

Chapter 9

Paradise Valley Community College: General Education Case Study

Paul A. Dale

Overview of the Institutional Culture

Paradise Valley Community College (PVCC), located in Phoenix, Arizona, is part of the Maricopa County Community College District (MCCCD). There are a total of 10 colleges in the MCCCD serving 222,174 credit students on an annual basis. PVCC was founded in 1987 and in fall 2005 served 8,717 students in credit courses. The full-time student equivalent (FTSE) in the same semester was 3,888. The college's service area—one of the fastest growing areas in metropolitan Phoenix with an expected population increase over the next 10 years to exceed 250,000—includes northeast Phoenix and northern Maricopa County and currently serves approximately 500,000 residents.

The student population at PVCC is generally representative of typical community college demographics: enrolled predominately in a part-time status (73% enrolled in 11 credit hours or less), comprised of a wide age-range distribution with roughly half of the student population under the age of 24, and becoming more ethnically diverse with students of color representing 32% of the total population. Our students are also entering the college experience at notably high levels of underpreparedness, with 67% of entrants completing placement tests scoring into developmental mathematics and 43% scoring into developmental writing.

Approximately 75% of incoming students state that transfer to a four-year university is their primary goal of attendance. Almost half of the college's total credit hours come from the following six academic areas: mathematics, English, biology, psychology, computer information systems, and communications.

Students who plan to transfer are encouraged to complete the Arizona General Education Curriculum (AGEC). AGEC is a 35-semester credit general education program of study that fulfills lower-division general education requirements for students who intend to transfer to any Arizona public community college or university. Courses are selected from the following six areas: composition, literacy and critical inquiry, mathematical studies, humanities and fine arts, social and behavioral sciences, and natural sciences. Once completed, courses transfer as a block without loss of credit.

In 1997, PVCC adopted learning as its core value and has committed itself to becoming a more learning-centered college. The college has adopted 12 indicators of a learning-centered college that focus efforts on student learning, organization, and structure that support student, employee, and organizational learning and implementation of the processes and procedures of student learning. The first three indicators focus specifically on student learning:

• Learning outcomes have been identified and made explicit.

• Learning outcomes serve as the centerpiece for program and curriculum development.

• Learning outcomes are measured for the purpose of intervention, remediation, and continuous improvement.

The college also reaffirmed that learning is not restricted to the classroom experience and that all student learning in and out of class is valued. Also in 1997, the student affairs division began using student learning as a "mental model" for program development and implementation. The division adopted the use and practices suggested in two seminal publications: *The Student Learning Imperative: Implications for Student Affairs* (American College Personnel Association, 1996) and *Powerful Partnerships: A Shared Responsibility for Learning* (American Association for Higher Education, American College Personnel Association, & National Association for Student Personnel Administrators, 1998). For example: 1) significant professional development activities were developed and implemented to create a foundation for the delivery of student affairs programs in the context of a learning-centered college, 2) each area identified how their respective areas contribute to student learning, and 3) student learning outcomes and assessment plans were developed for each area.

PVCC realigned its organizational structure to more fully support student learning with three primary divisions: learning, learning support services (replacing the traditional student affairs division), and administrative services. College leadership did not think that the traditional organizational model placed learning as the core of its being, embraced or accepted that student learning involves the whole student, and allowed for trailblazers to prosper and sustain new learning agendas. This realignment process recognized and acknowledged the role of student learning in the out-of-class environment including learning within the general education context. All student and academic support areas have adopted learning outcomes and are engaged in the assessment process. Five areas—Learning Support Center, Student Life and Leadership, Counseling, and Service-Learning—are also measuring student learning within the general education outcome context.

Given the college's commitment to becoming a more learning-centered college (including the assessment of out-of-class learning), its high level of student enrollment in general education courses, and the curricular alignment with the Arizona General Education Core curriculum, PVCC has placed an emphasis on the delivery and assessment of student learning in the context of general education.

Overview of the General Education Program

The following is the MCCCD general education statement:

> The general education core of the program of study for an associate degree or a certificate helps students develop a greater understanding of themselves, of their relationship with others, and of the richly diverse world in which they live. The general education experience provides students with opportunities to explore broad areas of commonly held knowledge and prepares them to contribute to society through

personal, social, and professional interactions with others. General education fosters students' personal development by opening them to new directions, perspectives, and processes.

Through its general education requirements, the Maricopa County Community College District is committed to helping students develop qualities and skills that will serve them throughout their lives. General education opportunities encourage students to:

• Build self-awareness, self-respect, and self-confidence

• Recognize and respect the beliefs, traditions, abilities, and customs of all people and all cultures

• Consider the local, global, and environmental impacts of personal, professional, and social decisions and actions

• Access, evaluate, analyze, synthesize, and use information wisely

• Communicate effectively personally, socially, and professionally

• Think critically, make informed decisions, solve problems, and implement decisions

• Consider the ethical implications of their choices

• Value the learning process throughout their lives

• Integrate and connect ideas and events in a historical perspective, and see relationships among the past, the present, and the future

• Develop a personal sense of aesthetics

• Use technological resources appropriately and productively

• Work cooperatively and respectfully with others to serve their communities

The general education experience at MCCCD is composed of specific elements across the curriculum designed to provide the learner with essential knowledge and skills. These include:

• Communication

• Arts and Humanities

• Numeracy

• Scientific Inquiry in the Natural and Social Sciences

• Information Literacy

• Problem-Solving and Critical Thinking

• Cultural Diversity

(MCCCD, 2005)

The faculty at PVCC have further defined general education outcomes in the context of critical thinking. The desired student outcomes include the ability to:

• Respond to material by distinguishing between facts and opinions, judgments and inferences, inductive and deductive arguments, and the objective and subjective;

• Generate questions, construct and recognize the structure of arguments, and adequately support arguments;

• Define, analyze, and devise solutions for problems and issues;

• Collect, organize, classify, correlate, analyze and present materials and data;

- Integrate information and identify relationships; and

- Evaluate information, materials, and numerical and/or graphical data by drawing inferences, arriving at reasonable and informed conclusions, applying understanding and knowledge to new and different problems, developing rational and reasonable interpretations, suspending beliefs and remaining open to new information, methods, cultural systems, values, and beliefs and by assimilating information.

(PVCC, 2005a)

The overall general education outcome of critical thinking is distributed among the following areas: communication (listening, reading, speaking, and writing), information literacy, problem solving, and technology. Under each of these general education categories, specific dimensions have been articulated. For example, under the communication/speaking general education outcome, the student "will be able to communicate orally his/her ideas on a topic objectively or subjectively in a competent and confident manner." For a complete listing of the Paradise Valley Community College General Education Outcomes see www.pvc.maricopa.edu/AI/outcomes.html

At this stage of the overall college implementation of the general education program and assessment, *cocurricular professionals* are not directly involved with the construction of general education outcomes; however, in selected areas they are very involved with the measurement of student general education learning in the out-of-class environment. (For clarity and consistency purposes the term *cocurricular professionals* will be used throughout this chapter to identify student affairs, learning support, and other professional staff who work outside the classroom.) Since PVCC faculty have made the general education outcomes explicit and easily accessible through the college web site, it has been relatively easy for cocurricular professionals to become aware and informed of the general education outcomes. Many of the cocurricular areas have faculty on either advisory or liaison teams and there is a high level of communication and sharing of information. The development of learning outcomes, integration of general education learning outside the classroom, and assessment are common topics of these teams.

Overview of Assessment of the General Education Program

At PVCC the overall academic assessment initiative is based on five central beliefs:

- Assessment is "good practice" at all levels within the college.

- Assessment contributes significantly to the enhancement of learning.

- Assessment informs good and continuously improving pedagogical practice.

- Assessment provides responses to two central questions and the evidence to support responses to the questions: What are our students learning? How do we know?

- Assessment is the "cornerstone" of PVCC's commitment to becoming a learning-centered college.

(PVCC, 2005b)

The college has an active Academic Assessment Team (AAT), which has developed a multiyear assessment plan, developed systems and structures to support the plan, and initiated the implementation of assessment activities. The AAT has also completed a course mapping matrix that identifies general study courses with the PVCC general education learning outcomes. This matrix indicates specific courses that meet general education outcomes.

Under the leadership of the AAT, general education assessment teams have also been established. Each team is charged with developing an assessment plan and strategy to measure the PVCC general education areas of communication (listening, reading, speaking, and writing), information literacy, problem solving, and technology. The roles and responsibilities of the general education team are to:

- Research pedagogy, best practices, and efforts at other schools relating to outcome area

- Use authentic student work to create General Education Learning Outcome rubrics capturing the criteria, progressions, and levels of achievement

- Prepare scoring guide

- Approve or refine the list of appropriate courses for initial implementation

- Enrich understanding of the outcome area through interdisciplinary discussions with colleagues

- Assist with college-wide training to increase understanding of the rationale and implications of assessing general education outcomes

(PVCC, 2006)

The academic general education assessment teams operate on an annual calendar cycle where fall semester activities include assessment planning and dissemination of previous year results, spring semester activities include actual college-wide assessment, and the summer is reserved for data analysis. In preparation for college-wide assessment, the following tasks have been completed: 1) cross-discipline rubrics have been developed for oral communication, written communication, information literacy, problem solving, and technology; 2) three-level rubric scales have been determined: meets minimum standards, needs some improvement, and does not meet standards; 3) specific core general education courses have been identified; and 4) training to orient faculty on the use of the rubrics. PVCC has completed its first round of institution-wide assessment of general education for the five areas noted above. Eighty-nine class sections used the general education rubrics and institution-wide frequency and mean scores have been calculated. Faculty leadership is currently in the process of developing strategies to improve student learning based on the findings.

The assessment of general education learning outcomes in the out-of-class environment evolved through a gradual and incremental process that began with the previously discussed organizational shift from a service-centered to a learning-centered delivery of cocurricular programs and services. This transformation, which still continues, began with a series of activities to refocus student and academic support services in the context of learning outcomes-based delivery of programs.

Each area was charged with identifying program and learning outcomes. According to Bresciani (2001), program outcomes measure whether the task was completed and learning outcomes address both cognitive and affective domains. This exercise was done at the department level. A simple stem sentence was used: As a result of students participating in _____, they will learn _____.

Our goal of this orientation shift was to ensure that:

• Learning outcomes were identified and made concrete.

• Learning outcomes were assessed and used to improve learning and service productivity.

• Student affairs policies and procedures were aligned to maximize student learning.

Out-of-class learning outcomes were compiled by departments, with each department identifying 8 to 10 learning outcomes. The departments' learning outcomes were then placed on a matrix and where appropriate aligned with the college's general education learning outcomes. The alignment was done by each of the department managers based on their appraisal of the relationship between the departmental learning outcomes and the description of the general education outcome. Additionally, selected cocurricular programs were inventoried to determine where activities could be mapped to the general education dimensions. Table 9.1 is a sample of the matrix from one of the out-of-class areas. This sample shows two of the Student Life and Leadership learning outcomes aligned with selected college general education outcomes.

Once the out-of-class learning outcomes were correlated with the college's general education outcomes, five areas with the greatest correlation between departmental learning outcomes and the overall general education outcomes volunteered to pilot assessment of general education outcomes in the out-of-class environment. The following areas are currently measuring general education outcomes: Student Life and Leadership, Service Learning, Learning Support Center, and Counseling.

Table 9.1
Out of Class General Education Outcomes Matrix

Learning Area	Com/ Listening	Com/ Reading	Com/ Speaking	Com/ Writing	Info Lit	Prob Solv	Tech
Student Life and Leadership Center students will:							
Identify and develop social, cultural, leadership values, and skills through club participation and leadership training.	X	X	X	X		X	
Develop and apply civic responsibility, leadership values, and skills with specific emphasis on leadership for social change.		X	X	X	X	X	

In the fall semester, each department submits an annual assessment plan which addresses the following elements:

• Area or program to be assessed

• Specific learning outcomes to be measured (including general education outcomes)

• Assessment strategy/methodology

• What you expect to learn from this assessment activity

• Samples of assessment instruments

The director in each area is charged with implementing the plan. Assessment activities are conducted either in the fall or spring semesters. The department managers work with the college's out-of-class assessment coordinator to develop the plan, identify assessment tools, and develop an implementation strategy. Assessment plans are an integral part of each department's operation and required as a part of the department's overall operational planning process. At the end of each academic year, each department then submits a summary report that includes the following elements:

• What did the area expect to learn as a result of the assessment activity?

- What were the results and how will the results be used?

- What are the plans for improvements, enhancements, and changes to help students achieve the learning outcome more efficiently and effectively?

- Samples of assessment tools and completed measurements.

The general education outcomes measured by departments vary based on their own departmental outcomes. For instance, the Office of Student Life and Leadership learning outcome "Develop and apply civic responsibility, leadership values, and skills with specific emphasis on leadership for social change" is aligned with the college's communication, information literacy, and problem solving general education outcomes.

To assist with the coordination of out-of-class assessment, an out-of-class assessment team, comprised of staff from cocurricular functional areas, meets on a monthly basis. The role of this group is to provide continuing professional development activities in the area of assessment; gather and review all the out-of-class assessment plans; provide consultation and peer support to encourage improvements in assessment strategies; and gather and evaluate the annual assessment plans. This ad hoc team is also charged with further linking the out-of-class assessment process with the academic assessment general education activities. For example, this team is currently exploring the use of faculty-developed cross-disciplined general education rubrics for use in out-of-class assessment.

Examples of Assessment and How Results Are Used

Emerging Leaders is a student leadership development program based on *A Social Change Model of Leadership Development* (Higher Education Research Institute, 1996) that provides an opportunity to increase historically uninvolved students' participation in cocurricular leadership activities. The overall outcome of the program is to provide an experience that increases students' ability to become more active as citizens and enact positive social change. In its seventh year, the program has graduated more than 500 students.

The Student Leadership Council serves as the student governance organization committed to the representation of student needs at PVCC, leadership development, and service. Students participate as elected executive board members or senators or appointed club representatives and volunteer commissioners.

The Office of Student Life and Leadership has aligned two cocurricular learning outcomes with the college's general education outcomes. The first learning outcome—identify and apply various leadership styles, skills, and values through club participation and leadership training—is aligned with the general education outcomes of communication, information literacy, and problem solving.

In order to measure this cocurricular student learning outcome in the context of the general education outcomes, a variety of assessment tools have been developed and two of these instruments will be highlighted: Student Leadership Council Grading Rubric and the Student Leadership Pre/Post Survey.

Students serving on the Student Leadership Council are enrolled in a leadership course that is embedded in the activities and functions of the council. Each week there is also a structured leadership class taught by the director of the student life and leadership office. The Student Leadership Grading Rubric was developed through primary trait analysis, to create objective criteria for the evaluation of students' leadership portfolios. Two outcomes are included: the general education written communication outcome and a leadership content learning outcome. Each trait contains a 0–100 scale. The written communications scale includes dimensions from the college written communication general education outcome. The students' leadership portfolios contain a purposeful selection of leadership assignments from throughout the semester including summaries of work samples, leadership goals, resumes, and conference and workshop information. Writing samples, which include the students' service-learning reflections, are assembled to measure progress in their critical thinking and problem solving abilities, as well as written communication outcomes.

During the pilot administration of this rubric, the objective data gathered (rubric scores) provided evidence of students' learning in the areas of written communications and critical thinking skills through their participation in the Student Leadership Council activities. This pilot also resulted in the following programmatic decisions: the relationship of the general education outcomes to the student leadership outcomes will be made more explicit to students; greater analysis of aggregate student rubric scores needs to be completed in order to evaluate the effectiveness of specific student leadership activities; the student leadership general education assessment findings need to be communicated with appropriate faculty; and additional staff time and support is needed to maintain the assessment activities.

The pre/post instrument, administered upon election into Student Leadership Council and following each semester of completion, is a self-reported survey designed to elicit students' beliefs if they have successfully met the following course objectives:

- Describe various styles of leadership.

- Apply event planning skills in organization of group dynamics.

- Demonstrate an understanding of group dynamics with diverse groups and in a variety of environments.

- Communicate orally his or her ideas in a manner appropriate for the audience and occasion.

- Communicate in writing his or her ideas on a topic in a competent manner

- Lead appropriate team-building activities.

- Apply problem-solving skill in leadership by defining, analyzing, and devising solutions for problems and issues.

- Apply appropriate decision-making skills to leadership challenges.

Comparative data have been collected from students in their first, second, and third (or more) semesters of involvement. After three administrations of the survey no consistent trends were found. This finding is attributed to the varying lengths of time of student involvement and the general turnover of student leaders between semesters. As a result of these findings, the pre/post methodology has been abandoned and will be substituted with a rubric-based evaluation of student leaders' work compiled in an e-portfolio.

The second Student Life and Leadership learning outcome— "Develop and apply civic responsibility, leadership values, and skills with a specific emphasis on leadership for social change"—is also aligned with the general education outcomes of communication, information literacy, and problem solving. In order to measure this student learning outcome in the context of the general education outcomes, two assessment tools are used including Emerging Leaders Final Project Rubric and the Emerging Leaders Oral Presentation Rubric. Primary trait analysis has been used to develop the Final Project and Oral Presentation Grading Rubrics.

The Oral Presentation Rubric is divided into three main topical areas: organization, delivery, and course-specific content. Under each of the main categories are specific dimensions that are evaluated on a 3-point scale: meets standards for competence, needs improvement, and does not meet minimum standards. These dimensions were taken from the college's oral communication general education outcomes. This rubric is used while students are making a presentation requiring them to demonstrate an understanding of the social change leadership model in the context of their service-learning project. During the student presentations, multiple course facilitators rate the student's competence in the three topical areas. The rubric assessment scores are then totaled among all the raters for an overall student rating.

The oral presentation rubrics have been used over several semesters and a number of program improvements have been made. It became apparent during the earliest use of the rubrics that the students were competent in describing the tenets of the leadership model, but the examples used to illustrate the concepts were often misapplied. One fundamental improvement during the Emerging Leaders program was to design activities where the leadership concepts were more explicitly linked to the course experiences and activities. Other improvements included provision of detailed structure to students regarding the oral presentation; greater effort to communicate to students the criteria used in the rubrics by adding the scoring system to the program syllabus; and greater emphasis on public speaking strategies integrated into the activities.

The Emerging Leaders Final Project Rubric contains writing criteria (thesis, supporting details, focus, coherence, and mechanics) and several dimensions related to content. Again, the items are rated using a 3-point scale: meets standards for competence, needs improvement, and does not meet minimum standards. Comparing the findings from the facilitator evaluations after the pilot use of the rubrics, the content of the students' papers and presentations were rated with a majority of the students meeting standards.

The development and use of the oral and written communication rubrics resulted from the facilitators' frustration that previous students' competence in understanding the premises of the leadership model and ability to communicate their understanding were not at acceptable levels. It became apparent that relying on a somewhat subjective, intuitive evaluation observation method was part of the problem. The development of the rubrics not only made the desired outcomes more explicit to the students, it also served as a more objective report card for the facilitators to determine whether or not the students were really "getting" the intended outcomes.

It is important to note that the writing and oral presentation assessment rubrics used by the Office of Student Life and Leadership have been adopted from faculty-developed rubrics used in academic settings and the dimensions parallel the dimensions of the college's general education outcomes.

Tips for Implementing the Process

Measuring out-of-class student learning in the context of general education outcomes is a challenging and complex process. Prior to beginning the assessment of program-specific learning outcomes or general education learning outcomes in the cocurricular environment, the alignment of cocurricular programs as learning centered must be established. In addition, the experience at PVCC has reinforced the notion of "walk before you run" during the assessment process. Measuring programmatic-based learning outcomes was found to be a prerequisite for measuring college-wide general education outcomes in the out-of-class environment. The following is a set of pragmatic recommendations that will lead to successful assessment of general education outcomes in the out-of-class environment.

Learning as the core organizational value and the foundation for the delivery of out-of-class programs and services needs to be established and sustained. Cocurricular professionals need to become grounded in the contemporary literature that supports the premise of student learning outside the classroom as a valued part of the students' total college experience. In addition to an individual understanding of learning-centered practices, the organizational divisions and departments serving students in the out-of-class environment need to adopt and implement learning-centered practices across the college. The following are several examples of these practices:

• In order to make student learning a central focus, cocurricular leaders need to make a significant investment on the front end of the assessment process for professional development activities for staff specifically related to learning-centered practices, identification of learning outcomes, and assessment practices.

• A structured assessment planning and reporting structure that provides a step-by-step process with criteria outlining key elements is essential. Department assessment notebooks, including elements of the assessment plans and reporting process, that are updated on a yearly basis are valuable tools.

• The provision of consultative support to department managers as the out-of-class assessment initiative is implemented significantly increases organizational capacity. An out-of-class assessment coordinator can provide centralized coordination, professional development activities, coaching, and facilitation of collaborative efforts with faculty academic assessment activities.

• When measuring general education outcomes in the out-of-class environment, start with a manageable assessment plan. The assessment of one or two general education learning outcomes is sufficient.

• Out-of-class learning outcomes should be established before measuring college general education outcomes. These department-specific outcomes can then be aligned with the overall general education outcomes.

• The measurement of general education outcomes in the out-of-class environment needs to be eventually linked with the general education assessment being done in the classroom. Ideally, this would occur as a holistic, coordinated effort.

• Where possible, integrate the use of faculty-developed general education rubrics.

• Faculty-developed dimensions of the overall general education outcomes can be integrated into cocurricular-developed rubrics.

At Paradise Valley Community College, the assessment of general education outcomes in the out-of-class environment began with a department-level, self-selecting bottom-up approach with little overall alignment at the divisional level. While the department-level leaders are best able to identify which programs and activities naturally align with college general education outcomes, a concerted effort at the divisional level needs to take place to target select general education outcomes. Out-of-class cocurricular professionals generally do not have the capacity or ability to design and implement complex assessment plans. The development of assessment plans and instruments at the department level is inefficient and generally not transferable to other cocurricular programs. A better approach would be for a student affairs division to focus on one or two general education outcomes, develop flexible assessment instruments, and gather division-level learning outcomes data. This would allow for the eventual folding of the out-of-class general education outcomes assessment findings into the academic general assessment findings.

Second, the assessment of general education outcomes should not be relegated as an add-on assignment. Assessment, as part of the core operations of the cocurricular program, becomes an integral part of overall program planning, staff development and orientation, budget planning, and a key linkage to fundamental learning-centered practices. Assessment needs to be a regular part of staff meeting agendas with updates and sharing of best practices, professional staff evaluation, and reward systems.

Finally, it is imperative that general education assessment begin only if there is fiscal and organizational support for assessment activities. It is critical to invest time and money for professional development for staff, hiring of an assessment coordinator, attendance at assessment conferences, and the provision of additional administrative support for assessment-related planning, analysis, and reporting.

Challenges to Assessing General Education and Strategies to Overcome Them

One specific barrier to assessing general education in the out-of-class environment merits additional discussion and comment. This final section will describe the challenges of implementing out-of-class assessment of general education outcomes with minimal coordination and collaboration between faculty and cocurricular professionals. Strategies to overcome this significant obstacle will also be discussed.

At PVCC, the lack of an organizational connection between faculty-driven academic assessment and the assessment initiative of cocurricular professionals was probably the most significant barrier to assessing general education. Ultimately, this leads to out-of-class general education assessment findings and recommendations that are never generalized outside of the singular cocurricular department and program. The obvious benefit to conducting general education outcomes assessment in the out-of-class environment is to identify comprehensive college improvements that will improve the total college learning environment. This synergy cannot be realized unless faculty and cocurricular professionals collaborate on assessment initiatives.

Even though the initial intention and design of the overall out-of-class assessment plan was shared and communicated with the faculty-led academic assessment team, a faculty and cocurricular coordinated assessment effort did not materialize at PVCC. This lack of coordinated effort can be attributed to the following:

- While the college acknowledged that learning embraces the education of the whole student in a comprehensive college environment, a structure or model for comprehensive academic and out-of-class assessment was not available.

- Both the faculty- and cocurricular-led assessment teams were at different stages in the development of assessment planning and strategy implementation.

- There was some covert belief, albeit a very minority faculty position, that assessment should remain the purview of faculty and that cocurricular professionals did not have the qualifications or professional training to engage in assessment of general education student learning.

- With assessment still in a developmental stage at the college, faculty really did not have the time or capacity to integrate the work of the out-of-class assessment team with their in-class assessment activities.

• The initial out-of-class assessment initiative was not adequately supported with staff or fiscal resources to move the process at the same pace as the faculty-driven academic class assessment general education initiative.

Both the academic and out-of-class assessment coordinators collectively acknowledged at the outset that a coordinated effort would ultimately yield a greater positive impact on student learning and agreed early on that each side would gradually move closer to a more collaborative and coordinated model. While the college agreed to incrementally work through the issues just described, there were some notable strategies used to offset this barrier. The most effective strategies are discussed next.

The use of faculty and staff in linking or loosely coupled organizational roles that fostered sharing of general assessment practices and strategies was exploited. Faculty and staff who worked in programs that straddle student and academic affairs, such as service-learning, counseling, and instructional technology support, were able to serve as conduits between the two initiatives. Faculty with interest in cocurricular programs assisted staff in the development of rubrics, as well as sharing faculty-developed general education rubrics. In addition, two areas, Service Learning and Student Life and Leadership, provided stipends or arranged for faculty release time to assist with the out-of-class assessment initiative.

Even though there was not a coordinated effort, the leadership of the academic and out-of-class assessment teams maintained regular communication and shared progress updates. The frequency of communication between the groups became intensified as the college engaged in their self-study in preparation for reaffirmation of accreditation with the Higher Learning Commission. The reaffirmation process, with the new criteria focusing on assessment, also provided added validity for the need for out-of-class assessment. Additionally, one of the recommendations of the Higher Learning Commission visitation team was to integrate the efforts of the academic and out-of-class assessment initiatives. This directive has also provided further impetus toward the movement for a collective, college-wide assessment plan for general education outcomes.

Another strategy to address the lack of connectivity between the academic and out-of-class efforts toward general education assessment is to achieve cocurricular representation on the academic assessment committee. While this goal has not yet been achieved at PVCC, an active out-of-class assessment team with faculty representation has been formed. The out-of-class assessment team now has membership of the faculty assessment coordinator who is serving as a link to the general education assessment initiative. The role of the out-of-class assessment team is to provide continuing professional development activities in the area of assessment; gather and review all the out-of-class assessment plans; provide consultation and peer support to encourage improvements in assessment strategies; and gather and evaluate the annual assessment plans. This team is also charged with further linking the out-of-class assessment process with the academic assessment activities. More recently, the academic and out-of-class assessment initiatives have agreed to use parallel assessment planning and implementation structures. While the language is not exact, the general elements are fully aligned.

The ultimate goal at Paradise Valley Community College is to be able to assess student general education learning encompassing their full college experience including both academic and cocurricular out-of-class activities. Currently five out-of-class areas—Student Life and Leadership, Counseling, Learning Support Center, and Service Learning—have all completed at least one cycle of assessing student out-of-class learning in the context of the college general education outcomes. The out-of-class assessment planning is comprehensive, and notable efforts have been made to use faculty-developed general education rubrics. A number of program-level improvements have been made as a result of the assessment of general education outcomes, but additional time needs to be devoted to learn from the assessment findings and impact on student general education learning. Out-of-class assessment of general education outcomes at the college has not yet been integrated with academic assessment initiatives.

The assessment of general education outcomes in the out-of-class environment has provided greater focus for cocurricular professionals to develop programs with specific learning outcomes in mind. There is an overall greater clarity in the responses to the questions "What do we want students to learn in cocurricular programs?" and "How do we know what they have learned?" The alignment of out-of-class learning outcomes with the general education outcomes has served as a concrete way to begin to actualize the notion that the goal of higher education institutions should be "the integration of all domains of learning and involvement of all educators" (Baxter Magolda, 1999, p. 39).

References

American Association for Higher Education, American College Personnel Association, & National Association of Student Personnel Administrators. (1998). *Powerful partnerships: A shared responsibility for learning.* Washington, DC: American College Personnel Association.

American College Personnel Association. (1996). *The student learning imperative: Implications for student affairs.* Washington, DC: Author.

Baxter Magolda, M. B. (1999). Defining and redefining student learning. In E. Whitt (Ed.), *Student learning as student affairs work* (NASPA Monograph Series No. 23, pp. 35–49). Washington, DC: National Association of Student Personnel Administrators.

Bresciani, M. J. (2001). Writing measurable and meaningful outcomes. *NetResults.* Washington, DC: National Association of Student Personnel Administrators.

Higher Education Research Institute. (1996). *A social change model of leadership development* (3rd ed.). Los Angeles, CA: University of California–Los Angeles, Graduate School of Education and Information Studies.

Maricopa County Community College District. (2005). *Curriculum procedures handbook: A guide for curriculum development and processing.* Retrieved November 6, 2006, from the Maricopa County Community College District, District Curriculum Office web site: www.maricopa .edu/academic/curric/cphb/genedguide.php

Paradise Valley Community College. (2005a). *PVCC general education learning outcomes.* Retrieved November 6, 2006, from the Paradise Valley Community College, Assessment Initiative web site: www.pvc.maricopa.edu/AI/outcomes.html

Paradise Valley Community College. (2005b). *Report of the institutional self-study for reaffirmation of accreditation.* Retrieved December 4, 2006, from the Paradise Valley Community College web site: www.pvc.maricopa.edu/~selfstudy/report/index.htm

Paradise Valley Community College. (2006). *Paradise Valley Community College assessment handbook: 2006.* Retrieved November 6, 2006, from the Paradise Valley Community College, Assessment Initiative web site: www.pvc.maricopa.edu/AI/

State University of New York System Administration: General Education Case Study

Patricia L. Francis, Anne E. Huot

Overview of the Institutional Culture

The State University of New York (SUNY) is the largest comprehensive system of public higher education in the United States, consisting of 64 institutions offering 6,688 programs of study across New York state's 62 counties and categorized into four institution types: doctoral degree–granting institutions, comprehensive colleges, colleges of technology, and community colleges. Overall enrollment exceeds 414,000 students, with more than 373,000 undergraduates who must satisfy SUNY-wide general education requirements at the 57 institutions with general education programs. These institutions differ widely in location, mission, programs, and enrollment (i.e., from around 1,200 to more than 27,000), and include colleges and universities as varied as the Fashion Institute of Technology in Manhattan; Maritime College, formerly a nautical school which still features a Regiment of Cadets; SUNY Geneseo, SUNY's "public ivy"; and the University at Buffalo, which stands in the first rank among the nation's research-intensive public universities. This diversity, while clearly beneficial to the citizens of New York state, poses a serious challenge when attempting to develop and implement an assessment strategy that can be uniformly applied across institutions, is respectful of campus autonomy, and meets standards of good assessment practice.

SUNY is also the youngest system of public higher education in the continental United States, established in 1948 and made up at that time of 29 formerly unaffiliated institutions, 11 of which were serving as teachers colleges. Throughout its history, SUNY has attempted to serve dual functions—excellence and access—or, as stated in its mission statement, "to provide to the people of New York with educational services of the highest quality, with the broadest possible access, fully representative of all segments of the population" (SUNY, 2006). SUNY has clearly provided educational access to the state's citizens, enrolling 40% of all New York high school graduates. In addition, in 1995 the SUNY Board of Trustees launched a new planning initiative, *Rethinking SUNY,* which called for significantly higher academic aspirations throughout the system. Since that time, virtually every indicator of academic excellence has shown a marked upward trajectory, including applications, incoming students' academic profile, institutional selectivity, sponsored research activity, and fundraising. *Rethinking SUNY* also placed renewed emphasis on the quality of undergraduate education, and the SUNY Assessment Initiative—which includes the general education assessment process described in this chapter—is an integral component of that effort.

Overview of the General Education Program

In addition to institutional diversity, there are three other unique factors that require explanation when describing the implementation of general education assessment across the SUNY system. First, every SUNY general education program—regardless of the campus on which it is located—must address the same set of 30 student learning outcomes, organized under 10 Knowledge and Skills areas and 2 Competencies as shown in Figure 10.1. After these outcomes were developed in 1999 by a SUNY-wide task force created by university Provost Peter D. Salins, SUNY System Administration conducted a review process in which campuses had each of their general education courses approved as meeting the student learning outcomes in one or more of the 12 student learning outcome categories. This process ultimately produced a finite set of courses on each campus that would be appropriate for inclusion in the assessment of the SUNY general education learning outcomes.

Second, in 2000, Provost Salins formed another task force charged to make recommendations regarding those issues most central

Figure 10.1
SUNY General Education Learning Outcomes

Mathematics
Students will demonstrate the ability to:
- Interpret and draw inferences from mathematical models such as formulas, graphs, tables, and schematics.
- Represent mathematical information symbolically, visually, numerically, and verbally.
- Employ quantitative methods such as arithmetic, algebra, geometry, or statistics to solve problems.
- Estimate and check mathematical results for reasonableness.
- Recognize the limits of mathematical and statistical methods.

Natural Sciences
Students will demonstrate:
- Understanding of the methods scientists use to explore natural phenomena, including observation, hypothesis development, measurement and data collection, experimentation, evaluation of evidence, and employment of mathematical analysis.
- Application of scientific data, concepts, and models in one of the natural sciences.

Social Sciences
Students will demonstrate:
- Understanding of the methods social scientists use to explore social phenomena, including observation, hypothesis development, measurement and data collection, experimentation, evaluation of evidence, and employment of mathematical and interpretive analysis.
- Knowledge of major concepts, models, and issues of at least one discipline in the social sciences.

American History
Students will demonstrate:
- Knowledge of a basic narrative of American history: political, economic, social, and cultural, including knowledge of unity and diversity in American society.
- Knowledge of common institutions in American society and how they have affected different groups.
- Understanding of America's evolving relationship with the rest of the world.

Western Civilization
Students will:
- Demonstrate knowledge of the development of the distinctive features of the history, institutions, economy, society, culture, and so on of Western civilization.
- Relate the development of Western civilization to that of other regions of the world.

Other World Civilizations
Students will demonstrate:
- Knowledge of a broad outline of world history.
  Or
- The distinctive features of the history, institutions, economy, society, culture, and so on of one non-Western civilization.

Humanities
Students will demonstrate:
- Knowledge of the conventions and methods of at least one of the humanities in addition to those encompassed by other knowledge areas required by the general education program.

The Arts
Students will demonstrate:
- Understanding of at least one principal form of artistic expression and the creative process inherent therein.

Foreign Language
Students will demonstrate:
- Basic proficiency in the understanding and use of a foreign language; and
- Knowledge of the distinctive features of culture(s) associated with the language they are studying.

Basic Communication
Students will:
- Produce coherent texts within common college-level written forms.
- Demonstrate the ability to revise and improve such texts.
- Research a topic, develop an argument, and organize supporting details.
- Develop proficiency in oral discourse.
- Evaluate an oral presentation according to established criteria.

Critical Thinking (Reasoning)
Students will:
- Identify, analyze, and evaluate arguments as they occur in their own or others' work.
- Develop well-reasoned arguments.

Information Management
Students will:
- Perform the basic operations of personal computer use.
- Understand and use basic research techniques.
- Locate, evaluate, and synthesize information from a variety of sources.

to outcomes assessment in undergraduate education. This group's final report established the foundation for SUNY-wide implementation of outcomes assessment and what is now commonly referred to as the SUNY Assessment Initiative, which contains guidelines for campuses to follow in assessing both general education and academic majors. While the guidelines for assessing academic majors are relatively non-prescriptive, procedures guiding general education assessment are fairly specific, as detailed below.

A third unique factor is the strong presence of faculty governance in the SUNY system and its role in shaping SUNY's approach to assessment (e.g., *Assessment at SUNY,* 1992), with the four-year campuses represented by the University Faculty Senate (UFS) and the community colleges by the Faculty Council of Community Colleges (FCCC). As demonstrated throughout this chapter, the maintenance of close and collegial relationships with both these groups has been integral to the Assessment Initiative's success, a finding that is quite consistent with the literature attesting to the value of involving governance organizations in the assessment process (Morse & Santiago, 2000).

As a final related point, just as SUNY gives ultimate responsibility to its faculty in developing and delivering its curricular programs, it assumes that faculty members are in the best position to determine the most appropriate means of assessing student learning. As a result, at least 95% of the general education assessment that has taken place across SUNY to this point has been course embedded, with measures created by faculty and administered as part of the students' enrollment in a class. In addition to helping ensure student motivation and requiring less additional work by faculty, this strategy is beneficial because it provides specific feedback on student learning and can lead directly and quickly to teaching, course, and program improvements. Further, although participation in the general education assessment process by professional staff members and even students varies greatly across campuses, most institutions do involve representatives from these constituent groups. In fact, because a campus's general education assessment plan must be approved by the institution's local faculty governance body—many of which include professional staff and student members—these groups have direct input into the process in most cases.

Overview of Assessment of the General Education Program

Oversight for SUNY-wide general education assessment is the charge of the General Education Assessment Review group, or GEAR. Formed originally in spring 2001, GEAR developed protocols and templates for campus general education assessment plans and has responsibility for reviewing those plans and recommending their approval to the university provost. GEAR consists of 20 faculty and staff members, 2 students, 2 chief academic officers, and 2 System Administration staff. Faculty and staff membership is recommended by the UFS and the FCCC in consultation with the university provost, and always includes the UFS and FCCC presidents or their designee.

In developing its guidelines for campuses to follow, GEAR delineated eight criteria, with campus leadership assured that their plans would receive approval if they accomplished the following:

• Demonstrated a clear relationship between campus objectives for student learning in their general education courses and the SUNY student learning outcomes.

• Showed that programmatic activities for accomplishing the objectives for student learning were in place.

• Provided evidence that their measures of student learning were direct, valid, and reliable, and that representative sampling of students and courses would take place in the assessments.

• Proposed a priori standards to which student performance could be compared, with campuses specifically required to state how they would define student performance that "exceeded," "met," "approached," or "failed to meet" standards.

• Described appropriate processes for sharing assessment results with faculty and closing the loop based on assessment data as necessary.

• Demonstrated that the assessment plan had been reviewed and approved through appropriate curriculum and faculty governance structures, with a sign-off sheet that required the campus governance leader's signature.

• Adhered to the GEAR Group's timetable of completing an entire round of general education assessment every three years (i.e., meaning that campuses would, on average, assess four learning outcome areas each year).

• Included provisions for evaluating the assessment process itself and disseminating results to appropriate members of the campus community.

When creating these guidelines and in its subsequent reviews of campus plans, GEAR gave campuses considerable leeway in their actual approach to assessment, and encouraged campuses to use an approach that was consistent with their own assessment culture. As such, campuses were free to use qualitative and quantitative measures as well as course-embedded and stand-alone strategies; to use standardized tests or local measures; to assess all students enrolled in a particular student learning outcome area or to assess a representative sample of students; and to use common assignments across course sections in collecting assessment data or individualized assignments, although some external review of individualized assignments (e.g., by other faculty or a campus committee) was required to assure validity. In short, GEAR placed no inherent value on specific assessment methodologies, as long as it was convinced the campus met its criteria based on good assessment practice.

Similarly, GEAR was careful not to view itself—or be perceived by campuses—as the "SUNY Assessment Police," but instead emphasized its role as peer reviewers and colleagues in its evaluation of campus assessment plans. Notably, GEAR's review of campus general education assessment focused entirely on the process of assessment itself, not the results yielded by that process. In fact, although campuses are required to provide annual reports on their general education assessment results to System Administration, GEAR is not involved in the reporting process. GEAR also serves as an important resource role to campuses, with members available to visit campuses for consultation. Further, since 2001 GEAR has cosponsored, with System Administration and the UFS and FCCC, three conferences on the general education assessment process.

After GEAR distributed its guidelines to campuses in fall 2001, campuses began submitting general education assessment plans, and GEAR's review process proved to be rigorous, with few campuses receiving approval on their first attempt. Many campuses, in fact, submitted their plans multiple times before approval was achieved, with the last of the 57 plans approved in summer 2005. Actual data collection began in the 2002–2003 academic year, which means that 2004–2005 represented the third year of data collection, or the completion of the first full cycle of SUNY-wide general education assessment for most campuses.

Obviously, given the diversity of the SUNY campuses as well as the autonomy they were provided in developing and implementing their assessment plans, there are few commonalities in how these 57 institutions are going about assessing their general education programs. As previously described, campuses are using a wide range of strategies and measures to assess the same student learning outcomes. Similarly, some campuses have a relatively centralized assessment approach, often overseen by an institutional research or assessment office, while other campuses have assigned responsibility for coordinating the process to departments or committees. In the latter case, a common strategy has been to form committees for the different student learning outcomes areas (e.g., humanities, Western civilization), with these committees then responsible for reviewing assessment measures as needed, developing an assessment schedule (i.e., in the event that it is not practical to assess every course section at the same point in time), and reviewing and disseminating assessment data.

While such variability in assessment approaches and measures might be viewed as a weakness, it is important to remember that any system-wide assessment effort based on a one-size-fits-all philosophy would have inevitably failed. In addition, the flexibility of the GEAR guidelines confers maximum autonomy to individual institutions, helping to ensure that the campus's assessment plan is consistent with its own mission, goals, and objectives. Further, this flexibility filters down to the faculty and course level, thereby increasing the likelihood that faculty members teaching in the program actively participate in the assessment process, hopefully leading to the faculty buy-in that is so vital to successful assessment. Perhaps most important, despite the flexibility of the guidelines and resulting surface variations in campus assessment plans, features critical to good assessment are absolutely constant. That is, for each student learning outcome a campus must use valid and reliable measures and representative sampling, determine beforehand how it will define successful—and unsuccessful—student performance, compare the assessment results against these standards, and then feed that information back into the teaching and learning process, or close the loop.

Examples of Assessment and How Results Are Used

As stated earlier, each year campuses must submit to SUNY System Administration a report that summarizes their general education assessment results from that year, including quantitative data, a qualitative analysis of the findings, and planned adjustments for the future based on the results. Now that the first round of general education assessment has been completed for most campuses, they will be asked to submit updated plans to GEAR, which will review and evaluate them much as it did the first time, except there will be more emphasis on how campuses are actually using assessment data to improve teaching and learning.

A review of the existing campus assessment plans themselves reveals a plethora of useful and innovative examples of how campuses have approached the assessment of SUNY's 12 general education learning outcomes areas. Table 10.1 shows a sampling of assessment methods, measures, and criteria for several of these areas, taken from actual campus assessment plans.

There is also a wealth of information on how campuses are using data yielded through the general education assessment process, from their annual reports to SUNY System Administration as well as from a survey that was administered in fall 2005 to all campuses participating in the process. Overall, it appears that general education assessment has already led to many positive changes on SUNY campuses, in three key ways: 1) improving courses, programs, and teaching; 2) assisting in ongoing accreditation efforts; and 3) enhancing faculty communication and professional development.

Improving Courses, Programs, and Teaching

Campuses report multiple revisions to their general education programs and courses on the basis of assessment data. Some of these

Table 10.1
Examples of Assessment Methods, Measures, and Standards
From Campus Assessment Plans

Learning Outcome		
Area	Method/Measure(s)	Standards
The Arts	A faculty team will rate students' portfolios (three works selected from each), on a 4–point scale, with reference to 12 criteria: the 5 formal elements of art (line, shape, color, texture, value), the 5 formal principles of design (unity and variety, rhythm and movement, balance, dominance, economy), technical proficiency in the medium, and communication of concept.	*Exceeding:* 38–48 points *Meeting:* 34–37 points *Approaching:* 29–33 points *Not meeting:* 12–28 points
Critical Thinking	ACT Critical Thinking Test (CAAP)	*Exceeding:* Scores that are more than one standard deviation (SD) above the national mean *Meeting:* Scores that fall between 1 SD above and 1 SD below the national mean *Approaching:* Scores that are less than 1 below but greater than 2 SDs below the national mean *Not meeting:* Scores that are less than 2 SDs below the national mean
Foreign Languages (Outcome #2)	End-of-semester exam testing students' knowledge of social customs and practices such as those related to lifestyle, travel, shopping, dining, distinguishing features of countries and regions where the language is spoken, and key famous people in countries where the language is spoken.	*Exceeding:* 86–100% *Meeting:* 75–85% *Approaching:* 60–74% *Not meeting:* < 60%

Learning Outcome		
Area	Method/Measure(s)	Standards
Basic Communication (Writing)	Essay questions developed by faculty teaching in this outcomes area and administered as part of students' final exam, with questions scored independently by faculty at a summer retreat using a 6-point rubric developed by the college's director of composition.	*Exceeding:* 5–6 points *Meeting:* 4 points *Approaching:* 3 points *Not meeting:* 0–2 points
Basic Communication (Oral)	Student evaluates a famous public speech and critiques its effectiveness on the following components: introduction, proposition, outline, proof, refutation, and conclusion. Student evaluation is assessed using a rubric developed by communications faculty which assigns up to 4 points for each of the 6 components.	*Exceeding:* 21–24 points *Meeting:* 16–20 points *Approaching:* 11–15 points *Not meeting:* 6–10 points

revisions are relatively minor, such as placing more emphasis on all the student learning outcomes included under a particular category, increasing writing requirements, and updating syllabi. In a number of cases, however, institutions indicated significant benefits resulting from their general education assessment process. For instance, one college reported that, on the basis of assessment data, it applied for and received a Title III grant for the purpose of improving students' math and science proficiency, while another stated that it had developed an Information Literacy Across the Curriculum initiative because its assessment of information management revealed such uneven performance across students in this area. Other substantial changes reported by institutions include the following:

• Creation of a writing skills lab and extension of programs in the areas of math tutoring and peer tutoring at a doctoral degree-granting institution.

• Changes in the scheduling of math courses and in the size of language courses at a comprehensive college.

- The addition of an English course at a college of technology based on the assessment of student writing.
- Revision by a community college's mathematics, engineering, and computer science division of its algebra/pre-calculus/calculus curriculum.

Assisting in Ongoing Accreditation Efforts

It was also clear from the survey administered to campuses in fall 2005 that, for many institutions, SUNY's general education assessment process has proved to be extremely helpful in their accreditation activities, especially those related to Middle States. To illustrate, of the 45 institutions responding to the survey, 36 indicated that SUNY's assessment requirements had been at least "moderately" useful in their accreditation efforts (and 20 reported they had been "extensively" useful). Far more impressive, however, was the nature of campuses' comments in response to this item. For instance, one comprehensive college stated that "the fact that System Administration requires these assessments makes it more difficult for colleges to ignore assessment tasks on a regular basis," while another said "our involvement with the SUNY process has been valuable in ensuring compliance with Middle States standards for data collection and analysis." Similarly, a community college offered the following comment: "The SUNY assessment processes have helped the campus 'buy in' to the culture of assessment that is needed to meet Middle States requirements for an Institutional Assessment Plan." Speaking more generally, a college of technology reported that "external organizations have been generally pleased with the formal, institutionalized process of assessment provided for by General Education Assessment."

Enhancing Faculty Communication and Professional Development

From the outset of the SUNY Assessment Initiative, it was assumed that an effective student learning outcomes assessment process benefits an institution in numerous ways, far beyond "just" through the improvement of teaching and learning. As Palomba and Banta (1999) observe,

> Much of the value of assessment comes from the systematic way it makes educators question, dis-

cuss, share, and observe. As a result, assessment contributes greatly to the understanding of what educators do and to the choices they make about future directions for their work. (pp. 328–329)

Other authors have commented similarly on how assessment activity serves to facilitate communication among faculty (Hill, 1996; Rust, 1997).

Not surprisingly then, the fall 2005 survey yielded numerous examples of the positive impact the implementation of general education assessment had brought about with respect to these more "peripheral" issues. As one doctoral institution wrote,

The assessment process encourages faculty to consider how to examine learning outcomes across students. As the process continues, more and more faculty teaching general education courses will be involved in the process. Thus, the process itself becomes a vehicle for faculty development.

A comprehensive college offered the following thoughtful observation:

In our view, the major benefit of the general education assessment process has been in the area of faculty development. In meeting to design assessment instruments and to score them, faculty from various disciplines involved in general education have come to a better understanding of the different general education categories and of the place of their courses in the general education program. They have also learned how their peers in different departments handle various pedagogical issues and problems, and they have learned more about assessment. In more than one case, the assessment approach developed by an interdisciplinary team working on general education assessment has been adapted for use in academic program assessment.

In addition, many respondents to the fall 2005 survey described specific faculty development activities that have arisen directly from the assessment process, including workshops, mentoring sessions, departmental meetings that focus on improving pedagogy, writing across the curriculum programs, and presentations by nationally prominent assessment experts. Notable examples included the following:

• Institutional support to faculty for attending national general education and assessment conferences.

• Development of a unique course on technology and pedagogy that is offered online and required of all new faculty.

• Funding support that is given to faculty who have used the assessment process to identify professional development needs.

• Participation by faculty in a large-scale FIPSE grant examining how to improve the use of assessment of student learning outcomes to foster better student performance.

Tips for Implementing the Process

Despite the proliferation of available resources on the implementation of effective assessment programs in higher education, early on in the SUNY Assessment Initiative there was surprisingly little information from a state- or university-wide perspective to guide it. For instance, as concluded by Wellman (2001), statewide accountability systems for higher education have typically relied heavily on institutional measures such as persistence and graduation rates. Similarly, Ewell (2001) summarized the attempts of states to make standardized tests an element of their higher education policy, concluding that these efforts do not generally yield information leading to program improvement but instead serve to ensure quality control or publicly embarrass institutions.

The principal flaw from an assessment perspective in both of these approaches is the fact that the measures are totally disconnected from specific objectives for student learning. One fundamental tip to other systems or even large universities considering an assessment approach similar to SUNY's, therefore, is to make sure there are common student learning outcomes in place across institutions, schools, or departments, such as SUNY's 30 learning outcome statements for general education. Of course, some of these statements are necessarily wide ranging (i.e., in order to accommodate the wide variety of disciplines that exist on different campuses) and require operationalization at the department and even course level as appropriate. For example, "hypothesis testing" from the social sciences learning outcome area will be taught—and assessed—differently in a psychology course as compared to a sociology or economics course. Still, the 30 student learning outcome statements comprising SUNY's general education requirement serve as a basic, common blueprint uniting the general education programs on all 57 campuses offering such a program and, without this blueprint, meaningful assessment of student learning would have been impossible.

It is also important that systems and institutions attempting to implement effective learning outcomes assessment work with existing faculty governance bodies every step of the way, as well as with academic leadership and, as appropriate, governing boards. As an example from SUNY's own experience, in June 2003 the SUNY Board of Trustees recommended several changes to SUNY's general education assessment process that were intended to strengthen accountability through the use of a common testing instrument across the 57 campuses. Faculty across SUNY objected strongly to these changes, largely because they felt that existing assessment efforts were working and that campuses had not been given sufficient time to demonstrate their effectiveness.

In responding to this situation, System Administration formed a largely faculty discussion group which met during the 2003–2004 academic year to develop an alternative to the trustees' recommendations that would satisfy the trustees and prove acceptable to faculty. The results of that successful effort—Strengthened Campus-Based Assessment—represents the next phase of the SUNY Assessment Initiative and calls for the use of "externally referenced" measures for critical thinking, mathematics, and basic communication (written), which may include nationally normed tests or rubrics and standards developed by panels of SUNY faculty and approved by the UFS and the FCCC.

Additional tips to systems or institutions attempting to develop effective, large-scale assessment programs involve the importance of offering support, financial and otherwise, to participating campuses or departments and of providing ongoing communication about the assessment effort to participants. As described earlier, System Administration has sponsored three conferences on general education assessment in conjunction with GEAR, the UFS, and the FCCC, the first of which took place in June 2001 and focused on GEAR guidelines and strategies for developing campus assessment plans. The second conference, held in November 2003, featured best practices across SUNY, and the third took place in April 2005, focusing on strengthened campus-based assessment. As other examples of financial support, for the 2001–2002 academic year System Administration distributed approximately $100,000 to nine campuses as part of a competitive assessment incentive grant program, and in August 2004 SUNY created and filled a new assistant provost's position charged with overseeing system-wide assessment and offering assistance to campuses in their assessment efforts. Regular communication to campuses about new developments in the Assessment Initiative is provided through the GEAR web site (www.cortland.edu/gear), as well as through an assessment listserv, to which anyone at SUNY can subscribe.

It is also important to acknowledge components of SUNY's assessment efforts that could have been implemented more effectively. First, in retrospect the design of the SUNY Assessment Initiative should have been mapped more carefully to Middle States' assessment requirements and standards. Although, as suggested earlier, there is considerable correspondence between SUNY's and Middle States' expectations for assessment, a number of incongruities exist, which has proved problematic to institutions attempting to meet SUNY's requirements while simultaneously preparing for Middle States reaccreditation. A lesson that follows from this situation in implementing a large-scale assessment effort is to be mindful of other assessment and certification requirements and make every effort to ensure that campuses or departments can coordinate their assessment activities so as to meet all requirements in as non-duplicative and efficient manner as possible. In this regard, a recent meeting between SUNY System Administration staff and Middle States representatives is likely to lead to adjustments in the Assessment Initiative that will be beneficial to SUNY campuses and reduce their assessment efforts somewhat.

Other ways in which SUNY's approach to assessment might have been improved include building in from the outset an "assessment of the assessment" and ensuring more student input into the assessment process, at both the system and campus levels. With respect to the former point, it was not until the summer of 2005 that System Administration began a systematic attempt to evaluate components of SUNY-wide assessment, forming a task force to examine specifically SUNY's data collection and reporting requirements. Hopefully, from this point on there will be ongoing review of different aspects of the SUNY Assessment Initiative so as to better assure the quality of the overall effort. Finally, even though GEAR includes two student members and encourages campuses to include students in their assessment process, reports indicate that such inclusion across SUNY is uneven at best. Future plans to address this issue include calling for best practices for student involvement from campuses and featuring them on the GEAR web site.

Challenges to Assessing General Education and Strategies to Overcome Them

Not surprisingly given the intended scope of SUNY's Assessment Initiative, progress has been relatively slow and, at certain points, has almost come to a standstill, if only temporarily. To illustrate, in late 2004 SUNY System Administration received a Freedom of Information Request from a journalist requiring that campuses' general education assessment data be made public. Campuses reacted strongly and negatively, due to concerns that such disclosure would lead to inappropriate inter-institutional comparisons (i.e., because campuses were using different measures and standards). System Administration responded by working closely with the UFS, FCCC, and campus leadership to broker this situation, releasing the materials but providing enough contextual information so that it was clear that the data reflected a wide variety of different assessment approaches and measures. Ultimately, the newspaper articles that appeared were few in number—possibly because the inability to compare institutions made the data of less interest—and largely positive. This incident also helped stimulate the formation of the task force described earlier that has been charged to review SUNY's data collection and reporting requirements and to make recommendations for their improvement, at both the campus and system levels.

References

Ewell, P. T. (2001, March/April). Statewide testing in higher education. *Change, 33*(2), 20–27.

Hill, I. B. (1996). Case 1: Setting the context for assessment. In T. W. Banta, J. P. Lund, K. E. Black, & F. W. Oblander, *Assessment in practice: Putting principles to work on college campuses* (pp. 76–78). San Francisco, CA: Jossey-Bass.

Morse, J. A., & Santiago, G., Jr. (2000, January/February). Accreditation and faculty working together. *Academe, 86*(1), 30–34.

Palomba, C. A., & Banta, T. W. (1999). *Assessment essentials: Planning, implementing, and improving assessment in higher education.* San Francisco, CA: Jossey-Bass.

Rust, C. (1997, November/December). Assessing what really matters in the major and the degree: A British perspective on moves to better practices in assessment. *Assessment Update, 9*(6), 6–8.

State University of New York. (2000). *Provost's advisory task force on the assessment of student learning outcomes: Final report.* Albany, NY: Author.

State University of New York. (2006). *Mission statement.* Retrieved November 6, 2006, from the State University of New York, About SUNY web site: www.suny.edu/about_suny/Mission.cfm

State University of New York, University Faculty Senate. (1992). *Assessment at SUNY: Principles, process, and case studies.* Albany, NY: Author.

Wellman, J. V. (2001, March/April). Assessing state accountability systems, *Change, 33*(2), 46–52.

Chapter 11

The College of William and Mary: General Education Case Study

Susan L. Bosworth

Overview of the Institutional Culture

The College of William and Mary is a moderate-sized, highly selective public university located in historic Williamsburg, Virginia. Of the 7,650 students, approximately 5,700 are undergraduates and three-quarters live on campus. The student-faculty ratio is 12 to 1. Undergraduate, graduate, and professional programs are located in the Schools of Arts and Sciences, Business Administration, Education, Law, and Marine Science. With a nationally acclaimed undergraduate program integrated with selective graduate and professional programs, students experience the best features of an undergraduate education along with opportunities afforded by modern research universities. It has been described by media as one of the nation's prestigious "Public Ivies." This characterization aptly describes the mission of William and Mary to be a great *and* public institution of higher education. The college is dually committed to fulfilling its public responsibility and maintaining academic excellence.

Chartered in 1693, William and Mary is the second oldest institution of higher learning in the nation. In 1776, the college severed formal ties with Britain. William and Mary became a state-supported institution in 1906. It became coeducational in 1918 and achieved modern university status in 1967. This historic institution is the birth place of Phi Beta Kappa, the nation's premier academic honor society, and the honor code system of conduct. Reflecting on the college's rich history, President Gene Nichol highlighted such traditions in terms of a legacy and a challenge: "to pursue excellence; to explore, examine, probe, question, and contribute; and to teach and learn in the context of a small, life-changing liberal arts experience."[1] The college's curricula nurture this vision of the William and Mary experience, as does the cocurriculum. The general education curriculum introduces students to broad areas of knowledge and fosters skills necessary for advanced study and professional pursuits. Cocurricular student experiences enhance the general education curriculum. In a highly selective student body, students often bring required skills, values, and knowledge with them when they arrive on campus. Students live in residence halls, eat in campus dining facilities, attend lectures and cultural events, meet informally with other students and with faculty members, and participate in a vast array of cocurricular activities. A "liberal education" occurs within this broader context in a community of scholars.

It is within this rich environment that the faculty designed a formal general education curriculum. Courses that meet a general education requirement address a specific set of collectively defined learning expectations. As criteria for general education courses were being defined, the faculty also began to explore ways to monitor results of curricular requirements. Working with assessment professionals, faculty members tested strategies and ultimately created a system of reviews that focuses on course experiences and student learning. The college augments the course-based reviews with broad-based studies of general education.

Overview of the General Education Program

We define our public responsibility, in part, as fostering the very best in liberal education. In short, at William and Mary the aim of general education is to "help students develop critical judgment, imagination, and moral autonomy." In a report on the undergraduate curriculum, the faculty describes what this means for students in the 21st century: Students must be able to think clearly and communicate thoughts, understand and deal with numerical data, and comprehend the fundamental principles of the natural and social sciences, as well as their major accomplishments, possibilities, and limits. Students must be highly literate, and in an age of global interdependence, they must be knowledgeable about their own cultural heritage and about cultures very different from their own. Historical perspective can engender new ideas and creative possibilities and free students from provincialism and ingrained prejudice. Students also need to recognize possibilities of artistic creativity as a means of expressing human meaning and to know aesthetic forms and achievements that profoundly mirror and shape culture. Finally, students need to be able to discern and analyze competing values and understand how to deal responsibly with moral questions of personal and social importance.[2] The challenge is translating conditions of a liberal education to a carefully structured set of requirements. This is a hallmark of the general education program at William and Mary.

Working from this conceptual model, the faculty designed a curriculum that builds a strong foundation in the freshman year and addresses specific areas of liberal education in seven general education requirements (GERs). In the freshman year, students take a writing-, reading-, and discussion-intensive freshman seminar. Students may continue to meet the seven GERs throughout their tenure at the college.[3] Collectively, the definitions and elaborations of the GERs specify areas of knowledge and skills important to undergraduate liberal education at William and Mary. The purpose of each requirement and the expectations for student learning are shown in Figure 11.1.

The general education curriculum transcends disciplinary lines and allows students to pursue individual interests as they satisfy their freshman seminar and GER requirements. For example, courses that satisfy GER 1, Mathematics and Quantitative Reasoning, are taught in computer science, economics, kinesiology, mathematics, psychology, and sociology. Courses that meet GER 4, World Cultures and History, are taught in at least 15 disciplines at both the introductory and advanced levels. The curriculum balances the college's emphasis on developing independent learners and the importance of a coherent and intentional set of general education requirements. At William and Mary, general education is more than a set of courses; it reflects what the faculty expects students to learn so they can think about, interact with, and work within the human community and advance the human condition.

Figure 11.1
General Education Requirements

Freshman Seminars

The purpose of the freshman seminar program is to help students develop their capacity for critical thinking, independent learning, and effective communication.

Expectations for student learning:

- Students will engage in critical thinking on topics pertinent to the subject matter of the course.
- Students will work independently to understand texts and form judgments on topics pertinent to the subject matter of the course.
- Students will communicate effectively on topics pertinent to the subject matter of the course.

GER 1: Mathematics and Quantitative Reasoning
(one course)

The purpose of GER 1 is to expose students to analytical techniques and computational tools for addressing real-world problems.

Expectations for student learning:

- Students will carry out numerical calculations by hand or by using calculators or computers.
- Students will understand approaches and calculations used in the coursework.
- Students will apply mathematics to study real-world problems.

GER 2: The Natural Sciences
(two courses, one of which is taken with its associated laboratory)
- 2A Physical Sciences (one course)
- 2B Biological Sciences (one course)

The purpose of GER 2 is to introduce students to enduring principles in the physical and biological sciences and to foster an appreciation of the broader contexts of those principles.

Expectations for student learning:

- Students will recognize and understand guiding principles, concepts, and a body of knowledge associated with a scientific discipline.
- Students will recognize and understand the process of scientific investigation and its limitations.
- Students will appreciate the broader context of a particular scientific discipline through a basic understanding of at least three of the following:
  – the character of natural laws
  – the role of mathematics in science
  – the centrality of cause and effect reasoning to the scientific world view
  – the fundamental importance of change and evolution

– the characteristic scales and proportions of natural phenomenon
– the historical development of science and its cultural and intellectual context

GER 2 laboratories: Through hands-on activities, students will gain experiential knowledge associated with a scientific discipline. Students will also gain experience in data collection and analysis.

GER 3: The Social Sciences
(2 courses)
The purpose of GER 3 is to introduce students to the systematic observation and analysis of human behavior and interaction.

Expectations for student learning:
• Students will understand basic concepts, key theories, and methods used by social scientists.
• Students will describe important findings of social science research.
• Students will, where appropriate, explain implications of social science findings for public policy.

GER 4: World Cultures and History
(one course in category A, one course in category B, and one additional course in either category A, B, or C)
• 4A History and Culture in the European Tradition
• 4B History and Culture Outside the European Tradition
• 4C Cross-Cultural Issues

The purpose of GER 4 is to introduce students to major ideas, institutions, and historical events in European and non-European traditions that have shaped human societies and cultures.

Expectations for student learning:
• Students will understand important cultural and historical topics, issues, or themes in more than one period or in one critical period or in a movement or movements.
• Students will understand institutions, movements, or cultural practices in historical context.
• Students will understand critical historical and cultural events, institutions, ideas, or literary/artistic achievements.

GER 5: Literature and History of the Arts
(one course)
The purpose of GER 5 is to introduce students to important literary or artistic achievements and how those achievements should be understood in their cultural contexts.

Expectations for student learning:
• Students will become conversant with at least two major forms, genres, eras, cultures, or movements, or with at least two methods of analysis of art or literature.

- Students will become familiar with the vocabulary of the discipline and be able to apply the appropriate methodologies for critical analysis.

GER 6: Creative and Performing Arts
(two credits in same creative or performing art)
The purpose of GER 6 is to help students understand the process of artistic communication through experience-based learning.

Expectation for student learning:
- Students will develop and apply their artistic skills through a creative or performing art (music, art, creative writing, dance, theater, or debate/forensics).

GER 7: Philosophical, Religious, and Social Thought
(one course)
The purpose of GER 7 is to introduce students to important and influential approaches to philosophical, religious, or social thought and to cultivate reasoned analysis and judgment.

Expectations for student learning:
- Students will address some fundamental questions about what is good, worthwhile, valuable, desirable, holy, sacred, right, just, true, beautiful, and the like in philosophical, religious, or social thought.
- Students will identify and justify philosophical, religious, or social norms and values.
- Students will engage in active critical analysis of evaluative or ethical theories, concepts, and methods of reasoning and deliberation in philosophical, religious, or social thought.

Coupled with the formal general education curriculum is a carefully developed cocurriculum. The mission of the Division of Student Affairs

> is to develop, plan, and supervise an array of programs, services, and activities which encourage optimal growth and personal development of students; contribute to student academic and personal success and well-being; foster a sense of community; and support an environment which is personal in nature, intellectually and culturally diverse, and which encourages the interaction and integration of the in- and out-of-class experience of students. (College of William and Mary, 2004, p. 1)

The division plans and administers programs, services, and activities and conducts regular assessments of the cocurriculum.

Assessment results indicate the extent to which the cocurriculum contributes to student learning and development; help the division examine and change or reorganize the learning environment in response to the needs, concerns, and interests of students; and inform improvements in the delivery of services and implementation of programs.

Overview of Assessment of the General Education Program

Assessments of the seven GERs and the freshman seminars align with a broader model of institutional effectiveness recently adopted by the college. The model emphasizes a continual process of planning, evaluation, and evidence-based decision-making. As part of this university-wide process, each academic program, including general education, constructs a *Profile of Institutional Effectiveness,* or a PIE.[4] In this model, assessments link evaluations of student learning directly to planning and decisions about the curriculum, activities designed to enhance student learning, and resource allocations. Within this context, assessment results can be used to adjust curricular experiences within a course and to monitor the curriculum more broadly. For GERs and the freshman seminar program, the PIE specifies:

- A clearly stated *purpose* that links general education and each requirement to the institutional mission

- Clearly stated *faculty expectations for student learning*

- Clear descriptions of *experiences* associated with the learning expectations

- *Evaluations* of how well expectations are being met

- *Evidenced-based decision-making and planning:* Descriptions of how information from evaluations is used in decisions about the curricula, activities, and resources

The PIE model is represented graphically in Figure 11.2 to highlight the continual process of evaluation and decision-making to enhance student learning. For general education, the purpose of each requirement and associated learning expectations is collectively defined by the faculty. Experiences that address the learning expectations vary by course and are defined by individual faculty members. Methods of evaluation are determined collectively and include a review of course experiences and student work. Results of evaluations at the course and curricular levels inform decision-making and planning to enhance general education. A more specific description of each component follows.

Figure 11.2
Profile of Institutional Effectiveness

The *purpose* of each GER and the freshman seminars was presented earlier with associated *faculty expectations for student learning*. These components of the PIE are common across the curriculum.

Curricular *experiences* are documented by faculty members teaching GER courses or freshman seminars. Each faculty member identifies assignments and activities in his or her course that address the learning expectations. This approach emphasizes an intentional and transparent alignment of course experiences and learning expectations.

Evaluation of individual students continues to be the purview of each faculty member. Evaluation and oversight of courses and the curriculum rests with departments, programs, and faculty committees. This distinction is clear in the course portfolio methodology the faculty has adopted for the *evaluation* of the GERs and the freshman seminar program. Course portfolios offer rich information about student experiences and consequent learning outcomes. They provide authentic measures of student learning and shared standards without forced standardization.

Portfolios incorporate multiple sources of information, including results of a student survey, an instructor's narrative, course material, and student work. Each portfolio represents how the curriculum is being delivered within a course, and collectively, the portfolios indicate whether learning expectations are being met in the general education curriculum. In the current round of assessments, portfolios are constructed electronically. Faculty members may upload their portfolio information directly into their password-protected course portfolios, or they may submit paper versions of any or all information to the Office of Planning and Assessment to upload. Each component of a GER or freshman seminar course portfolio is described in Table 11.1.

Table 11.1
Components of a Course Portfolio

1) GER/Freshman Seminar Student Survey Report	• Conducted and posted to electronic portfolio by the Office of Planning and Assessment at the end of the semester (all other materials are supplied by the instructor). Surveys ask students to indicate what types of experiences they had in their GER or freshman seminar course.
2) Instructor's Narrative (a couple of paragraphs)	• Brief overview of the course design and aims. • Description of how each learning expectation is addressed in the course, with clarity about objectives of specific assignments and how they align with learning expectations.
3) Syllabus	• Included in each electronic portfolio.
4) Assignment, Tests and/or Instructions (e.g., tests, paper prompts)	• Alignment of assignments/tests to learning expectations. • Details about assignments/tests (instructions to students, copy of test/test items if blue books are used).
5) Two Examples of Student Work on All Major Assignments	• Examples that reflect the range of student work (e.g., marginally acceptable to excellent). Examples of what "excellent" and "marginal" work are in relation to what students are expected to learn as part of the GER or freshman seminar requirement.
6) Comments	• Instructors may include comments about survey results (available at the end of the semester) and/or other comments that would be of use to working group members as they review the portfolio and the requirement.

Portfolios are reviewed by working groups of three to six faculty members. Working groups for each GER and the freshman seminars are appointed by the dean for educational policy. Each working group includes a member of the Educational Policy Committee and/or the Assessment Steering Committee and faculty members in disciplines closely associated with the GER and those from disciplines less closely associated with the GER. For example, a member of the mathematics faculty and a member of the classical studies faculty might serve on the working group for GER 1, Mathematics and Quantitative Reasoning. The composition of working groups reinforces collective ownership of the general education curriculum and assessment process. After completing a calibration exercise, a working group reviews portfolios using a standard scoring guide. The guides address only those learning expectations associated with the requirement. Working group members use a 3-point scale (inadequate, adequate, exemplary) to rate the extent to which a portfolio provides evidence that each learning expectation was met in the course. Each portfolio is reviewed independently by two members of the group. After any scoring discrepancies are resolved, the completed rating guide is posted to the portfolio. Faculty members may access the rating guide for their individual portfolios.

The Office of Planning and Assessment summarizes portfolio ratings and survey responses in tables and charts. Summaries include the means and distributions of ratings for the portfolios and survey responses for each learning expectation of the requirement. The working group analyzes results and submits a report to the Educational Policy Committee, the dean's office, and departments and programs that offer the respective GER courses. Summary results also are included in appropriate reports to the State Council of Higher Education for Virginia. Reports of the working groups provide overall conclusions about the requirement and analyses by course and student characteristics. The general outline of each report includes the following:

- Description of the requirement

- Description of the methodologies and response rates (course portfolios, student surveys)

- List of courses included in the review

- Distribution of portfolio scores and overall analysis
- Correlation of portfolio and survey results
- Comparative analyses for each of the following:
  - Class size
  - Course level
  - Rank of professor
  - Student academic class status (survey only)

The working group reports inform decision-making and planning. The advantage of this methodology is that results can be used by individual instructors, departments and programs, faculty oversight committees, and deans. This methodology also is appropriate when a general education curriculum transcends disciplinary lines rendering content-specific methods, such as embedded test items or standardized tests, inappropriate.

The GERs and freshman seminar program are assessed on a five-year cycle. Each review begins in the fall term and ends in the spring. During a review, all instructors who teach courses that meet a requirement under review are asked to submit a course portfolio.[5] During the initial round of portfolio reviews, each working group was asked to suggest ways to improve the assessment process. Adjustments were made with each subsequent review. Most notably, as the process progressed through the first cycle, working groups relied increasingly on student work as authentic measures of student learning and reviewed course material to ensure the breadth of each GER was addressed in course experiences. Results of the first round of portfolio evaluations indicated that courses generally were providing experiences that resulted in the learning envisioned by the general education curriculum. The report format in the initial cycle intentionally precluded details of individual course sections. However, analyses revealed few or no differences by class size, course level, rank of professor, or academic class status of students enrolled in the courses.

Working group reports indicated general satisfaction with how the curriculum was being delivered and focused on clarifying the language of the requirements and ways to improve the assessment process. In one case, the working group recommended substantive changes to the requirement. Portfolios for GER 2 courses and laboratories (natural sciences) were meeting the GER criteria, but the GER 2 working group was concerned that the criteria did not emphasize the main focus of a science course: to present scientific knowledge related to that particular subject. Instructors spend the majority of their time teaching this scientific knowledge. As initially worded, a course also had to address additional areas such as the historical significance and cultural impact of the particular subject under study. The GER 2 requirement was rewritten to emphasize the importance of gaining scientific knowledge to master "concepts and the development of the viewpoint specific to a particular scientific discipline." The changes to GER 2 and modest word changes to other requirements were approved by the faculty.

In the first cycle of reviews, working groups were unanimous in the need to streamline the assessment process to reduce the workload of working groups and faculty members teaching GER courses and, at the same time, provide greater oversight of the curriculum at the course and course section levels. The process has been revised to address concerns expressed by the working groups. Details are provided in the next section.

The college has explored other methodologies for assessing general education. Early in the assessment process, the faculty developed a 71-item test of historical knowledge. The test was intended to be the first in a series to measure student learning outcomes. Eleven items were from a test conducted by the National Endowment for the Humanities, and the other items were constructed by a group of faculty members. William and Mary students performed much better than the national average on the subset of nationally comparative items. Even so, the methodology proved to be ineffective in identifying ways to enhance student learning at the course level and for promoting institutional effectiveness.

In addition to assessments of specific general education requirements, the college conducts periodic studies that support the more focused review of course portfolios. These types of studies reinforce results of the more specific initiatives. For example, comparative results of the 1992 and 2002 senior surveys showed that students graduating under the new general education curriculum rated their level of knowledge and skills in general education higher than students graduating under the old cafeteria-style system of general education (see Table 11.2).

Table 11.2
Complementary Initiatives: 1992 and 2002 Senior Surveys

Skills & Knowledge (1 = low to 5 = high)	1992 (N = 290)	2002 (N = 503)	Difference
Effective Writing	3.99	4.24	+.25
Computer	2.66	3.79	+1.13
Natural Sciences	2.83	3.31	+.48
Scientific Method	3.09	3.50	+.41
Mathematical	2.96	3.23	+.27
Critical Thinking	4.09	4.38	+.29
Effective Speaking	3.47	3.88	+.41

In 2003, a transcript analysis indicated that many seniors had completed more than the minimal requirements for each GER. Results suggest that students have multiple experiences which reinforce the learning expectations associated with GERs (see Table 11.3).

Table 11.3 Complementary Initiatives: Transcript Analysis

	Seniors: Took minimal number of GER courses	Seniors: Took more than minimum of GER courses
GER 1	657 (63%)	382 (37%)
GER 2a	859 (78%)	244 (22%)
GER 2b	607 (57%)	463 (43%)
GER 3	382 (32%)	808 (68%)
GER 4	342 (28%)	863 (72%)
GER 5	367 (36%)	746 (64%)
GER 6	826 (71%)	337 (29%)
GER 7	916 (79%)	238 (21%)

These studies increase confidence in conclusions drawn from the portfolio analyses. Although these indirect studies are not designed to specify ways to enhance student learning, results provide a broader perspective and may generate areas for further study.

Examples of Assessment and How Results Are Used

The college completed the first round of GER assessments in 2003, and the Educational Policy Committee made recommendations to the faculty based on assessment results. As noted earlier, working groups concluded that GER courses collectively were addressing the general goals of the requirements. However, each working group identified limitations with the course portfolio methodology as it was implemented, and each group was concerned with the work-load involved in such close monitoring of the curriculum.

Based on the working groups' recommendations, significant changes were made to the evaluation process. To streamline the process, portfolios are now constructed and reviewed electronically. The timeline was changed so that working groups meet in May to review portfolios, complete evaluations, and prepare recommendations for the Educational Policy Committee and the Assessment Steering Committee. The most notable change, however, is the level of aggregation at which information is shared. In the first cycle, only aggregate results were released. This policy was established to ensure that assessment results were used only to monitor the curriculum. This was in keeping with the college's long-standing tradition to prohibit the use of assessment results in tenure and merit considerations or as proxies for course evaluations. This intentional separation of faculty and course evaluations and assessments of student learning supports assessment as a shared process that ensures that curricular experiences lead to the types of learning faculty expect of students. However, these restrictions and the policy to release only aggregate results limited the ability of the working groups, departments and programs, and the Educational Policy Committee to monitor the curriculum and reduced the extent to which assessment results could be used to enhance student learning. Frustrated by these imposed restrictions, every working group and both oversight committees supported a change in policy. Based on recommendations of the faculty groups, the full faculty voted to release information at the course section level. The revision allows for more detailed analyses by working groups and more specific guidance and recommendations by the Educational Policy Committee and the dean's office. The change also gives departments and programs a much more active role in the assessment process. At the beginning of each semester, department chairs and program directors receive a list of all instructors who have been asked to construct portfolios for a review. Chairs and directors are also provided with periodic updates on the progress of each portfolio. At the end of the review, course section information can be used to guide discussions about general education courses taught within a department or program, and results can inform planning, decision-making, and educational policy at the department and program level.

The expanded role of departments and programs and release of information at the course section level represents a philosophical shift in the assessment program and greater faculty ownership of the process. Faculty are heavily involved in all aspects of the assessment process. Oversight of the curriculum was mandated by the faculty and is controlled by the faculty. The faculty adopted a work-intensive methodology, but one that best reflects the experienced curriculum and student learning outcomes. The unanimous faculty vote to adopt the policy change reflects a commitment to shared responsibility for the general education curriculum and trust among the faculty that the assessment process will be formative and academic freedom and pedagogical creativity will continue to be protected.

The planning and decision-making process draws from the Profiles of Institutional Effectiveness, or PIEs, and decisions are tracked over time. This important step in the assessment process documents how the college closes the loop in a continual process of institutional effectiveness. The process also ensures that the purpose of a requirement and learning expectations is reviewed on a regular basis. Faculty members align course experiences to the learning expectations and the purpose, and working groups, oversight committees, departments and programs, and the dean interpret assessment results based on learning expectations and the purposes of each general education requirement. Assessments are useful to the extent they are consequential.

Tips for Implementing the Process

All accredited institutions with undergraduate programs define general education and most have at least some way to assess learning outcomes. So why might an institution contemplate change? And why might an institution want to replicate how William and Mary defines and assesses general education? An administrator once observed that she believes assessment is a wasted effort in general education because curricula are cyclical. They are revised every 10 years or so. It may be that general education curricula have been revised periodically because faculty members lack confidence that their intentions are being achieved, and lacking good evidence, a reasonable alternative is to reinvent the process. It may be also that careful monitoring will allow increasing refinement and better approximation of the goals of a curriculum, and that changes may become more incremental and targeted. The challenge is in making assessments an integral part of the institutional culture.

William and Mary implemented a new general education curriculum in the mid-1990s. The new curriculum was a product of much research, lengthy debate, and multiple drafts. In the end there was considerable consensus about what it means to be liberally educated at William and Mary. Those exchanges engaged faculty members in discussions about student learning, and ultimately in discussions about how to monitor the curriculum. General education is most appropriately defined by an institution's faculty. There are many excellent models, and even if much is borrowed from other institutions, the faculty should share a joint sense of ownership and responsibility for general education.

William and Mary's PIEs are distinctive from other models of assessment. The PIEs deliberately link what faculty expect students to learn and what students experience in the classroom. When the connection between learning and experiences is intentional and direct, evaluations can be structured so individual instructors can identify which experiences work and which do not, and adjust courses accordingly. Similarly, departments and programs can monitor learning outcomes at the course level and pursue interventions as necessary, as can the Educational Policy Committee and the dean. The model does require transparency and involvement on the part of faculty; an office to organize collection and review of portfolios (electronic or otherwise), conduct surveys, and help working groups prepare reports; and a commitment to use results in making decisions and planning. Faculty members have commented very favorably on the ease of uploading material to the electronic portfolio, but this requires someone to maintain the database. The PIE model emphasizes the expertise of faculty to structure learning experiences and evaluate individual student learning. Samples of student work reflect the range of performance rather than achievements of an individual student. There are no issues with student motivation, as may be the case in post hoc, course-external assessments. The review process has had the additional and valued consequence of reminding faculty and students about the learning expectations in general education.

Institutions can benefit from some well-known practices in general education assessment, and from the experiences of others. Both are offered here in three major considerations of an assessment program: building a culture of assessment, organizing a structure of assessment, and nurturing healthy assessment.

Culture of Assessment

• Focus on mission.

• Emphasize cultural compatibility.

• Integrate from the beginning (not as an afterthought).

• Use results for planning and decision-making.

Structure of Assessment

• Establish a model or framework.

• Include multiple sources of information.

• Rely on existing structure (to extent possible).

• Keep faculty engaged.

• Determine a process for assessing the assessment.

Nurturing Healthy Assessment

• Be flexible.

• Be responsive.

• Keep a sense of humor.

Challenges to Assessing General Education and Strategies to Overcome Them

There are barriers to developing, implementing, and sustaining any assessment program, but they are perhaps most evident in assessing general education. Often one barrier is linked to another. Five common and somewhat connected barriers are described next.

Ownership

Who "owns" the general education curriculum, the courses, and assessment? General education implies agreement about what students should learn in a core curriculum. Expectations for student learning need to be explicit. When there is consensus about what students should know and be able to do as graduates of the institution, the faculty can determine how best to ensure those learning expectations are met. The general education curriculum—those knowledge and skill areas defined as important for all students—is owned by the faculty.

The key to delivering a general education curriculum is intentionality. Faculty need to determine how each component of general education will be addressed. At some institutions, the faculty will rely on individual departments to take responsibility for certain requirements. For example, a requirement in scientific reasoning might be defined and taught in one or more departments in the sciences, or a quantitative reasoning requirement might be addressed in a mathematics course. Other requirements, such as critical thinking or writing, might be integrated across the curriculum. Some requirements might be addressed in structured cocurricular activities. The mode of delivery is less important than the intentional link between curricular and cocurricular experiences and learning expectations in general education. Faculty need to be explicit about those links, and students should understand the coherence and relevance of their experiences to a liberal education. The faculty should be able to identify when and how students are developing skills and acquiring knowledge associated with general education. Ownership of the curriculum and courses rest with the faculty, even if individual instructors, department faculties, or student affairs professionals structure experiences that address learning expectations.

The faculty defines how students meet general education requirements, and ultimately, the faculty is responsible for ensuring experiences that result in the types of learning expected of students. The methodologies will vary from institution to institution, and often from requirement to requirement within the same institution. What is important is that the faculty agrees the methods selected are valid and reliable, and results can be used to monitor and improve general education. The faculty may rely on common tests or assignments, embedded test items, a shared rubric to rate various examples of student work, or some other method to measure results of general education. The method may be developed by an assessment committee, an office, a department, an individual faculty member, or others. But assessment is owned collectively by the faculty.

Regardless of institutional approach or the ways in which the curriculum is delivered and assessed, general education is a campus-wide responsibility, and ultimately, the faculty must be accountable for ensuring that learning expectations are met. The faculty as a whole owns general education, but an appropriate structure for monitoring the curriculum must be defined so oversight will not fall between the cracks.

Resistance to Assessment

Resistance is common, especially among faculty members who are uncertain about the purpose, process, and consequences of assessment. To help reduce resistance, make sure the purpose, process, and consequences are clear and communicated regularly to faculty. Work within existing structures to reinforce the importance of participating in assessment. For example, involve departments in the process. If courses in a department meet a general education requirement, make sure the department chair understands the assessment process and ask for assistance in encouraging faculty members to participate. Resolving ownership issues early makes it easier to emphasize collective responsibility for general education. If assessment requires faculty action (e.g., course portfolio methodology, embedded questions, common tests administered in class), contact faculty members early and often and follow up with personal telephone calls or emails to ensure that each faculty member understands his or her role in general education. Offer assistance at all steps in the process.

In the proverbial carrot-and-stick approach, use carrots. Often, faculty members resent yet another time-consuming task that takes away from their teaching and scholarship. We have found that faculty members will vent frustrations, even as they participate in assessment of general education. Rely on faculty members who have participated in the past to train their colleagues. If possible, reward faculty members for their effort, even with a personal thank you. Resistance to assessment may well stem from a resentment of oversight when none was necessary in early years of higher education. Some may view assessment as intrusive and a threat to academic freedom. These concerns are best addressed by being open about assessment and the use of results, and emphasizing faculty ownership of the process. Be sure to make explicit if and how general education assessment will be used in tenure and promotion decisions or to evaluate teaching, in resource allocations, and to address external reporting requirements

External Focus

Regional and professional accreditation requirements and state requirements may dictate, in part, definitions of general education and assessments. These external demands for accountability motivate institutions in the short run, but if general education and assessments are reactive and focused externally, efforts toward defining a liberally educated graduate and measuring student learning will not be sustained in the long run. An external focus relegates general education to mandated concern instead of a central component of undergraduate education. The faculty needs to "own" the process and define general education for the institution and for the academy. Initial momentum might well be in response to external demands. However, an external focus becomes a barrier if the importance of general education is not internalized and if the assessments do not inform local priorities and decision-making.

Competing Priorities

Faculty members are faced with competing demands. Often internal reward structures do not acknowledge contributions to general education. Institutions need to reflect on the importance of general education and determine how active and effective participation is encouraged on campus. An obvious starting point is to define how local commitments to general education are defined (e.g., service on an assessment steering committee, teaching general education courses, assessing learning outcomes) and acknowledged. Administrators and faculties can indicate how the scholarship of assessment or scholarly writing on teaching and learning are weighted in tenure and merit decisions. General education will not be prominent if there is no recognition of the time and effort involved in creating, implementing, maintaining, and enhancing general education.

Use General Education Assessment Results

Nothing deflates assessment faster than a perception that it is busy-work. Use of results should be part of the planning and structure of assessment. How results are used will determine, in part, appropriate methodologies and reporting formats. To enhance general education, results need to be useful to instructors. To monitor the curriculum, results need to be useful to oversight committees, departments, programs, and deans. To inform budgetary decisions, results need to be useful to those responsible for allocating resources at different levels within the institution. Use of results should not be an afterthought, nor should results necessarily be reported in a single format. Use of results should be planned carefully, subsequent decisions documented, and follow-up reports scheduled to ensure a continuous process of institutional effectiveness. Without a clear sense of how results will be used, assessment reports might well take up space on a shelf as general education drifts. Assessment involves a lot of effort, and if there is no demonstrable use of results, interest (and participation) will wane. Perhaps results show courses are having the intended effects on student learning and the faculty decides to continue current practices. The decision to do so is a use of assessment results. Likewise, if there are problems identified in delivering or defining the curriculum, appropriate action can be taken. Results and subsequent decisions should be circulated.

Author Note

Much of the information in this case study is summarized from the college's web site: www.wm.edu

Endnotes

1) This quote is from President Gene Nichol's introductory note that was included with the submission of the college's compliance certification to the Southern Association of Colleges and Schools (September 2, 2005).

2) This paragraph was extracted with minor modifications from College of William and Mary (1993).

3) This chapter focuses on the freshman seminars and courses that fulfill the GERs. However, each requirement addresses a specific general education objective. The Educational Policy Committee and the faculty may consider alternative means of fulfilling the requirement besides the completion of courses taken at William and Mary.

4) Administrative and support units also construct PIEs that focuses on unit objectives.

5) Faculty members teaching multiple *sections* of a course are asked to submit a single portfolio. Faculty members teaching multiple *courses* that meet requirements are asked to submit a portfolio for each course.

References

College of William and Mary, Curriculum Review Steering Committee. (1993). *Final report on the undergraduate curriculum.* Williamsburg, VA: Author.

College of William and Mary. (2004). *Division of Student Affairs assessment plan.* Retrieved November 8, 2006, from the College of William and Mary, Division of Student Affairs web site: www.wm.edu/sacs/accdoc/2/10/documents/StudentAffairsDivision-wideAssessmentPlan.pdf

Chapter 12

University of Central Florida: General Education Case Study

Martha Marinara, Kristina Tollefson

Overview of the Institutional Culture

The University of Central Florida (UCF), located 13 miles east of downtown Orlando, was founded in June 1963 as Florida Technical University. The name was changed by action of the Florida Legislature on December 6, 1978. Comprising nine colleges (Burnett Honors College, Center for Research and Education in Optics and Lasers, College of Arts and Humanities, College of Business, College of Education, College of Engineering, College of Health and Public Affairs, College of Molecular and Microbiology, College of Sciences), the University of Central Florida is 1 of 11 public universities in the state of Florida. The university houses 92 baccalaureate programs, 94 master's programs, 3 graduate specialty programs, and 24 Ph.D. programs. The Southern Association of Colleges and Schools rates UCF as a level-6 institution and the university's Carnegie classification is doctoral research intensive. The university serves an 11-county area, from Levy to Brevard counties, and its regional campuses include 12 sites in seven of those counties.

UCF's student/faculty ratio is 18 to 1, which is less than that of benchmark universities of comparative size and with a comparative mission. One of the university's five goals is a commitment to "become more inclusive and diverse." Since the university's founding, the student population has grown more diverse and more international. Fully 13% of the student population is Hispanic, 9% is African American and 6% is Asian. Currently, there are 1,624 international students, predominantly from Asia but also from Africa, South America, Europe, the Middle East, and Central America. International students make up almost 4% of the student enrollment and most often enroll in engineering, computer science, optics, and business.

In 1996, 27,411 students enrolled at UCF; just 10 years later, the university's enrollment has grown by more than 17,500 students. With approximately 44,953 students and 1,186 faculty, rapid growth has been one of the university's major accomplishments and certainly its principal challenge. The university has matched this growth, hiring more faculty, constructing more classrooms, and increasing the level of support services. In the last five years, the university has built additions to the College of Business, the College of Health and Public Affairs, and the College of Engineering, and built a Teaching Academy for the College of Education, constructed a fully wired classroom building, and a new Student Union building. In 2006, UCF broke ground to build a new psychology building and is currently building a new, 10,000-seat convocation center. A large portion of this growth can be attributed to the introduction of online courses in the 1996–1997 academic year. In the spring 2005 semester, 262 online courses were offered, and the enrollment in those courses exceeded 29,000 students.

The focus of UCF's mission concerns its role as a large metropolitan research university. Its primary mission is to provide intellectual leadership through quality undergraduate and graduate programs. UCF is dedicated to serving the surrounding communities by providing services that enhance the intellectual, cultural, environmental, and economic development of the region. Most certainly, the university's location in Florida's High Tech Corridor has helped shape its curricula, research programs, and policies. Rapid growth and a technology-rich environment have contributed to the academic culture of UCF. The university is future-directed and defines itself as "a dynamic university with opportunities to take risks; to investigate creative change; to develop collaborative, cooperative relationships; to form partnerships; and to implement technological innovation" (UCF, 2000). UCF is committed to integrating new research knowledge and creative expression into its curricula.

One faculty member has described the environment as fertile ground for entrepreneurship. Although the campus characteristics do not directly match this marketing analogy, UCF does support pedagogical innovation and academic transformation, as long as changes to the curriculum are well informed. Institutional assessments are meant to be transformative, and the changes to the General Education Program's assessment process help support practices that improve student learning.

Overview of the General Education Program

UCF's General Education Program (GEP) is designed to

> introduce students to a broad range of human knowledge and intellectual pursuits, to equip them with the analytic and expressive skills required to engage in those pursuits, to develop their ability to think critically, and to prepare them for life-long learning. The GEP curriculum provides students with the intellectual, ethical, and aesthetic foundations necessary to make informed choices; to accept the responsibilities of working and living in a rapidly changing world; and to lead a productive and satisfying life. (UCF, 2006, p. 46)

Although many faculty members perceive the GEP's purpose as providing students with the skills necessary to succeed in their upper-level courses and academic majors, others recognize that academic skills, ways of thinking, and disciplinary concepts are introduced in GEP courses and then further enhanced and reinforced as students work through their major courses. The GEP is organized around five learning foundations: communication, cultural and historical, mathematical, social, and science. Each learning foundation has a set of student learning objectives.

General Education Program Learning Objectives

Communication Foundation

• Demonstrate the ability to analyze the situational characteristics of a communication act: audience, purpose, and source/author.

- Demonstrate the ability to understand communication and speaking skills.

- Demonstrate the ability to write in a clear, logical, and appropriate manner.

- Demonstrate the ability to research academic topics and present the synthesis of that research 1) in speech with appropriate citations and 2) in texts with correct documentation.

- Demonstrate an awareness of diversity in American society.

Cultural and Historical Foundation
- Be able to gather, synthesize, and analyze information from appropriate resources and be able to critically evaluate information and sources for accuracy and credibility.

- Identify and deepen appreciation of common human themes and the richness of diverse cultures.

- Be able to analyze and discuss meaning of an artwork, performance, or text in diverse aesthetic, historical, and cultural contexts.

- Demonstrate knowledge and critical thinking of the concepts, styles, and aesthetic, theoretical, and critical principle in an art.

- Demonstrate knowledge of the chronology and significance of major events and movements in Western civilization, U.S. history, or world civilization.

Mathematical Foundation
- Demonstrate the skills needed to solve quantitative problems including choosing the proper technique and/or technology.

- Be able to solve real-world quantitative problems.

- Demonstrate qualitative understanding of mathematical, statistical, and computing concepts.

- Demonstrate knowledge and understanding of essential computing concepts common to academic degrees and their related professions.

- Demonstrate essential computing skills common to academic degrees and their related professions. In particular, skills relating to professional use of computers and application software.

Social Foundation

• Be able to gather and synthesize information from appropriate resources, and be able to evaluate information and sources for accuracy and credibility.

• Understand how an individual's place in the world is affected by social, economic, and political institutions.

• Gain a deeper appreciation of one's role and potential impact in social, economic, and political institutions.

• Demonstrate an understanding of the interaction among social, economic, and political structures and functions.

• Understand how individuals behave and interact with other individuals in their psychological, political, economic, and social environments.

Science Foundation

• Demonstrate an understanding of science as an empirical attempt to acquire information about the real world, develop possible explanations of these phenomena, and test the explanations by predicting the outcome of future observations.

• Demonstrate an ability to assess the extent to which claims presented as scientific satisfy the empirical character of scientific explanations.

• Demonstrate understanding of scientific knowledge and problem solving in a physical or life science.

The GEP requires completion of a minimum 36 credit hours from the five learning foundations and includes 41 courses organized in a "menu" or "cafeteria style" structure: Students choose courses from the list of courses in each foundation area. Some majors require a more advanced level of particular GEP courses. The faculty senate has approved a list that can be substituted for some of the requirements; departments or programs cannot make these substitutions on their own. The Common Program Requirements Oversight Committee, a cross-section of faculty from across the university and a subcommittee of the faculty senate, oversees the GEP and reviews applications for additions and substitutions to the GEP, which are then approved by the University Policy and Curriculum Committee.

The GEP is also responsible for introducing students to notions of cultural diversity. Recognizing the necessity of an awareness and understanding of societal diversity, including race/ethnicity, gender, social class, religion, age, sexual orientation, and physical ability, UCF requires that every student complete at least one course designated as a Diversity Course. Several courses within the GEP are classified as Diversity Courses so that the university's diversity requirement is also met by completion of the GEP.

As on many campuses, UCF's GEP courses are largely taught by part-time faculty and graduate students. The university administration and department leaders have made efforts to more closely involve the GEP faculty with pedagogical and assessment issues.

> The University of Central Florida is committed to the presence of a vital and effective General Education Program on-campus. Providing professional development to faculty who teach in the GEP is central to achieving this goal. To this end, the University encourages and supports faculty to acquire an ever-increasing knowledge of general education issues and to attend national meetings to maintain their professional acuteness. (UCF, 2005a)

This commitment includes funding faculty to attend national conferences focused on General Education.

In addition, the General Education Faculty Assembly provides opportunities for faculty teaching general education courses at UCF to discuss a wide range of issues affecting the GEP. The group meets sporadically throughout the year and is open to all faculty members who instruct in the GEP. "During the 2004–2005 academic year, the GEP Faculty Assembly held focus groups to discuss methods for further invigoration of the GEP as well as how to engage adjunct faculty in pedagogical issues tied to the GEP" (UCF, 2005b).

Overview of Assessment of the General Education Program

Assessing the General Education Program has been one of the greatest challenges of the university's entire assessment process. The first attempt at GEP assessment was encumbered by the scope of courses, lack of uniformity in different students' GEP program choices, technical difficulties associated with tracking due to a large transfer program as more than 40% of UCF's juniors and seniors are transfer students from area community colleges (Shoenberg, 2001), lack of uniformity in the timing of completion, differences in expectations of skill levels across majors, and a GEP culture focused on evaluating individual performance rather than effectiveness of programs (Gaff, 1999). At the time we first began our GEP assessment efforts, almost 70% of students enrolled completed their GEP elsewhere. Although the high percentage of transfer students who complete their GEP requirements at other universities and colleges is declining, this unique transfer situation added to the difficulty of gauging the timing and scope of GEP assessment.

Rather than tackling first the task of developing a consensus on how best to assess learning outcomes across the GEP for all the required areas, the GEP Assessment Committee made the decision to assess three target outcome areas that should be common to all students: proficiency in writing, proficiency in computational skills, and increased appreciation of cultural events. The last outcome was dropped after two years because the self-report of participation in cultural events was judged a weak measure and a better measure could not be designed. The committee retained and continued to hone the assessment of learning outcomes related to writing and mathematics. The target outcomes were identified by discipline faculty, agreed upon by the GEP Common Program Oversight Committee, and then evaluated through course-embedded assessment in these two areas (Marinara, Vajravelu, & Young, 2004).

Mathematics and composition represented the GEP in the university assessment process for the 2000–2001 and 2001–2002 academic years not only for the numbers of students involved, but because the competencies learned in those courses further students' academic success in other courses in the GEP. There are drawbacks to designing a course-embedded GEP assessment process, most notably the problem of assessing only "pockets of competencies" rather than learning outcomes that involve all the disciplines reflected in the GEP and across the university's colleges. Since that time, the GEP Assessment Committee has worked to transform the assessment process so that it more closely reflects the GEP's mission and specifically targets student learning outcomes for each course.

The first step in this transformation occurred in the 2003–2004 academic year and concerned establishing the GEP Assessment Advisory Board:

> The GEP Assessment Advisory Board consists of a small group of faculty and staff who support the Dean of Undergraduate Studies in the coordination of assessment activities related to UCF's General Education Program. Board members assist the Dean in assembling the annual assessment calendar and in designing workshops to assist faculty involved in GEP course assessments. As part of their Board service, each member serves as a point person providing support to one of the foundation-level assessment groups. (UCF, 2005c)

The second task was to establish common learning objectives for each foundation area. Faculty committees established the learning objectives through submissions from the individual faculty members teaching the GEP courses during the spring and fall 2004 semesters. Each course within a foundation area was required to meet one or more of the learning objectives. Each department offering a course within the GEP is then responsible for assessing its selected course objectives. Most departments elected or appointed a faculty representative who works in the larger foundation group, when it meets to discuss the foundation's learning objectives. Those representatives then work with their departmental GEP assessment committees to establish the assessment plan and measures for their course or courses within the GEP.

The GEP Assessment Committee consists of faculty members from across the university tasked with coordinating the assessment of general education courses within their respective departments. Committee membership is determined by individual departments that host courses encompassed by UCF's GEP. The Assessment Committee is organized into five sub-groups that mirror the established foundations of the GEP.

The design and evaluation of the assessment plan for each course is created and carried out by faculty within each department, with support in the form of workshops and individual consultations from the Faculty Center for Teaching and Learning (FCTL) and

Operational Enhancement and Assessment Support (OEAS). This support is crucial to the development of the assessment plan as many faculty have no experience in large-scale assessment practices or in assessing programs rather than students. FCTL and OEAS staff helped each department involved in the GEP to establish clear and concise direct and indirect measures appropriate to the learning objectives and convenient for data collection, to collect and analyze the data, and to make course revisions based on the results.

Each course is expected to have three outcomes selected from the unified list of objectives for each content, with two direct measures for each. Through this process, some departments have identified deficiencies and made revisions not only to their GEP course but to other courses within their major.

Assessment plans are revised and established in the fall of each academic year. These plans are posted on the Office of Institutional Research web pages. Sampling and assessment are done during fall and spring semesters; summer semester is optional. Results and interpretations are reported during the following fall and posted on their respective password-protected web pages. The process remains fluid: If at any time during the assessment process's yearly cycle, departments discover a better way to assess or discover a needed change from the data they have already collected, they are welcome to revise their plan toward increased student learning. Those changes become part of the annual assessment report. Once the reports are submitted, the GEP Divisional Review Committee, made up of a combination of faculty and deans, reviews all of the reports and provides feedback to the departments. This feedback becomes part of the assessment process as departments use the review board's comments to revise their plans.

Assessment of student learning objectives is part of UCF's reaffirmation of the accreditation process; as such, it is required that courses in the GEP be assessed. However, individual departments and the faculty teaching these courses decide how and what to assess. Faculty control of the process results in a healthy but diverse assessment process. Some departments are assessing all students, while others are assessing a random sampling of students. However, individual courses with multiple sections are assessing the same objectives in the same way.

Examples of Assessment and How Results Are Used

Composition 1101 and 1102

The Composition Program's assessment process involves a 10-member committee made up of faculty in the Composition Program who teach composition regularly; most are at the instructor or visiting instructor level. Committee members read close to 400 student portfolios twice each year—December and May—and assess the portfolios using a rubric that reflects the learning objectives and is written and approved by the committee. Each portfolio is evaluated by two faculty members; if there is a dispute, a third faculty member is called in. Portfolio evaluators are paid $100 dollars for approximately five hours of evaluating portfolios. There are no funds from the university to pay the evaluators. The funding comes from royalties the program receives from *Why Writing Matters: The Guide to First-year Writing at UCF,* made available for students to purchase in CD format.

First-year composition introduces students to the skills necessary for critical literacy. Students will be expected to practice and revise their writing in contexts that mirror tasks they will perform throughout their academic and professional lives.

The Composition Program's Assessment Committee reviewed the writing portfolios of 300–350 ENC 1102 students at the completion of spring 2004 and evaluated students' ability to analyze cultural texts and strategies of arguing with/about those same texts. In addition, the committee constructed a survey to assess how these same students perceived whether they met particular learning objectives:

• Students will demonstrate an understanding of writing a clear, analytical thesis.

• Students will demonstrate an understanding of specific textual support for a thesis and supply correct documentation for that support.

• Students will use a variety of sentence patterns and demonstrate grammatical proficiency.

The Composition Program has used its assessment results to increase staff development opportunities, revise its curricula, and fine-tune assignments. Assessment results have guided the program in making textbook selections, cocurricular planning, and increasing expectations and developing standards. Spring 2004 assessment results guided the committee in revising grading rubrics. Each of the four assignments in ENC 1101 and the four assignments in ENC 1102 now has its own grading rubric, carefully tailored to the assignment. The process—because it involved faculty who teach these courses, including a graduate teaching assistant and an adjunct—has helped shape the Composition Program into a more collaborative community of teachers and learners.

Theatre 2000

The Theatre 2000 Assessment Committee is comprised of faculty who teach the various sections of Theatre Survey and is led by the associate chair of the department. Most committee members are tenured or tenure-track faculty, but the makeup of the committee can change each semester as the instructors change. One of the challenges of teaching Theatre Survey is the diversity in size and type of sections. Theatre Survey is taught in small honors sections of 20 students who meet twice a week for one and one-half hours; in larger format, majors-only sections of 100 students which meet three times per week for one hour; and in large lecture format sections of 300 or more students who meet once per week for three hours.

Students will learn to recognize the significance, value, and development of theatre in a diverse society and to learn a context in which to understand and evaluate theatrical performance. Specifically, students will:

• Identify and deepen appreciation of common human themes and the richness of diverse cultures.

• Demonstrate knowledge of and be able to think critically about concepts, styles, and aesthetic, theoretical, and critical principles in an art.

• Demonstrate knowledge of the chronology and significance of major events and movements in Western civilization, U.S. history, or world civilization.

In order to achieve these goals, the Department of Theatre GEP Committee evaluates all students in every section in both the fall and spring semesters. Faculty who teach the course collectively administer and evaluate pre- and posttests and 3 two-minute papers that address the specific GEP student learning outcomes for the course as part of the cultural and historical foundation. Those materials are then reviewed and evaluated by the department GEP assessment committee.

The theatre department's assessment process has produced a great deal more discussion about core content and student competencies. This work has inspired the faculty to participate in conferences sponsored by the Faculty Center for Teaching and Learning, where they were able to establish a common list of goals and objectives, a unified topics list, and a unified reading list. The faculty who teach Theatre 2000 are also in the process of creating a unified course pack to be used by all sections of Theatre Survey.

Tips for Implementing the Process

- Establish faculty buy-in before beginning the assessment process. Bring faculty leaders into the process from the beginning so that faculty can help construct the assessment process and have a stake in the student learning outcomes.

- Start small; don't try to assess the whole program the first year. If possible, begin with a few courses. The next year, once the process is established and the support structure in place, courses can be assessed in groups or more courses can be added to the assessment.

- Involve faculty who teach the courses—including adjuncts and graduate teaching assistants—who know what student learning objectives are crucial to courses.

- Reward faculty leaders and/or faculty who are involved in assessment.

- Provide workshops to assist faculty in developing assessment plans. Faculty are very effective when helping each other and not so effective when "trained" by administrators or experts in institutional effectiveness.

- Provide support with data collection and analysis as many departments have neither the funds nor the expertise to do this themselves.

Challenges to Assessing General Education and Strategies to Overcome Them

The following are some of the assessment challenges we have encountered. We are working to identify strategies to overcome these challenges.

- Faculty buy-in continues to be a problem, and we've learned to be satisfied with grudging acceptance.

  - The addition of state-mandated Academic Learning Compacts (ALC) has made assessment more complicated but even more necessary. The courses and programs must assess in the areas of critical thinking, communication, and content knowledge. Faculty workshops were held to present how the ALCs would work with assessment plans already developed.

  - Most of those working on assessment are nine-month faculty, but the work of revising and reporting on plans takes place in the summer months. The point person in each department needs to be funded for the summer work.

  - UCF has added workshops at the Faculty Center for Teaching and Learning. Participants are given assistance in developing their assessment plans, a box lunch, and a $100 stipend. The FCTL holds two workshops per academic year.

- Often the new or least powerful faculty (i.e., instructor level) are put "in charge" of assessment in their department.

  - This problem has been solved. Those who teach the courses are still involved in developing the assessment plan; however, for the most part, tenured faculty direct and report on the assessment process.

- Enough faculty and staff to convince those involved understand how beneficial the process can be if valuable information is gathered and used for continuous quality improvement.

  - The workshops on assessment held at the FCTL have helped create a critical mass of faculty who understand the need for and conduct assessment because they find it useful.

- Departments have had trouble in the past submitting their complete results on time and then revising their plans for the next cycle.
  - UCF has changed its schedule for submitting plans and results and made the schedule more compatible with the academic year.
- We collect data by academic year and results are due the fall following the spring semester they are collected. New plans are written or revised based on data gathered the previous year. The assessment cycle causes results to be reported before forming a new plan. There is usually some data that goes uncollected during the fall semester while faculty are analyzing data and formulating a new plan.
  - There is still not enough time to digest and further evaluate results so that changes may be made to curriculum and assessment plans for the following year.
- Many faculty are not comfortable with the online interface for reporting results because a knowledge of HTML is necessary for many formatting changes such as bullets and spacing.
  - The institutional effectiveness web interface now includes *Help Links* and training is available.

References

Gaff, J. G. (1999). *General education: The changing agenda.* Washington, DC: Association of American Colleges and Universities.

Marinara, M., Vajravelu, K., & Young, D. L. (2004). Making sense of the "loose baggy monster": Assessing learning in a general education program is a whale of a task. *Journal of General Education, 53*(1), 1–19.

Shoenberg, R. (2001). "Why do I have to take this course?" or credit hours, transfer, and curricular coherence. In R. Shoenberg et al. (Ed.), *General education in an age of student mobility: An invitation to discuss systemic curricular planning* (pp. 1–10). Washington, DC: Association of American Colleges and Universities.

University of Central Florida. (2000). *UCF 1996–2001 strategic plan.* Retrieved November 16, 2006, from the University of Central Florida, Strategic Planning web site: www.ucf.edu/aboutUCF/strategic/plan/index.html

University of Central Florida. (2005a). *Conference notes and information.* Retrieved November 16, 2006, from the University of Central Florida, General Education Program web site: http://gep.ucf.edu/FacultyConference.htm

University of Central Florida. (2005b). *Faculty assembly.* Retrieved November 16, 2006, from the University of Central Florida, General Education Program web site: http://gep.ucf.edu/FacultyAssembly.htm

University of Central Florida. (2005c). *GEP advisory board.* Retrieved November 16, 2006, from the University of Central Florida, General Education Program web site: http://gep.ucf.edu/AdminGEPBoard.htm

University of Central Florida. (2006). *University of Central Florida 2006–2007 undergraduate catalog.* Orlando, FL: Author.

Chapter 13

University of Cincinnati: General Education Case Study

Janice Denton, Wayne Hall, Claudia Skutar

Overview of the Institutional Culture

The University of Cincinnati (UC) is a state-supported, Research I institution in southwest Ohio. It stands among the nation's top 25 public research universities, with a proud tradition of transformation and growth during its 190 years. UC offers students a balance of educational excellence and real-world experience. Within a dynamic community, the university nurtures rich cultural experiences and the intellectual exchange of ideas. The high quality of teaching and learning in its classrooms puts UC among the nation's top academic programs, while the university's research findings save and improve lives. Since its founding in 1819, UC has been the source of many discoveries creating positive change for society, including co-op education, the oral polio vaccine, the first electronic organ, the first safe anti-knock gasoline, and the first antihistamine. UC's commitment to building and improving community at home and abroad continues today.

Each year, this public comprehensive university, which enrolled 35,364 students in the 2004–2005 academic year, graduates 5,000 students, adding to more than 200,000 living alumni around the world. UC is the largest employer in the Cincinnati, Ohio, region, with an economic impact of more than $3 billion. Of the school's total enrollment, about 86% are Ohio residents. The full-time student body comprises 19,619 undergraduates and 5,002 graduate and professional students. Part-time students, a population growing quickly at schools nationwide, including UC, comprises 6,695 undergraduates and 3,048 graduate and professional students. The physical campus includes a main academic campus, medical campus, and two regional campuses located in area suburbs.

UC is accredited by the Higher Learning Commission (a commission of the North Central Association of Colleges and Schools). However, 35 other specialty associations such as the American Bar Association, the National Association of Schools of Music, the National League for Nursing, and the Accrediting Board of Engineering and Technology also accredit specific programs within the university's 15 colleges.

Overview of the General Education Program

The UC General Education Program was designed and approved by the faculty in 2000. It was put into place and took effect with the class entering in 2001 and graduating in 2005. Students now share a common educational experience that comprehensively links undergraduates in every program at UC and prepares them for active participation in their communities.

The program complements the traditional academic major and can be readily transferred from one college to another within UC. The program is outcomes-based in part because UC recognizes that undergraduate students will follow many different paths at the university. The goal of the program is that, by the time they complete their degree programs, all undergraduates are able to demonstrate the baccalaureate competencies: critical thinking, effective communication, knowledge integration, and social responsibility. The program works to develop these through breadth of knowledge (BoK) and program/major requirements (see Figure 13.1).

Description of Baccalaureate Competencies

The first baccalaureate competency is *critical thinking,* which addresses the analysis, synthesis, and evaluation of information and ideas from multiple perspectives. The educated individual thinks critically and analytically about subjects. Critical thinking includes the capability for analysis, problem solving, logical argument, the application of scholarly and scientific methods, the accurate use of terminology, and information literacy.

Figure 13.1
UC General Education Program Requirements

I. BoK Requirements	
	What Courses Fulfilled the BoK Requirements? *List BoK Courses*
■ English Composition	
Distribution Areas	List 8 Courses from a Minimum of 5 Distribution Areas
■ Fine Arts	
■ Historical Perspectives	
■ Humanities	
■ Literature	
■ Natural Sciences	
■ Social Sciences	
	What Courses/Experiences Fulfilled the BoK Requirements? *List BoK Courses or Qualifying Experiences*
● Quantitative Reasoning	
● Diversity & Culture	
● Social & Ethical Issues	
II. Program/Major Requirements	
	What Courses/Experiences Fulfilled the BoK Requirements? *Check with your Advisor or College Advising Center*
● Methodology	
● Capstone	

Note
- ■ Must be fulfilled by a course (3-credit minimum)
- ● May be fulfilled by either a course or an experience

- A *breadth of knowledge course* is for undergraduates (100 level and above), is a minimum of three credit hours, and develops at least one of the baccalaureate competencies.
- A *methodology course* is a course in the major that teaches the how-to or provides an understanding of the systematic methods and history of the discipline/major.
- A *capstone course* or experience provides students the opportunity to demonstrate mastery and integration of baccalaureate competencies and the content/skills of the program/major.

The second competency is *effective communication,* which fosters competence in aural, visual, and language arts—including the ability to read, write, speak, and listen—and the use of communication resources and technology for personal and professional expression. The educated individual must be able to understand and convey ideas in diverse contexts using appropriate communication and information technology resources and skills.

Knowledge integration comprises the third baccalaureate competency, which promotes student linkage of information and concepts from multiple disciplines for personal, professional, and civic enhancement. The UC General Education Program seeks to do this by integrating study between disciplines, thereby helping students become familiar with multiple subjects. The ability to evaluate critically one's own views and those of others requires the individual to be able to access, judge, and compare diverse fields of knowledge.

The fourth competency is *social responsibility,* which requires of students the ability to apply knowledge and skills gained through their undergraduate experiences for the advancement of society. Awareness and service are characteristic of a socially accountable, well-educated individual.

A Coherent Educational Vision

For a general education program to succeed, it must accommodate the complex and diverse paths taken by all baccalaureate students toward graduation. The UC General Education Program ensures that the university's undergraduates will have a common educational experience and was designed to accommodate the curriculum demands of the UC professional colleges, such as the College-Conservatory of Music, the College of Engineering, and the College of Design, Architecture, Art, and Planning.

One way the program accommodates diverse curricula is to allow a student to use the same course to satisfy multiple UC academic requirements. For example, for a College of Arts and Sciences major in history, a course in Western Civilization might fulfill not only the UC general education historical perspectives requirement, but also a College of Arts and Sciences history requirement.

The UC General Education Program also affords opportunities to use faculty-supervised experiences to satisfy diversity and culture, social and ethical issues, and quantitative reasoning requirements rather than satisfying them simply through designated courses. For example, the diversity and culture or the social and ethical issues component of the BoK requirements can be fulfilled by field trips, study abroad, or co-op in a foreign country. The program also encourages students to participate in service-learning opportunities to fulfill diversity and culture and social and ethical requirements.

To ensure a smooth transition, students may enter the university with advanced-standing credits such as transfer courses and advanced placement credits. When advanced-standing credits are equated with UC courses, the student will have fulfilled the general education BoK credit(s) that have been assigned to the UC course.

For courses to be designated as fulfilling a BoK requirement, they must be at least three credit hours and offered at the 100 level or above. However, courses less than three credit hours can be linked together if they collectively account for at least three credit hours. For example, in the College-Conservatory of Music, three quarters of a one-credit hour course on World Music Lab, when taken in sequence, will fulfill the diversity and culture requirement.

The strength of the university's General Education Program is that it provides students with a vast array of courses that meet the BoK requirements. The certification process for graduating students takes place at the college level; therefore, colleges also have the right and discretionary authority to review petitions for BoK waivers and substitutions. Appeals of college decisions on these requirements are handled within the college's normal appeals process. At the end of each academic year, each college is asked to submit to the provost a summary of general education student waivers or substitutions granted (the numbers of which have, so far, been small). This enables the UC General Education Advisory Committee to identify problem areas in availability of courses and to make appropriate recommendations to faculty.

If a student changes majors or baccalaureate colleges within the university, all courses taken in any UC department to fulfill a BoK requirement transfer and retain the general education credit.

Finally, UniverSIS, the student degree audit system, will automatically track that a particular general education requirement has been met. This information is recorded in the student's degree progress audit, which a student can access at any time to track his or her own progress.

Overview of Assessment of the General Education Program

The program capstone—the one course or experience common to every advanced undergraduate at UC—serves as the vehicle for university-wide general education assessment. The capstone permits evaluation on two levels. Departments or units use the capstone to judge student achievement in a particular discipline. In addition, the capstone functions as a place where faculty members use common guidelines to assess student achievement of the four baccalaureate competencies. This analysis occurs through use of discipline-specific rubrics.

Faculty teaching the capstone experience use discipline-specific rubrics to assess student learning and to provide comments on student achievement of the baccalaureate competencies. These evaluations stay within the unit. Each year an appropriate group within the unit/department (e.g., the Faculty Curriculum Committee) reviews these assessment data. Considered over time, the data provide faculty with detailed evidence of student achievement and suggest curricular issues meriting review or revision. This completes the first (internal unit/department) assessment feedback loop.

The second feedback loop occurs when unit/departments submit an annual report to the UC General Education Advisory Committee. Units and departments answer a questionnaire to provide detailed information on their assessment of student learning outcomes and on any proposed or accomplished program revisions.

Each year the Advisory Committee, with assistance from the UC Office of Institutional Research, analyzes data received from the unit/departments and the colleges and issues a report to the provost and to the faculty. Topics include analysis of faculty evaluation of student achievement of the baccalaureate competencies, examples of curricular revisions occurring in units/departments and colleges, and problems with course availability and resources. This information allows the Advisory Committee to make program revision recommendations to the UC faculty.

Examples of Assessment and How Results Are Used

The class of 2005 was the first group of students to graduate under the UC General Education Program, and data for this year reflects a first attempt at measuring achievement of the baccalaureate competencies. Interpretation of aggregate data collected over time will unleash the real power of assessment in UC's program. Figure 13.2 is a sample of a report form sent to the Advisory Committee reporting student achievement of the baccalaureate competencies.

Tips for Implementing the Process

Although at the time of this writing the UC General Education Program had assessment data from only one academic year, the pilot project and first year of the program already have yielded useful information for strengthening general education at the university. Feedback gleaned and lessons learned reveal:

- General education outcomes, whatever they may be, should be embedded in coursework that is part of a student's academic program requirements.

- All university units and departments involved in undergraduate education should avoid making general education an add-on or marginalized part of a student's experience.

- Disciplinary capstone courses are powerful learning experiences for students, and they generally have strong faculty buy-in.

- The program offers no specially designated group of general education courses. Rather, it guides students to multiple courses that fulfill the BoK requirements and through which students can develop the skills needed to successfully demonstrate baccalaureate competencies in the capstone course/experience before graduation.

- At some point, having a committee run the program will no longer be the most efficient way to move the university's general education initiative forward. The university should consider appointing a faculty director to work in tandem with an advisory committee.

- Some programs have large numbers of graduates, and assessment of the baccalaureate competencies in the capstone experience has been challenging. It has been proposed that those programs assess a statistically significant sample of students and report those results.

Figure 13.2
General Education Assessment of the
Four Baccalaureate Competencies

Composite Capstone Student Assessment Form

College: College-Conservatory of Music
Administrative Unit: Electronic Media Division
Baccalaureate Program/Major: BFA
Capstone Requirement(s): Presentation
Academic Year: Spring/Summer 2005
Faculty Assessor(s):
Number of Students Assessed: 12

Using the 1–5 scale of your rubrics, enter the average of all individual student ratings for the four baccalaureate competencies.

Critical Thinking   Average Scale Number: 2.8

Comments: Discuss here any changes to the capstone or rubric that will be made as a result of this first round of assessing students' critical thinking skills. Deemphasize the length of showcasing projects. Insist on students reflecting on projects and integration of class material from outside of major.

Effective Communication   Average Scale Number: 2.9

Comments: Discuss here any changes to the capstone or rubric that will be made as a result of this first round of assessing students' communication skills. Students will need more time, need to begin earlier with their projects. Deemphasize technology, shorten length of presentation.

Knowledge Integration   Average Scale Number: 3.0

Comments: Discuss here any changes to the capstone or rubric that will be made as a result of this first round of assessing students' knowledge integration. Insist on more integration of course material from outside of major; meeting with faculty required.

Social Responsibility   Average Scale Number: 2.4

Comments: Discuss here any changes to the capstone or rubric that will be made as a result of this first round of assessing students' social responsibility. Stress ethical component, and hold students liable for content of presentation.

One final but very important lesson learned is that a general education program must fit the culture of the institution. Faculty cannot adopt another institution's model and expect it to work without modification. UC faculty must be involved at every level of the UC General Education Program, from development to implementation and assessment.

Challenges to Assessing General Education and Strategies to Overcome Them

In achieving a coherent approach to general education, UC needed to address the challenges and barriers that had emerged from its earlier and incomplete program. Following an accreditation visit in April 1999 by the Higher Learning Commission, UC began to review the earlier program and concluded that it was limited by its lack of adaptability to existing UC curricula. Bottlenecks included the emphasis on designated "general education courses," student difficulty in fulfilling requirements, and poor articulation among colleges.

Within the original General Education Program, students needed to take a designated number of general education courses that would be taught in a manner to enhance learning. While the goal was admirable—to encourage faculty to rethink pedagogy, as well as to increase student discussion and writing assignments in smaller classes—the number of classes with a general education designation remained limited. The fact that general education courses had a class size limit also created resource and staffing difficulties for a number of departments. And students in some colleges, including engineering and the College-Conservatory of Music, were not able to fit these new course requirements within their existing programs.

The new General Education Program eliminates the earlier bottlenecks of the previous program. It provides for the diversity of undergraduate paths at UC, for changes of majors, and for transfer students. The ultimate goal is outcomes based, not one linked to student completion of a predetermined set of courses. The program challenges faculty who teach every undergraduate course to contribute to student development of the general education baccalaureate competencies, and the competencies are measured in a discipline-specific capstone, so assessment is embedded, not added on. The two fundamental strengths of the new program are clear: It has intellectual integrity and it enhances the undergraduate student experience.

Chapter 14

University of South Florida: General Education Case Study

Teresa L. Flateby

Overview of the Institutional Culture

Context is critical for the focus of assessment. Thus, context provides the backdrop for this chronicle of the evolution of both our general education assessment processes and the general education curriculum itself at the University of South Florida.

The University of South Florida (USF) is a multi-campus national research university that supports the development of the metropolitan Tampa Bay region, Florida, the United States, and the world. Building on unique strengths inherent in Florida's population, location, and natural resources, the university is dedicated to excellence in:

• Teaching and lifelong learning in a student-centered environment

• Research to advance knowledge and promote social, cultural, economic, educational, health, and technological development

• Service based on academic excellence and the ethic of community responsibility

• Community engagement to build university-community partnerships and collaborations

The complexity of USF, a research-extensive institution with more than 43,000 students, 10 colleges, a college of medicine, and three regional campuses, affects the general education curriculum.

Overview of the General Education Program

When the official assessment of general education was initiated, it was based on a distributed model, with both general education and liberal arts exit courses forming the liberal arts curriculum. Breadth and depth were central features of the program, which stressed thinking and communication skills. Five contemporary issues, which were termed *dimensions,* include gender, values and ethics, global perspectives, environmental issues, and race and ethnicity. These were addressed in courses in the areas of English composition, quantitative methods, natural sciences, social sciences, fine arts, and African, Latin American, Middle Eastern, or Asian perspectives. In an effort to ensure a liberal arts education for both first-time and transfer students, students must complete 36 semester hours of coursework in these areas, most of which are required by legislative mandate, during their first 60 hours, and 6 hours in major works and major issues courses and 3 hours in a literature and writing course during their junior and senior years.

More specifically, USF's (2006) liberal arts requirements specify:

> Courses in the liberal arts requirements should incorporate the following components whenever they are relevant to the specific discipline: the learning skills of conceptual thinking, analytical thinking, creative thinking, written expression, oral expression, and the dimensions of values and ethics, international perspectives, environmental perspectives, race and ethnicity, and gender. When warranted by the subject matter, each course must incorporate consideration of at least one of the dimensions and one of the thinking skills to meet the liberal arts requirements. . .
>
> Whenever possible courses will encourage creativity and discipline in the written and oral uses of language. The writing experience for students will emphasize the qualitative aspects of developing writing skills. Writing requirements will entail substantive feedback for students rather than merely

> the correction of spelling and punctuation. The goal is to include a writing component in all appropriate liberal arts course requirements, even if this component is not equivalent to the Gordon Rule requirement. Courses will also encourage the development of oral expression skills.

Clearly, this description remains relevant.

When this curriculum was introduced, or rather revised in the late 1980s and early 1990s, the General Education Council was established to ensure that courses fulfilled these requirements. For reasons that are unclear, the council dissolved in the late 1990s. Following this dissolution, the feeling across campus was that a random proliferation of courses had occurred. Additionally, the original developers of the courses were often no longer teaching the courses nor were they involved with the courses in any way, resulting in a drift away from the original syllabi and our general education focus.

Overview of Assessment of the General Education Program

Related to the general education outcomes, in the mid-1990s, concerned faculty and administrators began investigating specific general education learning outcomes as a consequence of changes in accountability mandates. For approximately 10 years before this time, all students in state-funded institutions were required to pass the College-Level Academic Skills Test (CLAST), a reading, writing, and mathematics exam, before completing 60 semester hours. Although in retrospect the measures and approaches used to assess writing were misaligned with encouraged and acceptable writing practices, we believed that the timed writing assessment would identify students who could benefit from additional writing instruction. In fact, additional instruction was provided, even required, for students who did not pass the essay subtest. However, in the mid-1990s, political reasons provided for exceptions to this requirement, and a 2.5 GPA in Composition 1 and 2 exempted students from the CLAST writing and essay tests. Concern about this change led us to investigate grades assigned in freshman composition courses and to evaluate the performance of students who were required to complete college preparatory (remedial) work prior to enrollment in

Composition 1. This study revealed a wide range of grading practices, from giving nearly everyone in a class As, with the exception of two or three Fs, to assigning normally distributed grades. In addition, a survey was distributed to the course instructors to assess their perception of students' level of preparation for freshman composition. The responses to this inquiry also varied considerably. Expectations for writing were unclear.

In addition to the change in the testing requirement, another event prompted the systematic study of general education outcomes: A two-year learning community model was introduced in 1995. A critical component of this interdisciplinary team-taught general education program was writing across the curriculum, a new instructional strategy for USF. Partially funded by a grant from the Fund for the Improvement of Postsecondary Education, assessment was initiated and became an integral part of the learning community program.

To address concerns of students' writing competency and to assess USF's General Education Learning Community, a timed writing assessment was administered to students in the learning community and to students in selected sections of English composition near their completion of Composition 2 (again, in hindsight, a different assessment method should have been used). These essays were evaluated with the CLAST holistic scoring criteria by official CLAST readers external to the university. As a result of this comparison and related evidence about writing instruction in the learning communities, instructional changes were implemented in the learning communities.

Because of our concern about student writing and its importance, we continued our assessment of writing and began focusing on other key student learning outcomes. Several factors affected our assessment efforts. Even though the learning community's learning outcomes were not well specified, other outcomes in addition to writing emerged as we observed the learning community. For example, because team teaching, interdisciplinarity, and active learning were features of the learning communities, students were reaching higher-order thinking levels in these classes. In addition, their intellectual development, as defined by William Perry's (1970) Scheme of Intellectual and Ethical Development, appeared to be positively affected by the learning community environment. We decided to assess intellectual development levels and cognitive levels exhibited in students' papers. Although the Measure of Intellectual Development (Moore, 1991) was available to assess students' intellectual development, we were unable to identify an instrument to assess writing and cognitive levels. Thus, a collaborative team of faculty, teaching assistants, measurement specialists, and the learning community coordinator created the Cognitive Level and Quality of Writing Assessment (CLAQWA). This two-part rubric provides faculty whose discipline is not English with a method for assessing papers on 17 skills relevant to effective writing. It encourages faculty users to consciously consider the cognitive level expected for an assignment, enables self- and peer review, and facilitates a multidisciplinary approach to writing assessment.

Even though our assessment results were consistent over three years—we identified important formative information that had the potential to contribute to the writing, thinking, and intellectual outcomes we were studying—the results were generally ignored by faculty and administrators. Frustrated, during an end-of-year learning community retreat, representatives of the learning community were asked to form an assessment team. All critical stakeholders, including faculty, advisors, administrators, and students, volunteered to participate in the assessment processes. This group, which referred to itself as the A Team, was extremely active and contributed to all aspects of the assessment, including formative and summative elements. We developed instruments, observed classrooms, conducted focus groups, helped collect data, wrote reports, and communicated our activities and findings across all learning communities. Changes were made as a result of our efforts, and participation became a meaningful faculty and staff development activity. Assessment was expected and, in fact, became an integral part of the learning community. This truly was an early example of a culture of assessment.

Concomitantly, in late 1999, partially in anticipation of our Southern Association of Colleges and Schools reaffirmation visit, we began an assessment of the general education curriculum. Recognizing the value of collaboration from the learning community assessment experiences, an ad-hoc team of faculty devoted to general education was formed. The group, composed of faculty and the director of evaluation and testing, reviewed the goals and dimensions of the general education curriculum and offered recommendations for focusing the assessment. Concerned specifically with student writing, we continued to assess students' quality of writing at matriculation, during ENC 1102 (as we had in the learning communities) and writing at the completion of their general education courses. Liberal arts mathematics courses also were targeted for study due to students' performance in these classes. Although not a recognized concern, faculty felt strongly about the importance of intellectual development and cognitive levels reached and wanted growth in these areas also to be assessed. Because we had a distributed general education curriculum, with students taking classes from a vast array of courses without specified and standard learning outcomes, we decided not to tackle assessing outcomes in the core areas. Since most of our general education classes included one or more of the general education dimensions (values/ethics, race/ethnicity, environmental and gender issues, or global/international perspectives), we concurred that we should also assess students' perceptions concerning their understanding of and exposure to, and change in their attitudes toward, the dimensions.

After meeting for a nearly a year, the ad-hoc assessment committee recommended establishing a more formal group, one that might have more influence. Consequently, during the 2001–2002 academic year, the provost appointed a general education assessment committee. Members of the ad-hoc committee, faculty representing all colleges, administrators, advisors, and representatives from institutional research and evaluation and testing, formed the General Education Assessment Advisory Committee (GEAAC). This group provided advice about assessment until the 2005–2006 academic year, at which time a subcommittee of the newly formed General Education Council assumed a similar but more active role. In fact, this committee is beginning to assist faculty beyond the committee with assessment activities.

When we launched our initial general education writing assessment efforts, our method resembled a standardized test, with students writing on a specific standard topic under timed conditions at particular points in the curriculum. We applied the same strategies we used in the learning community, with CLAST raters external to the university. We followed a standardized scoring procedure and assigned scores of 1–6, ranging from "little command of the language" to readiness to "progress to upper level"—the last two years of coursework.

Our assessment practices were acceptable, but we were not satisfied. We knew some students were competent writers, but many more were not. Even after using this approach for several years, we had summative results but little formative information to help us identify specific student writing weaknesses. In short, we were able to assess students' writing proficiency levels on a holistic level; however, we were unable to identify the elements of writing which were more or less deficient, the information essential for making programmatic changes. Although determining the achievement levels of our students is important, assessment's major contribution to learning is providing the information needed to enhance student learning outcomes. In addition to having little formative data, our assessment process was further flawed by its lack of inclusion of our faculty.

Examples of Assessment and How Results Are Used

When we consulted with the GEAAC about these concerns, we agreed to maintain our assessment focus on writing, but believed we needed new methodologies. Assignments were retooled. To assess writing more authentically, we eliminated the timed writing and prompted students to complete assignments out of class. In addition, the committee recommended adopting the CLAQWA rubric, initially created in response to needs identified in the learning community program. Before CLAQWA was adopted in the program, faculty graded writing with problematic variation. Along with offering a more consistent approach to writing assessment, the instrument measures cognitive levels attained by the student. After adopting CLAQWA, faculty assessed writing with greater consistency.

This rubric, which had been used at the Community College of Baltimore County in Maryland to assess their preparatory writing classes, was refined and introduced to assess student writing outcomes. CLAQWA's 17 writing elements are organized into the following five major categories:

• *Assignment parameters* represent the degree to which students fulfill the requirements of the assignment presented, maintain a main idea, and consistently address the appropriate audience.

- *Structural integrity* is related to the organization revealed in papers and includes skills such as the adequacy of the opening and closing and the unity within and across paragraphs.

- *Reasoning and focus* pertains to the development of ideas and relates to writers' thought processes and evidence used when developing their ideas.

- *Language* focuses on appropriate word choice, level of vocabulary, sentence construction, and comprehensibility of sentences.

- *Grammar and mechanics* represents the degree to which students observe standard edited English.

Each element within the five categories is assessed using a 9–point scale with 5 defined levels. Although the scale at the time it was initiated for use in assessing the general education curriculum had only end- and midpoints defined, we have since further defined each of the 5 scale points. Now 16 elements (grammar and mechanics have been combined) provide more consistent scoring.

CLAQWA's Cognitive Scale, based on the work of Benjamin Bloom (1956) and his colleagues, provides a means to assess the cognitive level reached in students' essays. These essays are assessed according to the four levels of the; Cognitive Scale: Level 1: Knowledge; Level 2: Comprehension; Level 3: Application; and Level 4: Analysis, Synthesis, and Evaluation. For example, one of our general education prompts is written to elicit Level 4; if a paper is judged to be Level 2, the paper falls below expectations.

Teams of graduate and undergraduate assistants as well as faculty, representing many disciplines and majors, have been trained over several years to assess student writing, thinking, and intellectual development each semester using CLAQWA and other assessment techniques. We have been gratified to discover that undergraduates assign scores as consistently as more experienced graduate students and faculty. Meeting weekly, writing team members score assignments completed at three key points in the curriculum with the CLAQWA instrument. Rescoring previously read papers at the beginning of each scoring session helps achieve stability over time and agreement among scorers. If a scorer is unable to interpret the scale consistently with all other scorers, we have dismissed the scorer, since the reliable use of the rubric is critical to effective assessment.

When the two scorers assessing each essay assign scores varying more than .5 on the 9-point scale, they further examine the paper, discuss the discrepancy, and adjust one or both scores.

Two other teams also assess the same essays; in both teams, two faculty members score each essay. One faculty team assesses the cognitive level reached in students' essays with the CLAQWA Cognitive Scale, and another faculty team assesses students' intellectual development levels reflected in essays, based on the work of William Perry (1970). Trained in the use of William Moore's (1991) Measure of Intellectual Development (MID), the faculty team determines the intellectual development level exhibited in students' essays. The MID reflects students' intellectual development as they progress from a dualistic perspective focused on receiving the "truth" from authorities, through multiple perspectives in which knowledge becomes more uncertain and students take increasing responsibility for learning, to a contextual perspective in which students are self-reflective and self-motivating, value others' perspectives, and know the difference between opinion and supported opinion. While many of our students arrive at USF expecting passively to receive information from experts that will be relevant to the next test, we hope to cultivate the ability to think in context and value multiple perspectives.

In addition to writing, cognitive levels, and intellectual development levels, we also have been targeting mathematics achievement in liberal arts mathematics courses and perceived and actual knowledge about our general education dimensions. Even prior to the formal assessment of general education outcomes as part of a placement testing study, we discovered failure and withdrawal rates of 50% or higher in many of the lower-level math courses. In response to the low passing rate in math courses and because students who earned Cs or below in these courses were required to pass the state-mandated CLAST exam, the mathematics department hired instructional coordinators for the lower-level mathematics courses before the 2000–2001 academic year. We worked with the coordinator of finite mathematics, one of the primary general education math courses, to develop a common course final. This exam reflected the content of the course and the skills on the CLAST examination consistent with the course. During subsequent years, results remained level, and only minor changes were introduced in the math courses; therefore, our assessment efforts were ineffective in producing change.

We also developed a questionnaire to assess students' understanding of the general education dimensions. The questionnaire was designed to elicit both students' knowledge and attitudes about the five general education dimensions. It included closed-response questions about knowledge levels and the importance of each dimension, and open-ended questions asking students to describe each dimension. We asked students in upper-level courses about the knowledge gained in each dimension as a result of the general education curriculum or other influences.

Over the several years of data collection, the results indicated very little difference in self-reported levels of knowledge between freshman and upper-level students. Upper-level students, however, were more likely to acknowledge the importance of the dimensions. Students' responses to the open-ended questions revealed differences between entering students' and upper-level students' understanding of the dimensions. We concluded that when students enter USF, their perceptions about the dimensions are compartmentalized and often superficial. Although, by the time they are in upper-level courses, many students have a broader and deeper understanding about the dimensions.

Attempting to gather formative data regarding students' classroom experiences, best practices in pedagogy, and additional elements of the general education curriculum, we developed the freshman academic survey. Designed to provide further insight into what students gain from the general education experience as well as which classroom activities they find most beneficial and effective, this survey asks students to reflect on their academic experiences during their first year at USF. Much of these data further supported findings from both the general education dimensions surveys and the essay prompts. For example, students were asked to respond to questions about the effectiveness of various common classroom activities. The responses, similar to the content analysis of students' essays, emphasized a desire for interactive classrooms. The following academic year, we administered the National Survey of Student Engagement to freshmen and seniors, which also corroborated our findings.

To garner support for a mostly institutionally coordinated assessment, we have developed an approach that is both efficient and focused on outcomes of concern to the faculty. Because of the nature of our assignments, we have been able to assess writing proficiency and cognitive and intellectual development levels. While maintaining the basic structure of the writing assignments, we encourage faculty to adapt assignments to reflect their courses or disciplines, and we recently began providing individual student reports as well as aggregated reports for each faculty member. In addition to assessing learning outcomes, we also have content-analyzed essays to summarize students' impressions of the learning environment. These summaries are provided to each faculty member participating in the assessment. Early on, we realized that our 60-page reports were not widely read. Instead, we began tailoring individual college reports that included writing, intellectual development, cognitive level, general education dimensions, math outcome results, and a summary of what students experience as a favorable learning environment and where they believe deficiencies in the curriculum may exist.

The data collected revealed weaker student performance and other problems with the general education curriculum. The university chose general education reform as the focus of our quality enhancement plan, a requirement of the Southern Associations of Colleges and Schools to show improvement in student learning. Specifically, our assessments revealed areas of weakness in students' performance, most notably the underdevelopment of students' ideas, the lack of details to develop the main ideas, and the lack of cohesion in their essays. These and other results, such as missing elements in the curriculum and inadequate teaching strategies to support deep thinking, have guided general education curriculum review and reform decisions. The revised curriculum reemphasizes writing and thinking, and not just more writing but writing to facilitate learning and reader-centered writing in which feedback and revision, beyond editing, are major components. A newly required capstone course will stress writing either within a student's discipline or within an interdisciplinary context. In addition, graduate and undergraduate students will be trained to assist faculty members in our increasingly larger courses to provide break-out sessions to foster thinking and allow for more writing and revising. Additional courses are being developed to emphasize global and international perspectives, and inquiry-based learning is also a major component in the revised curriculum, which will be directed and monitored by the newly formed General Education Council.

Other changes have occurred as a result of our assessment efforts. The process of using CLAQWA to assess writing has had a variety of instructional effects. For example, faculty scorers have begun using the instrument in their classes and have expressed benefits in student writing. They consider the cognitive levels in their assignments more carefully than before, and they better understand areas to target in student writing. In addition, many faculty members report improvements in their own writing.

Our writing assessment focus has initiated other campus writing efforts. The Department of English has introduced the CLAQWA instrument in Composition 1 and 2 first-year classes in an effort to increase consistency in assessment across online and face-to-face classes. The College of Engineering is planning to train teaching assistants to assist faculty with assessing writing and providing feedback to their students. In addition, a campus-wide effort is under way to train beginning students to provide each other with feedback regarding writing and the thinking revealed in writing in most writing genres, from essays to lab reports. A modified CLAQWA for peer review supplies students with a systematic, nonthreatening structure to give feedback to each other. Resource constraints required us to become more creative to achieve the writing and thinking student learning outcomes we expect. We believe that developing peers as partners in the learning and assessment processes may help achieve our goals.

As evidenced in the increased participation in our assessment activities, more faculty and administrators support our efforts and value the results. In fact, faculty are requesting that we assess writing in their classes and speak with their students about their writing performance, and faculty have embraced the peer-review process.

Tips for Implementing the Process

Our experience and discoveries may help institutions planning to implement an institution-focused assessment of general education. For example, it is important to focus on outcomes faculty members find central to the curriculum. If faculty are concerned about student achievement levels of these outcomes, their interest should be heightened. This should in turn elevate the level of participation. If a standard prompt is developed, allow faculty to adapt it to their specific courses or disciplines while maintaining the fundamental features of the prompt. It is especially important for the cognitive levels of the prompts to be consistent if comparisons will be made over time or across groups.

Try not to force faculty participation. It is acceptable to start with a sample that is less than ideal. Work with the faculty participants and help make the assessment a meaningful experience. Provide results they can use in their classes, such as aggregating and summarizing their students' results and suggesting ways they might be able to use the results to improve student learning outcomes. Also, give each student his or her results. Feedback is essential. Realize that the assessment processes will evolve as results are gathered, more faculty and administrators value assessment, and more is learned about assessment approaches.

Challenges to Assessing General Education and Strategies to Overcome Them

Because of our institution-focused general education assessment process, faculty willingness to participate was critical for its success. Generating sufficient participation levels was often a challenge. We wanted faculty to be supportive partners, thereby communicating to students the importance of the assessment process and encouraging a level of student seriousness. At first, we relied on associate deans in each of the colleges to help identify faculty, but other motivators became increasingly more important. We encouraged faculty to tailor the assignments to their courses or disciplines and we began providing feedback to their students and a summary of the results for their classes. By giving them relevant and timely results, they realized the benefits of assessment. Faculty have begun using the results in their classes, which is useful information for recruiting additional participants. We hope that by recognizing the benefits of assessment and achieving greater participation, as an institution, we will self-reflect more and become more learner centered.

References

Bloom, B.S. (Ed.). (1956). *Taxonomy of educational objectives: Book 1: Cognitive domain.* New York, NY: Longman.

Flateby, T. L., & Metzger, E. A. (2003). *Cognitive level and quality of writing assessment: Building better thought through better writing.* Tampa, FL: University of South Florida.

Moore, W. S. (1991, April). *The Perry scheme of intellectual and ethical development: An introduction to the model and two major assessment approaches.* Paper presented at the annual meeting of the American Educational Research Association, Chicago, IL.

Perry, W. G., Jr. (1970). *Forms of intellectual and ethical development in the college years: A scheme.* New York, NY: Holt, Rinehart, & Winston.

University of South Florida. (2006). *The liberal arts requirement.* Retrieved November 16, 2006, from the University of South Florida, Liberal Arts web site: www.ugs.usf.edu/gec/facappdoc.htm

Chapter 15

A Summary of Good Practice Strategies for Assessing General Education

Marilee J. Bresciani

The good practice case studies for general education assessment contained in this book have outlined several helpful tips for implementing outcomes-based assessment in general education. These tips are not intended to be prescriptive; rather, they are intended to encourage the reader to consider practical advice when implementing outcomes-based assessment of general education.

In summarizing the advice listed in each case study, the following points are shared to emphasize the need for readers' consideration of these aspects as they implement general education assessment on their campuses.

Institutional Culture and the Purpose of General Education

The institutions profiled in this book implemented outcomes-based assessment of general education in different ways. As discussed in Chapter 1, assessing general education cannot be done without paying attention to how general education is delivered. The delivery of general education must be done in accordance with its purpose. And the purpose of general education is often intertwined with the institutional culture and mission. All these facets are inseparable. When you try to separate them, you will find that you have the opportunity to experience further challenges in demonstrating how general education is contributing to student learning. It is not necessary to endure those increased challenges if you tend to these intertwining facets.

Similarly, as you consider the purpose of general education, it is wise to do so in light of the purposes of each discipline's education and within the context of your institutional core learning principles (e.g., what you want every student to be able to know and do once they graduate from your institution, regardless of discipline). In addition, it is important to understand how the cocurricular learning opportunities contribute to general education. Figure 15.1 illustrates this interaction and interrelationship.

Figure 15.1
**The Interrelationship of Institutional Culture on Student
Learning-Centeredness of General Education**

Institutional culture is a complex, multifaceted reality that impacts the ability of faculty and administrators to maintain student learning-centeredness and to practice its purposeful reflection (Mentkowski & Associates, 2000). It is within the institutional culture that faculty and administrators will recognize their ability to reform general education or develop a genuine reflection process that involves faculty in a systematic way to improve student learning within general education.

The faculty and administrators represented in each case study have learned what works best for their institutions by paying attention to their institutional culture and the interplay of the institutional mission, purpose of general education, the design for its delivery, and the plan for implementing assessment of general education. Monitoring these factors, in addition to disciplinary education, cocurricular learning, and core student learning principles, while designing a good practice approach to outcomes-based assessment, allows each institution to implement an assessment plan for general education that is effective, efficient, and enduring. Thus, the faculty engaged in the process can actually use the results to improve student learning.

Good Practice in Outcomes-Based Assessment

Each case study institution utilizes good practice in outcomes-based assessment. By implementing variations of the *Nine Principles of Good Practice for Assessing Student Learning* (Astin et al., 1991), each institution demonstrates sound outcomes-based assessment practices. Although this is not a how-to on assessment book (there are several fine resources for that; see Bresciani, Zelna, & Anderson, 2004; Diamond, 1998; Huba & Freed, 2000; Lusthaus, Adrien, Anderson, & Carden, 1999; Maki, 2004; Michelson, Mandell, & Contributors, 2004; Nichols, 1995; Palomba & Banta, 1999; Stevens & Levi, 2004; Suskie, 2001, 2004; Tanner, 2001; Upcraft & Schuh, 1996; Wergin & Swingen, 2000), this book is intended to provide the reader with characteristics of good practice on which to reflect while implementing outcomes-based assessment of general education.

One of the key characteristics of that practice is the ability of faculty and administrators to engage in meaningful and purposeful reflection about what the general education program is supposed to accomplish in regard to what students are able to know and do as a result of general education. In addition, once those engaged in general education are able to articulate the intended end results of student learning, they are able to plan for the outcomes to be delivered, evaluate how well the outcomes are achieved, and identify what needs to be improved so that student leaning can be maximized.

Involvement of Faculty, Cocurricular Professionals, and Students

Each good practice institution recommends a transparent outcomes-based assessment process where faculty can participate fully and observe what is happening with general education and its evaluation each step of the way. Such transparency builds trust in the self-reflection process and encourages faculty to become more involved as they see how they are contributing to improving student learning in a direct and valuable way (Huba & Freed, 2000; Maki, 2004; Mentkowski & Associates, 2000).

Similarly, the involvement of cocurricular professionals ensures a more integrated learning experience for students, allowing them to more easily connect their classroom learning with their out-of-classroom learning (Kuh, Kinzie, Schuh, Whitt, & Associates, 2005). When students have a better understanding of what they are to get out of the general education experience, enhanced learning will occur and they will take greater responsibility for their own learning (Mentkowski & Associates, 2000).

Commitment of Resources and Leadership to Student Learning

Resources are needed to ensure intense reflection of deep learning and consensus building for the purpose and process of general education and its evaluation. Faculty and staff development opportunities need to be provided in order for faculty, administrators (including cocurricular professionals), and students, where appropriate, to identify how to:

• Determine the purpose of general education.

• Articulate goals and outcomes for general education.

• Design or refine the delivery of learning outcomes.

• Align learning outcomes to the delivery of the general education (e.g., connect the learning to teaching and course and curriculum design).

• Align education outcomes with the discipline outcomes, cocurricular outcomes, and overarching student learning principles, if applicable.

• Identify the means to evaluate learning outcomes (both direct and indirect methods) and do so in a manner that will help inform decisions or recommendations to improve learning.

- Gather, analyze, and interpret results in a manner that will lead to decisions and recommendations for improvement at all levels.

- Discuss the recommendations for improving student learning in a collegial manner and with regard to the resources that will be needed to improve student learning.

- Report the results in a manner that will invite feedback from those involved in the learning process, including students and cocurricular professionals.

- Align the evaluation processes of general education with those of the disciplines and professional accreditors, where appropriate.

- Build consensus at each step.

- Explore additional opportunities to collaborate for improving student learning in general education.

- Have conversations about removing barriers to improving student learning.

This process of improving student learning in general education does not happen overnight, as each case study in this book illustrates. It requires a commitment of leadership from both the administration and the faculty. It also requires a commitment to the value of improving student learning, which means creating an environment that celebrates student learning and one where faculty and administrators feel the time they invest in this discussion will not be demeaned, but rather rewarded, and at the very least recognized.

Again, although outcomes-based assessment must be done in the context of the institutional culture and the purpose of general education for that institution, integrity of the self-reflection process must be upheld as well as the commitment to creating an environment where varying perspectives are respected and flexibility is the norm. Nothing upsets a genuine self-reflection process more than a beaurocratic mandate to follow inquiry rules step by step. Rather, individual discipline perspectives, as well as cocurricular involvement, must be acknowledged and incorporated as the community as a whole engages in conversation and analysis of student learning.

Use of Results

The ability to gather data using good practice in outcomes-based assessment to improve student learning requires that assessment results be used to inform decisions, recommendations, and policies that will lead to the improvement of student learning. The use of results to improve student learning in general education is not always as straightforward as it may appear when compared to using results to improve student learning within the major academic discipline. While variations of general education delivery are one of the reasons this may look so different among particular institutions, institutional culture and demands by the state legislature, state governing boards, or institutional governing boards are other factors to consider.

Good practice in outcomes-based assessment encourages the practitioner and scholar to utilize the data to inform decisions and recommendations to improve student learning at the point of delivery of the student learning (Astin et al., 1991; Palomba & Banta, 1999). In other words, if student learning outcomes are associated with student learning expectations and if you identify means to evaluate that student learning in a way that allows you to gather data to identify where improvements can be made, then you will more readily be able to inform decisions to improve student learning on your campus. While this concept is logical, it is not visibly shared by all. Some constituents desire to have readily comparable student learning data across institutions and across institution types. In order to obtain this type of data, there may need to be compromises in the way it is gathered. Such compromise can mean a looser alignment of the means for evaluating student learning with the articulated student learning outcomes. The less associated the means to evaluate student learning is with the intended learning or with the means in which the learning is delivered, the less likely the data can be used to inform decisions and recommendations for improving student learning (Mentkowski & Associates, 2000).

This brief illustration reinforces the importance of institutional reflection on how general education assessment results are to be used. Do faculty and administrators intend to implement assessment in ways that allow them to make informed decisions and recommendations for improvement? Or are they trying to gather data that allows them to compare or attempt to compare learning across programs or institutions? If the latter, how can comparable learning data be used to better or more accurately determine which areas of student learning need closer attention as opposed to a more in-depth evaluation of student learning?

Consider the following example of how institutional cross-comparison data can be used to improve student learning at the program level. If an institution chooses to use a nationally available standardized test for examining student learning in a subject area such as math, the institution could understand how its students' scores compare with other institutions who also administer that exam. Regardless of the scores, however, the test results will not allow the institution to determine how to improve student learning unless the faculty and administrators fully understand what the test is examining and how well it aligns with their general education knowledge constructs and learning outcomes for math. In addition, the faculty would also have to determine how well these constructs are being learned and where they are intended to be learned so that improvements can be made where needed. This type of evaluation is akin to using benchmark indicators to investigate where the problems and successes are occurring. However, additional outcomes-based assessment must be administered so that genuine improvements can be made. Note, however, that using comparable data may be more complicated when attempting to test for skills and abilities, rather than subject area knowledge. In order for decisions and recommendations to be made for improving student learning, organized, systematic, and ongoing outcomes-based assessment still has to occur, even though nationally standardized tests may be used for cross-institutional comparisons.

State Mandates

Many states have standards for general education, which can cause concern among faculty and staff as they may assume that their own standards or outcomes for general education are not in alignment with state or governing board mandates. When this occurs, it may be helpful for the institution to first consider what it values in regard to student learning in general education, then consider what the state may value and work to align the two.

Although the case studies in this book were not analyzed to determine similarities or differences in state mandates and how those characteristics may affect the improvement of student learning, it is safe to assume that a state may have mandates because the constituents, similar to many faculty, are also concerned about the quality of student learning. The concerned state may go so far as to articulate student learning objectives for subject areas, as the state of Texas does. Even in this example, however, the state does not indicate which objectives must be learned, nor do they indicate at what level. Such flexibility allows each institution to determine how to best align with state values given their own learning values for general education. Thus, institutional culture prevails as it aligns itself with state values.

While many states have caps on credit hours required for general education and/or degrees, requirements for articulation agreements, and time-to-degree mandates, none of these types of policies typically center around conversations on student learning. Rather, these conversations are typically motivated by attempts to control costs and manage the learning environment. These types of conversations and restraints may be harmful to an institution's ability to move its focus from the administration of the learning environment to the actual student learning itself. It is important for an institution to acknowledge these potential conflicts in appearance of values; however, it is equally important for the institution to maintain the belief that legislators and other institutional constituents do care about the quality of student learning. The more an institution can demonstrate what it takes to have its students master the appropriate level of competencies, the more informed the public and the legislators will become about whether there are actual conflicts in values between the quality of student learning represented in articulation agreements and other such mandates.

Many of the good practice institutions illustrated how they were able to connect what their faculty value about student learning with what they understand the state to value in terms of expected student competencies and skills and abilities. This connection can effectively be illustrated at the outcomes level where faculty can articulate student learning outcomes that align with state learning goals and objectives. In addition, this alignment can be further illustrated as faculty, administrators, and students report out results with decisions and recommendations that are tied to their own articulated learning outcomes and the state learning goals or objectives.

Valuing the Process

Regardless of whether the results are being used as comparative indicators or to inform specific decisions and recommendations to improve student learning, it must be made clear to all involved that institutional faculty and administrative leadership value this process. It must also be made clear how the results will be used and by whom and for what. While faculty and administrators who are involved early on in this process may not fully understand how the results will be used, it is important to keep the process as transparent as possible and to keep communication open so that all involved can see the value of engaging in purposeful reflection. In other words, it is extremely valuable for those gathering the data and using the results to keep the process transparent so that faculty are reassured as to how the results will be used to improve student learning.

The case studies further articulate the importance of acknowledging those who are involved in the process. Finding ways to meaningfully reward those who use results of general education assessment to examine ways to improve student learning or to implement the means to improve learning is important to the sustainability of the efforts (Bresciani, 2006; Palomba & Banta, 1999). Results need to be used to improve learning, or at the very least to inform policy discussions, so that barriers to improving student learning can be removed. Faculty, administrators, and students must be acknowledged for their work in this area, for if they believe their efforts to improve student learning are not valued, it will be difficult for them to continue to commit their time to the process.

The good practice institutions also emphasize the importance of ensuring that students understand the purpose of general education, how it is evaluated, and how the results are used. Student understanding of the importance of general education assessment may help faculty and administrators better understand student motivation around learning and evaluating general education. If students better understand what they are to learn and how they are to learn it, they can become better partners in the learning and the evaluation of that learning (Mentkowski & Associates, 2000).

Remain Flexible and Embrace Ambiguity

Each case study has emphasized that evaluating and improving student learning cannot be done overnight, nor can it be done in a prescriptive manner. While these case studies have been shared to promote reader reflection of good practice, none are designed to be picked up and placed exactly as they appear within another institution.

These case studies have come to be what they are because the faculty and administrators involved in implementing student learning–centered general education have learned valuable lessons about what works for their campus culture. They have paid attention to their own assessment data and have used that data to inform practice and improve their models, and they have done so in their own way. While good practices for outcomes-based assessment have been followed and while many of them have "borrowed" evaluation tools and methods from other institutions, adopting the process into their own culture, which involved their own faculty, administrators, cocurricular professionals, and students, has made their process unique.

Remaining flexible and allowing for expressions of concerns and ideas from the faculty governing units, discipline leaders, cocurricular professionals, students, and state bodies ensures transparency of the process and open communication. Each case study indicates that this process was imperative to the long-term success of the institution's ability to improve student learning.

Flexibility cannot be maintained without embracing ambiguity and a commitment to working out the kinks in the process. Trying to plan the perfect process will most likely render the institution immobile. Pilot studies and an understanding of flexibility within a systematic model are imperative for long-term success. It is important to implement and refine as you go, providing opportunities for faculty, administrators, and students to reflect on how well student learning is being improved and how much better general education is being understood.

Engage in Meta-Assessment

It is important to provide flexibility to the general education assessment process to ensure its adoption into institutional culture. It is also important to do so in a framework of structure. Several books outline the necessity of evaluating your assessment process so that you can ensure effective, efficient, and enduring engagement in becoming more student learning–centered. Such books include those by Bresciani (2006), Palomba and Banta (1999), and Suskie (2004); all provide a meta-assessment framework for the improvement of student learning.

The good practice case studies represented in this book strongly encourage those implementing a general education assessment process to incorporate feedback from faculty, administrators, and students to improve how general education is evaluated. It is the evaluation of general education that will inform decisions and recommendations to improve student learning in general education, as well as improving student learning where general education connects to discipline learning, cocurricular learning, and overarching student learning principles. The meta-assessment of this general education evaluation process will help you obtain the information needed to improve student learning via the general education assessment process. It is the evaluation of the general education assessment process itself that will help you, among other things, identify where data collection methods may be cumbersome or where outcomes are unclear.

The meta-assessment process also allows you to identify how well this self-reflection process ties back to the campus culture and provides opportunities for the university to better understand the purpose of general education and therefore to better deliver general education. In revisiting Figure 15.1, it is clear that engaging in the meta-assessment process allows you to demonstrate, through evidence, how the culture of the institution is interrelated with the desire to improve student learning via general education and other learning avenues.

An effective meta-assessment process requires timely responses to faculty concerns about how well the process is working. As mentioned in several of the good practice case studies, the general education assessment process must make sense to the faculty. It must be provided in a manner that is not overly burdensome but meaningful enough to provide faculty with information on how to specifically improve student learning. This means that these aspects have to be evaluated in the meta-assessment process.

Furthermore, the good practice case studies emphasize the importance of providing resources and opportunities for cross-disciplinary discussions as well as discussions with the cocurricular professionals and other faculty and administrators committed to student learning–centeredness. Therefore, the meta-assessment process must evaluate how well these opportunities are presented and how well they are providing the kinds of discussions and results that are required to make the entire assessment process work for improving general education.

Finally, the good practice case studies emphasize the resources that must be provided in order for the refinement of student learning in general education to occur. A meta-assessment must focus on how well these resources are provided and how well they accomplish what they intend to accomplish—the further refinement of student learning in general education.

It is crucial that the meta-assessment evaluate all that is important to the institution's process to ensure a student learning–centered environment that promotes, evaluates, and refines student learning in general education, however general education is to be defined and delivered on campus. A flexible meta-assessment process that responsibly incorporates the feedback of all involved in delivering and evaluating general education will result in an improved assessment process.

As demonstrated by the good practice case studies in this book, creating a student learning–centered environment that promotes general education learning principles requires time, collaboration, flexibility, communication, commitment of leaders and resources, responsive and responsible use of data, and, possibly, a sense of humor.

References

Astin, A. W., Banta, T. W., Cross, K. P., El-Khaswas, E., Ewell, P. T., Hutchings, P., et al. (1991). *Nine principles of good practice for assessing student learning.* Sterling, VA: Stylus.

Bresciani, M. J. (2006). *Outcomes-based academic and co-curricular program review: A compilation of institutional good practices.* Sterling, VA: Stylus.

Bresciani, M. J., Zelna, C. L., & Anderson, J. A. (2004). *Assessing student learning and development: A handbook for practitioners.* Washington, DC: National Association of Student Personnel Administrators.

Diamond, R. M. (1998). *Designing and assessing courses and curricula: A practical guide* (Revised ed.). San Francisco, CA: Jossey-Bass.

Huba, M. E., & Freed, J. E. (2000). *Learner-centered assessment on college campuses: Shifting the focus from teaching to learning.* Needham Heights, MA: Allyn & Bacon.

Kuh, G. D., Kinzie, J., Schuh, J. H., Whitt, E. J., & Associates (2005). *Student success in college: Creating conditions that matter.* San Francisco, CA: Jossey-Bass.

Lusthaus C., Adrien, M.-H., Anderson, G., & Carden, F. (1999). *Enhancing organizational performance: A toolbox for self-assessment.* Sterling, VA: Stylus.

Maki, P. L. (2004). *Assessing for learning: Building a sustainable commitment across the institution.* Sterling, VA: Stylus.

Mentkowski, M., & Associates. (2000). *Learning that lasts: Integrating learning, development, and performance in college and beyond.* San Francisco, CA: Jossey-Bass.

Michelson, E., Mandell, A., & Contributors. (2004). *Portfolio development and the assessment of prior learning: Perspectives, models, and practices* (2nd ed.). Sterling, VA: Stylus.

Nichols, J. O. (1995). *A practitioner's handbook for institutional effectiveness and student outcomes assessment implementation* (3rd ed.). New York, NY: Agathon Press.

Palomba, C. A., & Banta, T. W. (1999). *Assessment essentials: Planning, implementing, and improving assessment in higher education.* San Francisco, CA: Jossey-Bass.

Stevens, D. D., & Levi, A. J. (2004). *Introduction to rubrics: An assessment tool to save grading time, convey effective feedback, and promote student learning.* Sterling, VA: Stylus.

Suskie, L. (Ed.). (2001). *Assessment to promote deep learning: Insight from AAHE's 2000 and 1999 assessment conferences.* Sterling, VA: Stylus.

Suskie, L. (2004). *Assessing student learning: A common sense guide.* Bolton, MA: Anker.

Tanner, D. E. (2001). *Assessing academic achievement.* Needham Heights, MA: Allyn & Bacon.

Upcraft, M. L., & Schuh, J. H. (1996). *Assessment in student affairs: A guide for practitioners.* San Francisco, CA: Jossey-Bass.

Wergin, J. F., & Swingen, J. N. (2000). *Departmental assessment: How some campuses are effectively evaluating the collective work of faculty.* Sterling, VA: Stylus.

Suggested Resources for Assessing General Education

Compiled using information gathered from
good practice institutions by:
Marilee Bresciani
Matthew B. Fuller
Catherine Tonner
Texas A&M University

Resources

The variety and breadth of information and resources available to those fording the seemingly rough waters of general education assessment is both exhilarating and overwhelming. The exhaustive efforts of those dedicated to the assessment movement has fostered a plethora of valuable resources providing guidance, tools, and information for assessment champions. Colleges and universities alike have established helpful electronic resources housed within their institutional web sites that provide snapshots of the many approaches to general education and assessment as well as links to practical tools for assessment initiatives.

Keeping abreast of the good practices of peer institutions is a great way to see how and what institutions are doing in their general education and assessment programs. North Carolina State University's web site offers a virtual gold mine of assessment and general education information, providing an exhaustive and well-maintained list of Internet resources (www2.acs.ncsu.edu/UPA/assmt/resource.htm). In addition, the Association of American Colleges and Universities web site (www.aacu.org/) is a useful resource for understanding general education and the academy (see especially, the Greater Expectations initiative—www.aacu.org/gex/index.cfm—and the General Education page—www.aacu.org/issues/generaleducation/index.cfm).

The following are some additional resources that may be beneficial to those searching for assistance when assessing general education:

American Educational Research Association, American Psychological Association, & National Council on Measurement in Education. (1999). *Standards for educational and psychological testing.* Washington, DC: American Educational Research Association.

Anderson, R. D., & Thelk, A. D. (2005, March). The back translation: A good practice in instrument selection. *Assessment Update, 17*(2), 14–15.

Banta, T. W. (1991). Contemporary approaches to assessing student achievement of general education outcomes. *Journal of General Education, 40,* 203–223.

Crocker, L. (2003, September). Teaching for the test: Validity, fairness, and moral action. *Educational Measurement: Issues and Practice, 22*(3), 5–11.

Dawis, R. (1987). Scale construction. *Journal of Counseling Psychology, 34*(4), 481–489.

Eubanks, D. (2004). *Assessing the elephant.* Paper presented at the Assessment Institute Conference, Hartsville, SC. Retrieved December 18, 2006, from the Coker College, Assessment ASAP web site: www.coker.edu/assessment/elephant.pdf

Evans, G. G., & Anagnos, T. (2004, March). *Embedded assessment of student learning in general education.* Paper presented at the Association of American Colleges and Universities Conference on General Education and Assessment, Long Beach, CA. Retrieved December 18, 2006, from www.aacu.org/meetings/ppts/Anagnos.ppt

Ewell, P. T. (1999). Assessment of higher education quality: Promise and politics. In S. J. Messick (Ed.), *Assessment in higher education: Issues of access, quality, student development and public policy* (pp. 147–156). Mahwah, NJ: Lawrence Erlbaum.

Ewell, P. T. (2002). An emerging scholarship: A brief history of assessment. In T. W. Banta & Associates, *Building a scholarship of assessment* (pp. 3–25). San Francisco, CA: Jossey-Bass.

Ewell, P. T. (2004). *General education and the assessment reform agenda.* Washington, DC: Association of American Colleges and Universities.

Leskes, A., & Wright, B. (2005). *The art and science of assessing general education outcomes: A practical guide.* Washington, DC: Association of American Colleges and Universities.

Meacham, J. (1994). *Assessing general education: A questionnaire to initiate campus conversations.* Retrieved December 18, 2006, from www.aacu.org/publications/pdfs/AssessingGenEdMeacham.pdf

Pellegrino, J. W., Chudowsky, N., & Glaser, R. (Eds.). (2001). *Knowing what students know: The science and design of educational assessment.* Washington, DC: National Academies Press.

Sundre, D. L., & Miller, B. J. (2005, November). *Continued refinement of an assessment instrument: JMU's scientific and quantitative reasoning tests.* Paper presented at the annual meeting of the Virginia Assessment Group, Virginia Beach, VA.

Learning-Centered Resource Suggestions

The following is a list of resources for developing learning-centered practices and implementing assessment strategies in the out-of-class environment:

Allen, M. J. (2006). *Assessing general education programs.* Bolton, MA: Anker.

Alverno College Faculty. (1994). *Student assessment-as-learning at Alverno College* (3rd ed.). Milwaukee, WI: Alverno College Institute.

Angelo, T. (1997, June). The campus as a learning community: Seven promising shifts and seven powerful levers. *AAHE Bulletin, 49*(9), 3–6.

Barr, R. B., & Tagg, J. (1995, November/December). From teaching to learning—A new paradigm for undergraduate education. *Change, 27*(6), 12–25.

Blimling, G. S., Whitt, E. J., & Associates. (1999). *Good practice in student affairs: Principles to foster student learning.* San Francisco, CA: Jossey-Bass.

Boyer, E. L., & Kaplan, M. (1979). *Educating for survival.* Somerset, NY: Transaction.

Carnegie Foundation for the Advancement of Teaching. (1977). *Missions of the college curriculum.* San Francisco, CA: Jossey-Bass.

Chickering, A. W., & Gamson, Z. F. (1987, June). Seven principles for good practice in undergraduate education. *AAHE Bulletin, 39*(7), 3–7.

Cross, K. P. (1999). *Learning is about making connections.* Mission Viejo, CA: League for Innovation in the Community College.

Dale, P. (2003). A journey in becoming more learning-centered. *NetResults.* Washington, DC: National Association of Student Personnel Administrators.

Eder, D. J. (2004). General education assessment within the disciplines. *Journal of General Education, 53*(2), 135–157.

Ender, S. C., Newton, F. B., & Caple, R. B. (Eds.). (1996). *New directions for student services: No. 75. Contributing to learning: The role of student affairs.* San Francisco, CA: Jossey-Bass.

Filer, A. (Ed.). (2000). *Assessment: Social practice and social product.* London, UK: Routledge.

Gerretson, H., & Golson, E. (2005). Synopsis of the use of course-embedded assessment in a medium sized public university's general education program. *Journal of Education, 54*(2), 139–149.

Harvard University, Task Force on the Core Curriculum. (1978). *Report on the core curriculum.* Cambridge, MA: Author.

Huot, B. (1996, December). Toward a new theory of writing assessment. *College Composition and Communication, 47*(4), 549–566.

Loacker, G. (Ed.). (2000). *Self assessment at Alverno College.* Milwaukee, WI: Alverno College Institute.

Loacker, G., & Rogers, G. (2005). *Assessment at Alverno College: Student, program, institutional.* Milwaukee, WI: Alverno College Institute.

National Association of Student Personnel Administrators, & American College Personnel Association. (2004). *Learning reconsidered: A campus-wide focus on the student experience.* Retrieved December 18, 2006, from www.naspa.org/membership/leader_ex_pdf/lr_long.pdf

Nichols, J. O. (1995). *Assessment case studies: Common issues in implementation with various campus approaches to resolution.* New York, NY: Agathon Press.

Pet-Armacost, J., & Armacost, R. L. (2003, July). *Blueprint for program assessment success: Organization and support.* Paper presented at the annual meeting of the Southeastern Association for Community College Research, St. Petersburg, FL.

Ratcliff, J. L., Johnson, D. K., & Gaff, J. G. (Eds.). (2004). *New directions for higher education: No. 125. Changing general education curriculum.* San Francisco, CA: Jossey-Bass.

Riordan, T., & Roth, J. (Eds.). (2005). *Disciplines as frameworks for student learning: Teaching the practice of the disciplines.* Sterling, VA: Stylus.

Schroeder, C. C. E. (Ed.). (1996, March/April). The student learning imperative [Special issue]. *Journal of College Student Development, 37*(2).

Shoenberg, R. (2001). *General education in an age of student mobility: An invitation to discuss systemic curricular planning.* Washington, DC: Association of American Colleges and Universities.

Singleton, R. A., Jr., Garvey, R. H., & Phillips, G. A. (1998, May/June). Connecting the academic and social lives of students: The Holy Cross first-year program. *Change, 30*(3), 18–25.

Slevin, J. F. (2001, January). Engaging intellectual work: The faculty's role in assessment. *College English, 63*(3), 288–305.

Stevens, A. H. (2001). The philosophy of general education and its contradictions: The influence of Hutchins. *Journal of General Education, 50*(3), 165–191.

Thompson, R. J., Jr., & Serra, M. (2005, Summer). Use of course evaluations to assess the contributions of curricular and pedagogical initiatives to undergraduate general education learning objectives. *Education, 125*(4), 693–702.

Todd, C. S. (2005). Assessing math and English general education courses with results applicable to advising. *Journal of College Student Retention: Research, Theory and Practice, 6*(2), 209–224.

Index